SCARECROW PRESS, INC.

Published in the United States of America
by Scarecrow Press, Inc.
A wholly owned subsidiary of
The Rowman & Littlefield Publishing Group, Inc.
4501 Forbes Boulevard, Suite 200, Lanham, Maryland 20706
www.scarecrowpress.com

Estover Road
Plymouth PL6 7PY
United Kingdom

British Library Cataloguing in Publication Information Available

Library of Congress Cataloging-in-Publication Data

Casement, Rose.
    Black history in the pages of children's literature / Rose Casement.
        p. cm.
    Includes bibliographical references and index.
    ISBN-13: 978-0-8108-5843-5 (alk. paper)
    ISBN-10: 0-8108-5843-6 (alk. paper)
    1. African Americans in literature—History and criticism. 2. Children's
literature, American—History and criticism. 3. African Americans in literature—
Bibliography. 4. Children's literature, American—Bibliography. 5. African
Americans in literature—Study and teaching. I. Title.
PS173.N4C37 2008
810.9'352996073—dc22

2007018137

⊚™   The paper used in this publication meets the minimum requirements of
American National Standard for Information Sciences—Permanence of Paper for
Printed Library Materials, ANSI/NISO Z39.48-1992.
Manufactured in the United States of America.

Contents

Preface

$\mathcal{I}$n spite of the month of February being designated as Black History Month, few students, Black or White, leave school with an understanding of the depth and breadth of historical Black experiences in America. Originally intended to celebrate the accomplishments of great Black Americans, curriculum during the month of February has often included stories of individual accomplishment; however, these stories are seldom contextualized historically. *Black History in the Pages of Children's Literature* presents a narrative timeline of Black history that can serve as a reference point. Each book chapter provides an introduction to one historical period as well as an annotated bibliography of outstanding children's literature that can be used to introduce and teach the history of the period. These children's books provide stories and information that can help students develop deeper understandings of the distinct history of African Americans within the encompassing history of the United States of America.

One reason there has been little understanding of Black history is that, too often, it has been largely ignored in American history studies for children. Yet people of African descent were present on this continent even before America began to be colonized in the early 1600s, and without their presence, American history would be a different story. As the history in this book unfolds, it will be clear that no major event in America's history could be authentically represented without the inclusion of the African Americans who were here every day in every way as part of the drama of our nation's history. So, as this book offers stories and history to share during Black History Month, it also offers the stories that can be used in any American history lesson during the period being studied. These stories can also be woven through language arts at all levels. The works included in each chapter bibliography are good books for children, and many of them have won national awards for excellence.

Chapter 1 begins the story before Europeans and Africans began to inhabit North America with the intention of staying and developing colonies in this raw and rough landscape. It provides a background: the often lost history of how the exploration of the world crossed racial lines and how the phenomenon known as slavery had its existence for centuries before African slaves were introduced here in the New World. The chapter also describes the greatness and variety of cultures on the continent of Africa that contributed to the legacy of strength, resourcefulness, resilience, and creativity that would be found in the Africans who immigrated to America, some of their own free will and many in a horrifying bondage that would mean enslavement for centuries.

Chapters 2 through 11 are organized chronologically, from the 1600s to the present. Chapters 2 through 4 address the years of slavery. Although we recognize slavery as a part of our history, we seldom think of it as occupying at least two hundred and fifty years, lasting from the earliest settlements to the end of the Civil War, the span of at least a dozen generations. Within those two hundred and fifty years, slavery quickly emerged as an acceptable cultural phenomenon as settlements were established. It then continued through the years of America's Revolutionary War and through much of the nineteenth century, until the end of the Civil War, when the practice of slavery finally ended in this country.

Chapter 2 looks at the beginning years of settlement in the New World, when issues of race were not prominent. During this very early history, much of the hard labor was provided by indentured servants from a number of countries, including people of different races. In time, however, race became the distinguishing feature that differentiated the roles that most people would play in the early years of this new nation.

Chapter 3 tells the story of the years when slavery had become a common feature in the fast-growing agricultural economy, and when even America's heroes of the Revolution, whose voices were raised in indignation that they would never be "slaves to the British," owned slaves themselves. By this time, fewer indentured servants were employed to do the hard and menial jobs that were done in harsh conditions, which made the demand for slaves more pronounced. It was around this time that slaves, alert and listening to the growing calls to freedom within this country, began to express their anger and frustration at their enslavement with plans for revolt from their conditions. Many joined forces with American patriots or with the British forces in hopes of gaining their freedom.

Chapter 4 tells of Harriet Tubman and Frederick Douglass as well as the Underground Railroad—the incredible network of routes through forests and over rivers, and dotted with homes, that provided safe passage for escaped slaves. Abolitionists, both Black and White, became conductors on these escape routes. Tubman, a conductor with a reward on her head, returned time after time to the South to lead three hundred slaves to freedom. Douglass, an escaped slave himself, was a brilliant orator who fought for the freedom of all slaves as he voiced eloquent arguments with both the pen and the spoken word.

Chapter 5 looks at the years leading up to and during the Civil War. By this time, the influx of slaves from Africa was to have ended with the stipulation in the Constitution to only allow the importation of slaves until 1808. Nevertheless, the number of slaves in America was in the millions as the slave trade continued illegally and as generation after generation after generation of slaves were born into families whose members had little hope of ever being free, who were owned and traded, and who were being regarded as less than human even in our Constitution that declared all men to be created equal.

Although refusal to allow the South to secede from the Union, not slavery, prompted the nation to go to war with itself, by war's end, slavery also ended. The Emancipation Proclamation, signed by Lincoln in 1863, ended the practice of slavery in the slave states, which had limited effectiveness because of the ongoing war. However, the practice soon ended in the entire nation with the passage of the Thirteenth Amendment to the Constitution. But because slavery had so clearly been a racial phenomenon and had literally been our history since the earliest days of our nation, it had scarred that history with an institution of injustice and inequity, one that continues to have an impact on our country during all the years that have followed the Civil War.

Chapter 6 looks at the years between the end of the Civil War and the onset of the Jim Crow years. In this short time period, identified historically as Reconstruction, freed slaves began to hope that they would have opportunities to reach their dreams of education and success. These dreams were to meet the realities that still existed in the larger context of America. Although slavery had been pronounced over, the economic and social realities of the times quickly awakened the nation to a new era of oppression.

Chapter 7 explores the experience of African Americans in the American West. African American soldiers, miners, cowboys, and pioneers helped settle the West. In spite of racial prejudice that was reflected in the laws in every region of the country, those who traveled west in hopes of a better life worked under tremendous pressure to make a home for their families. Some formed communities of all Black citizens so that they could live without the humiliation of the Jim Crow laws and ordinances.

Chapter 8 takes a deep look at the Jim Crow years, when court-ruled separation of the races was legitimized with the Supreme Court decision in *Plessy v. Ferguson* and racial injustice dominated the nation. During this time, lynching of African Americans became so common that songs were written about it. Terror and intimidation were used to maintain racial separation in much of the country, along with the enforced supremacy of White citizens at the expense of Black citizens.

Chapter 9 takes another look at the Jim Crow years and the outstanding accomplishments of African Americans that marked this era. This was a time when, in spite of violence and discrimination, Black men and women thrived with talent and creativity and courage that simply could not be suppressed. It was the time of the Harlem Renaissance, the Negro Baseball League, and the beginning of the Jazz Era. During the turn of the century to the beginning of the civil rights years, the country would be engaged in two world wars, and African Americans would again fight as they had in the nation's earlier wars, even as they were denied civil rights: rights that were denied in spite of the fact that African Americans had served valiantly in the armed forces. But, while the repression and oppression of Black Americans were protected by law, the emergence of Black talent and wisdom was evident in every area of American life.

The participation of African Americans had always had a profound impact on the accomplishments of this country, for without their contributions the prosperity that was being enjoyed would not have existed. Individuals who had contributed as explorers, scientists, scholars, artists, and writers had received individual recognition, but this time was different. In spite of the overwhelming injustices that presented themselves, the light of genius shone through and could not be suppressed.

Chapter 10 brings us to the civil rights movement. As our nation began to question the separation of races, the notion of "separate but equal" laws began to be questioned. As the Emancipation Proclamation had done at the end of the Civil War, the legal challenges of the civil rights movement moved the country forward in its promise of equal rights. Finally, in 1954, the Supreme Court decided that separate but equal was not fair, and with their decision on *Brown v. Board of Education*, laws came into effect that would again provide a dream of equality of opportunity and freedom from oppression. Just as in the past, however, changes were not without conflict, and the stories included in this chapter show the drama of this important movement in American history. Many of the events and heroes of this era are more familiar to children today because grandparents, parents, aunts, and uncles have personal stories to share about them.

Chapter 11 highlights the present. The many stories included in this chapter show the breadth of life in America today. Because of the contemporary nature of these stories, they may serve as a catalyst for bringing personal experience into classroom discussions. They can also serve as a point of reflection on the many changes we have seen in American history with regard to the Black experience. Our nation has come a long way since its beginnings. Imbedded in that experience, Black Americans have, through many years of inequality and oppression, managed to show remarkable resilience, courage, and creativity that can be told in the works of children's literature.

Certainly, looking at any piece of literature that we bring to children in the hope of increasing their understanding of a time in history, there needs to be a critical analysis to interrogate it for reliability, authenticity, and completeness of its depiction of Black history. Just having Black representation in history books does not guarantee that the representation will be fair and accurate. Because the Black experience has long been ignored or misrepresented in history books, it is now important to look at the representation in children's books to ensure its quality. Chapter 12 examines several books on the same subject, looking specifically for the depiction of the topic through the lens of what we know about African Americans' experience. This example works to address two significant questions: What questions can we reliably ask of any American history text that will be inclusive of how African Americans contributed to that time? How can we use our knowledge of Black history to enhance a lesson in American history that is presented without the consideration of the Black experience?

Chapter 13 highlights some of the authors and illustrators who have grown in prominence for their work with children's literature and have contributed to a strong and solid collection of quality books that relate specifically to the Black experience of history, family, and individual accomplishment. These authors and illustrators have worked in a variety of genres so that it is possible to speak to the Black experience in America through poetry, historical fiction, contemporary realistic fiction, and informational books, all written for children. The chapter concludes with a list of the Coretta Scott King Award winners, many of which are discussed in this book.

A glossary at the conclusion of the book defines words and phrases that may be unfamiliar to the reader. Notes at the end of each chapter refer to the source material and enhance the reader's understanding of where relevant sources may be found for future reference. Books are listed as early elementary (K–2), later elementary (3–5), and middle grades (6–8), according to their reading level and their concept load. Obviously, these are subjective suggestions, and you know best the reading ability and maturity of the young reader you are working with, but I would caution you to read any book before you share it with a child and only use my suggestions as an approximate guide. So much depends on the student's reading ability, his or her ability to deal emotionally with difficult topics, the context in which the book is being used, and the purpose for which it is being read.

In writing this book, I faced two obstacles. The first is that of naming. The names for groups of individuals are always in a state of flux, as individuals come to choose what name best fits their individual identity and the identity of their people. I frequently use "White" and "Black" here, but I also use "African American." Certainly none of these terms is ideal or considered by all to be the most accurate, but they are those most commonly in use as I write. Similarly, when describing those people whose ancestors lived on this continent for centuries before others arrived, I use the terms "Native Americans" and "indigenous peoples," as well as "American Indians" in a few circumstances when that term seems most appropriate. The second obstacle is that many more excellent books exist than I could possibly mention within this text. This is truly a wonderful circumstance, as more and more authors and publishers are beginning to include Black experiences in their historical and contemporary offerings. One can find Black history in historical fiction, contemporary realistic fiction, fantasy, nonfiction, biography, autobiography, and poetry works written for children of all ages.

So, with the realization that there are many more books and there is much more to say about every event and person mentioned in each chapter, what I share here is a beginning. It represents a hope that a more complete understanding of our history, the history that includes all of the people who participated in it, will help as we move into the future with an understanding that can only be gained from an honest look at our past.

Acknowledgments

$\mathscr{F}$irst, I would like to thank my family for the incredible personal support I have received as I have worked on this book, for which I am deeply grateful.

The authors and illustrators in this book have given us an important opportunity to include stories of Black history in American history lessons throughout the year. Serious research is woven into works of fiction, plays, and poems. Nonfiction works, both of historical events and biographies, that are included in this collection present scholarly studies of the topics that they cover. Even as they are accessible to young readers, they are no less accurate and thorough in their content than text for adult readers, and in many ways are ageless. Many provide a rare glimpse into the stories of people we might never have otherwise met or opportunities to understand how African Americans have helped shape the events that are included in the traditional American history curriculum. I thank these authors and illustrators for the thoroughness of their investigations into a history that is not always easily accessible, and for the creativity, beauty, and genius of their shared work.

Of course, for each of these books to come to fruition, publishers had to have recognized this talent and supported it through their publishing houses. I thank the publishers that provided support for the nearly two hundred and fifty books included here and for this book, too. Random House; Hyperion Books for Young Readers; Lee and Low; Henry Holt; the Penguin Group; Front Street Press; Scholastic; Lerner Publishing; Henry N. Adams; Chelsea House; Grosset and Dunlap; Grolier Publishing; Jossey-Bass; Oxford University Press; National Geographic; Harcourt; Houghton Mifflin; HarperCollins; Farrar, Straus and Giroux;

Candlewick; Carolrhoda; Benchmark Books; Bridgestone Books; Children's Book Press; Lothrop, Lee & Shepard Books; Clarion; Cinco Puntos; and Albert Whitman are some of the presses that have made this collection possible. My thanks also include the individual authors who responded to my requests for their support: Maya Angelou, Faith Ringgold, Angela Johnson, Christopher Paul Curtis, and Marilyn Nelson.

Finally, I wish to dedicate this book to the millions of African Americans who worked in every way possible, in spite of often overwhelming oppression, to support the goals of this nation despite remaining essentially invisible in the written history of the country.

Please note that all of the excerpts shared in this book are cited twice: once in the text and again in the bibliography. The quotes are also identified in the notes at the end of each chapter. Several publishers required specific citations, and these can be found in the Credits sections before the index.

• 1 •

Africans in the Americas
before Colonization

Some scholars think that some West African peoples had established trading relationships with the native peoples of the Americas before the arrival of Columbus in 1492. Such contacts may have begun as early as the 7th century B.C.[1]

$\mathscr{B}$efore we begin looking at African American history from the beginning of colonization on the North American continent to the present, it is important to contextualize the events of these initial years of our country's history with what we know about the ancient world and Africa before any settlement had begun on the eastern shore of North America. First, Africans were in the Americas hundreds of years before being forced here as slaves. Second, slavery existed all over the world and had for hundreds of years. Third, Africa had ancient civilizations that led the world in the development of government, farming, education, and art. Finally, these civilizations had often gone undiscovered, since Africa's vast dimensions made exploration into the interior of the continent very difficult.

"Contrary to popular belief . . . the first Africans came to the New World, not in bondage, but accompanying the explorers."[2] Many Africans arrived with Spanish explorers who had sailed from Europe to Africa and then across to the Indies, eventually moving north in their exploration of trade routes and search for riches. Little is known about many of these early contacts and expeditions, but it is believed by some historians that Pedro Alonzo Niño, the pilot of Columbus's *Santa Maria*, was Black,[3] and that "when Balboa discovered the Pacific Ocean in 1513 there were in his party thirty Black men."[4] For those individuals who were able to establish some reputation with extraordinary deeds, their stories are recorded and their names are known.

1

One such person was an African slave born in Morocco, named Esteban. After surviving an attack on the expedition led by Panfilo de Naraez in Florida in 1528 in which only a handful of men survived, Esteban continued along with three other men on "an extraordinary odyssey that took him through Texas and eventually ended in Mexico City."[5] It took them eight years to complete their journey.

In 1539, Esteban set out on another expedition, and by some accounts, he went forward when others wearied. Along with Indian guides, he explored west as far as Arizona and New Mexico. This exploration played a significant part in opening up that area, with all its riches, to European settlement. After his many amazing accomplishments, he was killed by Zuni Indians.[6]

Much of what happened in these early centuries is lost to the oceans, forests, plains, and deserts that were the only witnesses. The continent of Africa, too, during these years remains something of a mystery. Even now, except for the ancient culture of Egypt that is frequently studied, here in America little is known about Africa. But, to understand the Africans who were forced to migrate here in the early years of our country, it is important to recognize the many different cultures they were forced to leave behind.

In the era when European explorers were looking for new riches, ancient civilizations were present on the African continent: from the Egyptian empire in North Africa to the southern region of Great Zimbabwe, and from the western country of Mali to the eastern tip of the Horn of Africa. By 1000 CE, the kingdom of Ghana had developed in the Sudan, "with wide streets, stone buildings and weapons of gold and silver."[7] Along the Niger and Nile rivers, civilizations thrived. The ancient cities of Timbuktu, Gao, and Jenné on the Niger River "were then intellectual centers to whose universities came scholars from Europe and Asia and from which teachers journeyed to Arabia, Egypt and across the Mediterranean to Spain."[8]

In fact, as historian James Haskins points out in *Against All Opposition: Black Explorers in America*, "Before the European exploitation of Africa, African culture and civilization matched and often surpassed that of Europe. The empire of Mali was not unique in Africa. The empire of Songhay in West Africa, which succeeded the Malian, enjoyed similar wealth and educational levels."[9] Indeed, Haskins goes on to point out that the slave trade destroyed sophisticated cultures: "with the development of the African slave trade, the art, music, culture, and knowledge of these civilizations were virtually erased and the black African relegated to the role of slave and servant to the white person."[10]

As the second largest continent in the world, Africa's vast physical expanse is daunting. From north to south, the continent stretches over 5,000 miles, and at its widest points it is nearly that broad. Covered with rainforests and deserts, mountains and valleys, rivers and waterfalls, grasslands and lakes, some of which are the tallest, longest, or largest in the world, the many different countries on this huge continent share one feature: they all comprise an extraordinary land full of resources and wonders.

Long ago, as today, the diversity of Africa's physical characteristics were not the only areas of difference across the continent. "In Africa their cultures were rich and varied, as different from one another as were the African peoples themselves. Their colors, their languages, their food, their clothing differed in a range as great as the difference in size between the pygmies and the giant Watusi of Africa."[11] Later, these differences would add to the confusion and isolation of those captured to be slaves. When they were gathered for the voyage to the New World, they found themselves alone in many ways, imprisoned in the small spaces they were assigned in the dark, dank, and severely overcrowded area below deck.

The coastal regions of Africa had been explored more than the interior, primarily because of their accessibility to the merchant ships that came to trade and transport goods to other parts of the world. As early as 1441, it is recorded that two Portuguese ships dispatched by Prince Henry sailed to Cape Bianco on the western coast of Africa, looking for greater geographic knowledge, a new sea route to the Orient, possibly other Christians, and gold. The two captains returned to Portugal with some gold dust and a dozen Africans they had captured to show Prince Henry. Later voyages from Portugal would begin the deliberate acquisition of Africans for the purpose of making them slaves.[12] Unfortunately, after these Portuguese expeditions and acquisitions, the west coast of Africa soon became the area most exploited for kidnapped victims who became human cargo transported across the Atlantic to be sold as slaves in the Americas.

Slavery was not new with colonial America; rather, it had existed for centuries on nearly every continent. In most ancient civilizations, slavery was a common practice. As wars raged and ended, the victors often became the masters and the defeated became their slaves. There were White slaves, Black slaves, Asian slaves, and Indian slaves. As Palmer points out, "The foundations of the Atlantic slave trade were established in the 16th century by Spanish colonists, who were no strangers to the institution of slavery. Prior to Columbus's voyages to the Americas, the Spaniards held Muslims, Black Africans, Slavs, and even other Spaniards as slaves."[13]

The conditions under which slaves lived and the possibility of them ever having freedom depended on the cultural mores and needs of the victors and often on the individual slaves and their relationship with their "owner," along with their own resourcefulness. But by all accounts, regardless of the treatment or location, the condition of being a slave was tragic and dehumanizing.

The books included in this chapter present well-researched material that will help students better understand what the world was like as settlers began to form our new nation. These books provide support for the concept that slavery existed in the world well before we had slavery here. They look at the different civilizations from which slaves were taken, and they show the great diversity of the incredible continent of Africa. Citations within the annotations come from the book being cited unless otherwise noted.

EARLY ELEMENTARY

Feelings, Tom, ed. and illus. *Soul Looks Back in Wonder.* New York: Dial, 1993.

> My soul looks back in wonder at how African creativity has sustained us and how it still flows—seeking, searching for new ways to connect the ancient with the new, the young with the old, the unborn with the ancestors.[14]

This collection of poems includes the work of Maya Angelou, Lucille Clifton, Langston Hughes, Walter Dean Myers, and other great poets who are African American. In his introduction, Feelings speaks of the contemporary dangers for children of African descent who have been "removed from the benefits of ancient initiation rites—rites of passage designed to ease young people into manhood and womanhood, into the responsibilities and protection of full communal life."[15]

With the ancient symbols of the drumbeat, fire, and earth that are woven into the lines of poetry and create a flow of passionate energy that touches the ancient African spirits, Feelings uses his book to show the enduring creativity that is part of the African experience. In poems entitled "History of My People," "Mother of Brown-Ness," and "Africa You Are Beautiful," children are called to read of their connections to the ancient cultures. Poets speak of ancient poise, ancient fires, fires of pure knowing, consciousness and wonder, inviting children to feel those connections deeply. Along with the powerful poetry included in the text, the author includes a brief biographical sketch for each poet whose work appears in the book, and beautiful illustrations.

Genre: Poetry

Awards: Coretta Scott King Illustrator Award; Jane Addams Children's Book Honor

Grifalconi, Ann. *The Village That Vanished*. Illustrated by Kadir Nelson. New York: Dial Books for Young Readers, 2002.

> All the women and the strong young girls quickly packed up their great cooking pots, too heavy for the long trek into the woods, and filled them with their most precious things. Then they buried them. One day they would dig them up again![16]

This picture book takes the form of a legend being shared by a griot, or African American folkteller, of an African tribe, the Yao, that is anticipating the arrival of slave catchers. One mother in the village, Njemile, prays for safety, and hearing that the men of the village have been captured, she quickly devises a plan to save the women, children, and old men. With the brave help of her own mother and daughter, Njemile is able to organize the villagers to escape.

Those who have been lost to slavery include the men of the village and a neighboring village. The sad fact is that once captured, they never return. This story of bravery is one worth sharing. It is also a rare picture book that provides this information in a way that is accessible to even young children. The author's notes make clear that the story is more than just the story of the escaping village; it is also a lesson about the importance of faith and courage.

Genre: Historical Fiction

Award: Jane Addams Children's Picture Book Honor

MIDDLE GRADES

Haskins, James, and Kathleen Benson. *African Beginnings*. Illustrated by Floyd Cooper. New York: Lothrop, Lee & Shepard, 1998.

> Much of Africa's past was ignored or misunderstood by the Europeans who arrived in the 1400's in search of trade routes to India. Their search led them to the treasures of Africa, and it was these treasures, not Africa's rich history, that occupied their minds. At first, these traders sought gold, ivory, and spices. Later, after European colonization in the New World of the Americas, European traders undertook a huge commerce in human lives.[17]

This book is an important contribution to understanding that Africa was a continent rich in culture long before the North American continent began to be explored and colonized by European settlers. Businesses thrived and farms prospered. This book gives a glimpse into the many cultures that existed in different parts of the continent of Africa and a long history of the civilizations there. It takes the reader from 3800 BCE, when the ancient Nubian culture thrived with plentiful resources and successful businesses, to the years between 1500 and the 1800s CE, when much of West Africa was the source of slaves for the slave trade with the New World. Although slavery had existed on the continent for centuries, Haskins and Benson point out that the slaves in Africa had rights and responsibilities, while the "New World slavery was chattel slavery, in which slaves were regarded as property, not people, and had no rights at all."[18] During this time, West Africa suffered from the depletion of natural resources and the loss of "millions of its youngest, strongest, and healthiest people."[19]

Genre: Nonfiction/Informational

Palmer, Colin A. *The Young Oxford History of African Americans*. Vol. 1, *The First Passage: Blacks in the Americas, 1502–1617*. New York: Oxford University Press, 1995.

> The history of African-Americans begins on the African continent, a huge and varied land bounded by the Atlantic and Indian oceans. It was home to people with different languages, traditions, histories, and religions. They called themselves Twi, Yoruba, Ethiopian, Zulu, Ashanti, and Kumba, among other names. Some lived in large an-

cient kingdoms as old as the annals of recorded history, and others lived in small family groupings. . . . Some lived in societies headed by powerful men, and others in societies headed by powerful women.[20]

This is truly a remarkable book about this memorable period of history. It is well researched and well written, providing young readers with some of the best historical information available about the world events that led to the eventual enslavement of Africans in North America. As with other books that cover this period in history, it tells difficult truths.

While we know that the forced migration of slaves from the continent of Africa took the lives of untold thousands—hundreds of thousands, perhaps millions—many of us don't know that the journey to the coastal departure points also destroyed the lives of many through injuries sustained during their capture, abuse, disease, and wounds inflicted by their captors. Palmer also clears away the common myth that Africans kidnapped and sold their fellow countrymen, pointing out that although Africans captured and enslaved Africans, it was between different countries and that kidnapping fellow citizens would be considered an atrocity.

Genre: Nonfiction/Informational

CONCLUSION

The next four chapters will chronicle the two hundred and fifty years of slavery in America. Chapter 2 will cover the beginning of slavery in the colonies. Its continuation in spite of a war for independence and freedom that created a new nation will be covered in chapter 3. Chapters 4 and 5 address approximately the same post–Revolutionary War years, with chapter 4 looking specifically at the Underground Railroad, Harriet Tubman's work to free slaves, and Frederick Douglass's powerful antislavery oration and writing. Chapter 5 includes some of the events prior to and during the Civil War that raged between the southern states and the northern states. This war began over whether we would remain one country or divide into two, and it ended with the abolition of slavery.

It is important to remember through the reading of these next four chapters that Africans had been in the Americas before European colonization and worked in many different capacities, that slavery existed long before slavery was introduced here in America, and that the people who were enslaved and forced to come to America came from a remarkable continent rich in ancient civilizations, leaving homes and families they would never see again.

NOTES

1. Palmer, *First Passage*, 22.
2. Hughes and Meltzer, *Pictorial History*, 8. When I saw Langston Hughes's name as the author of this history collection in pictures, I was surprised. I know him as a poet of extraordinary ability. I was surprised again when, exploring this book, I found another book about Africa authored by Hughes, *The First Book of Africa* (Danbury, CT: Franklin Watts, 1960). I will be citing the pictorial history book that Hughes and Meltzer created together in later chapters. Although it is out of print, it is a book with a comprehensive look at history and is well worth finding.
3. U.S. National Park Service, "Did You Know?" *Boston African-American National Historic Site*, www.nps.gov/archive/boaf/didyouknow.htm. This National Park Service site provides several interesting facts about African American history.
4. Hughes and Meltzer, *Pictorial History*, 8.
5. Palmer, *First Passage*, 47.
6. Palmer, *First Passage*, 48.
7. Hughes and Meltzer, *Pictorial History*, 8.
8. Hughes and Meltzer, *Pictorial History*, 8.
9. Haskins, *Against All Opposition*, 8.
10. Haskins, *Against All Opposition*, 8.
11. Meltzer, *Black Americans*, 3.
12. Public Broadcasting Service, *Africans in America*, www.pbs.org. This comprehensive site for the PBS series *Africans in America* (1998) offers incredible historical information. This site follows the story as it was presented in the program and has easy links to additional information.
13. Palmer, *First Passage*, 23.
14. Tom Feelings, *Soul Looks Back*, author's note.
15. Feelings, *Soul Looks Back*.
16. Grifalconi, *Village That Vanished*.
17. Haskins and Benson, *African Beginnings*, 7.
18. Haskins and Benson, *African Beginnings*, 42.
19. Haskins and Benson, *African Beginnings*, 44.
20. Palmer, *First Passage*, 6.

BIBLIOGRAPHY OF BOOKS FOR CHILDREN

Feelings, Tom, ed. and illus. *Soul Looks Back in Wonder.* New York: Dial, 1993.

Grifalconi, Ann. *The Village That Vanished.* Illustrated by Kadir Nelson. New York: Dial Books for Young Readers, 2002.

Haskins, James, and Kathleen Benson. *African Beginnings.* Illustrated by Floyd Cooper. New York: Lothrop, Lee & Shepard, 1998.

Palmer, Colin A. *The Young Oxford History of African Americans.* Vol. 1, *The First Passage: Blacks in the Americas, 1502–1617.* New York: Oxford University Press, 1995.

BIBLIOGRAPHY OF REFERENCE WORKS

Haskins, James. *Against All Opposition: Black Explorers in America.* New York: Walker Books for Young Readers, 1992.

Hughes, Langston, and Milton Meltzer. *A Pictorial History of the Negro in America,* new rev. ed. New York: Crown, 1963.

Meltzer, Milton, ed. *The Black Americans: A History in Their Own Words.* New York: HarperCollins, 1984.

Public Broadcasting Service. *Africans in America.* www.pbs.org/wgbh/aia/home .html.

U.S. National Park Service. "Did You Know?" *Boston African-American National Historic Site.* www.nps.gov/archive/boaf/didyouknow.htm.

• 2 •

The Beginning of
Slavery in the New World

One of the most serious consequences of slavery was that it destroyed marriage and the family for the Black American. He had been part of an ancient African tradition of family life, but the forced migration from his homeland to the New World had disrupted his culture. In the Americas he met with an alien culture of European origins. Being sold on markets mixed him with many other tribes of different languages and traditions. . . . Not only was he cut off from his own world; he was not allowed to assimilate the new culture in a free way open to other immigrant peoples. As time passed, he was farther and farther removed from his African roots. He became property, and as property he was enslaved for life. His condition was passed on to his children and to his children's children.[1]

My own experience demonstrates how one might easily become misinformed by omission of important information regarding the role of people of color in the early days of this country. As a teacher of more than twenty years, I have looked at many informational books on colonial America, and I have rarely seen people of color. Yet, by 1708, there were approximately twenty-eight thousand African slaves in the United States, and Black slaves actually outnumbered Whites in the Carolinas.[2] I grew up believing that when Africans first came to America, they arrived as slaves. I did not know that for hundreds of years before a slave culture was created, Africans, Europeans, and Native Americans worked side by side exploring, developing, and building a New World. And, sadly, I would find out that Black families who worked hard and achieved a measure of prosperity in the early years in the New World could lose their land and fortunes as America began to identify slavery with race.

11

The story of Anthony Johnson, as described by James Haskins in *Black Stars of Colonial and Revolutionary Times*, illustrates the frightening loss of human rights that began to take place in some of the earliest years of colonization. Sold into slavery in 1621, Johnson worked hard, purchased his freedom, and established his own farm.[3] But while his success was evident, the earned status of African Americans was changing. By the time his grandson John died, "the legal situation for blacks in the region was becoming more and more tenuous,"[4] and it is believed that the legacy of his grandfather was not able to be passed down in the family. In fact, according to James Haskins and Kathleen Benson in *Building a New Land*, "the legal rights that free black men like Anthony Johnson had once enjoyed were slowly and steadily being taken away."[5]

By 1660, Virginia and Maryland had passed laws declaring that a child born of a slave mother inherited her slave status.[6] Such laws meant that not only would a child born of a slave man and slave woman be a slave, but so would a child born of a slave-owning man and a female slave. This was the situation for even the children born to prominent slave owners. For example, the slaves fathered by Thomas Jefferson would remain slaves for most or all of their lives. By 1682, Virginia had passed laws that denied blacks "the opportunity to own land," and "they were also barred from meeting in large numbers, from carrying arms, and from attacking 'any Christian.' "[7] Clearly, the era of slavery, with all of its dehumanization, was now firmly established.

These and other laws that were definitive by race created a hostile environment for Black people in the colonies. Such laws established the beginning of legalized discrimination that would continue almost uninterrupted for nearly three hundred and fifty years. For two hundred and fifty years of that time, slavery would be legal, and even when it was not legal, the discrimination would be imposed by Black Codes—state and local laws that maintained segregation and subjugation.

These early years have been oversimplified in the taught history of our country. Further, the lack of historical focus on the important contributions of African Americans to the settlement of this country has caused many to dismiss these contributions. The consequence of this historical omission and dismissal has been to continue the injustice.

This chapter brings into focus for contemporary history lessons the complexity of the early years of this nation's relationship to African Americans. Because our history lessons often do not include the stories of the Black explorers, traders, sailors, and colonists in the early settlements, they have perpetuated the perception that all Blacks were slaves in early America and that few African Americans lived in colonial America. In reality, "in the 40 years between 1680 and 1720, the proportion of blacks in Virginia's population jumped from 7 percent to 30 percent, as white landowners shifted from a labor system of indentured servitude to one of chattel slavery."[8]

The accomplishments of Black men and women in the very early years of this country and the turn of events that so dramatically impacted on the hundreds of years that followed are critical to understanding our nation's history. They also help us to correct the misunderstandings of this history.

The books described in this chapter provide stories of people and events that will give even younger students an understanding of the events of these early years. The content can be very intense, and although all of them are written for children, these books represent different developmental levels. I have suggested possible grade appropriateness for each book, but the adults who share them with children will need to decide the suitable concept load for the students who are reading them or having them read to them. All of the books are good background reading for the adult sharing and discussing this time in history. The recommendations begin with books for the youngest readers and move to those best shared with students in the sixth grade and beyond. Several of the books cover a broad swath of time and may also be referred to in a chapter that is focused on a later period.

EARLY ELEMENTARY

McGill, Alice. *Molly Bannaky*. Illustrated by Chris K. Soentpiet. Boston: Houghton Mifflin, 1999.

> In time she had a grandson, born of her eldest daughter, Mary, and her husband, Robert. In her Bible, Molly wrote her new grandson's name: Benjamin Banneker. She taught this young boy to read and write. She told him about his grandfather, a prince who was the son of a king in Africa, and about her days as a dairymaid across the ocean in England.[9]

In the late 1600s, Molly lived in servitude to a lord of a manor in England. When the cow that she was milking kicked the pail over for the second time, Molly found herself in court. She could have been put to death for this minor infraction. Instead, because she could read the Bible, "Her life was spared, but the justice sentenced Molly to seven years of bondage, to be served in a colony across the ocean. Having no family, Molly Welsh, age seventeen, said goodbye to England and boarded a ship."[10] She would soon find herself an indentured servant in the American colony in Maryland.

For most elementary school children, the concept of indentured servitude is unfamiliar. Historian Colin Palmer provides a simple explanation of this institution:

> Under what was known as the indentured labor system, the English colonists paid the passage of an assortment of people—farmers, laborers, servants, artisans, convicts, and the unemployed—who were interested in immigrating to North America. In return, these individuals signed an indenture, or contract, to work for the person who paid the passage, usually for a period of four to seven years.[11]

On her release from the contract, Molly staked a claim on some wilderness property and began to farm. Reading a posting that a slave ship was coming, Molly went to the ensuing auction and purchased a slave named Bannaky. Working together on the farm, they fell in love, and after she freed him, they were married. Although colonial laws might have forced Molly into slavery herself for marrying a Black man and former slave, she was not prosecuted. The couple had four daughters. In 1831, one of these daughters bore a son, Benjamin Banneker, who grew up to become a respected mathematician and scientist.[12]

Many parts of Molly's story will interest and inform students about life in England and early colonial experiences in the New World. Her story is particularly informative as it describes one of the conditions that could lead to indentured servitude. In England, Molly might have been punished with death for accidentally spilling the milk from a cow she was milking. However, an important consideration was that she had the ability to read the Bible.

Students may be surprised that women could be indentured servants. It may also surprise students that an indentured servant, at the end of the contract, would be provided with an ox and cart, a gun, farming implements, and seeds for tobacco and corn, and that she would have the means to purchase a slave. The legal prohibition to Molly and Bannaky's marriage, with the threat of her enslavement or death, although it was not exercised, illustrates the severity of the laws during that period, and particularly with respect to interracial marriage.

The book's illustrations go beautifully with the story and are especially striking in their use of light highlights in evening scenes.

Genre: Biography

Award: Jane Addams Children's Picture Book Award

LATER ELEMENTARY

Hamilton, Virginia. *Many Thousand Gone: African Americans from Slavery to Freedom*. Illustrated by Leo Dillon and Diane Dillon. New York: Knopf, 1993.

> Indentured servants grew to hate their lives and began to run away. The Native American indentured servants knew the countryside. They would vanish within the forests and find their way back to their own communities, often taking the former Africans and the white servants with them. This caused grave problems for the colonists. And it wasn't long before they adopted regulations governing the institution of servitude.[13]

Hamilton's reflection on indentured servitude, as well as slavery, takes the conversation beyond definition. She informs the reader about an institution that children might never have heard of, but one that was prevalent in the first years of colonial settlement (see McGill's *Molly Bannaky*, above).

Throughout the book, Hamilton introduces individuals whose lives were dramatically impacted by the condition of slavery or who were involved in resisting slavery. Some of the names are familiar, like Frederick Douglass and Harriet Tubman, but many more are unfamiliar and are part of the large number of people who made history in their times and whose stories are fascinating but silenced by time and inattention. The Society of Friends, more commonly known as Quakers, opposed slavery in the late 1600s and declared their stand in an antislavery publication. The Underground Railroad is introduced in the story of Tice Davids, who decided in 1831 that he could not stand being a slave one day more. Daniel Drayton, who captained a ship called the *Pearl*, provided passage to escaped slaves, but his exploits came to a dramatic and tragic end. And Margaret Garner's desperate resistance to her slavery and that of her children is a story you will not soon forget.

The stories Hamilton shares of the lives of slaves reveal much of the historical context that impacted their lives. The slaves she writes about start with African names as they are children born in Africa, kidnapped, and brought to America. Gradually, over time and generations, their names become European. The loss of their African family name was one way slaves were separated from their African roots, and as time passed and slaves were second, third, or fourth generation children born in slavery, they were named for and by their masters.

Hamilton's book is included here because it shares stories of people from the 1600s and early 1700s. Many of the stories in this book, though, speak of later eras and will be revisited as we move through the history of slavery in the next two chapters.

Genre: Nonfiction/Informational

Raven, Margot Theis. *Circle Unbroken*. Illustrated by E. B. Lewis. New York: Farrar, Straus and Giroux, 2004.

> Once, your old-timey grandfather lived in a village by a fine flowing river, across a wide, deep ocean, in faraway Africa.[14]

Thus begins the story of a present-day grandmother to her young granddaughter as she begins to share with her the art of making Gullah baskets with sweetgrass. This craft was brought with slaves who had learned to make them from their ancestors. The grandmother shares that, in the southern states, their distant relatives found grass similar to that in their home in Africa. Captured, enslaved, and sold for plantation work, they kept the skill alive by teaching their children, but more than that, they kept their memories alive by continuing to weave the Gullah baskets.

This book for young children is beautifully illustrated by E. B. Lewis, and the grandmother in the book introduces the concept of slavery to a young granddaughter as one might share the concept with young children in a classroom.

Genre: Realistic Contemporary Fiction

Haskins, James, and Kathleen Benson. *Building a New Land: African Americans in Colonial America*. Illustrated by James E. Ransome. New York: HarperCollins, Amistad, 2001.

African slaves were the largest single group of non-English-speaking people to enter the North American colonies before the Revolutionary War. The proportion of blacks to whites has never again been as high as it was during the eighteenth century. These blacks were pioneers: Whether free, servant, or slave, they were instrumental in building America.[15]

With the sharing of stories of individual early Black settlers, Haskins and Benson highlight times when Blacks were protected by law, and the tensions between those who believed in slavery and those who did not gave way to times when the perceived need for slaves was stronger than many individuals' antislavery sentiments.[16] This change in sentiment led to the establishment of the "1755 English slave code, which ended the protection of a slave's life, listed numerous crimes for which slaves could be executed, placed severe restrictions on a slave's everyday movements, and made it very difficult for slaves to gain their freedom."[17]

As conditions became more and more harsh, slaves resisted. One act of resistance chosen by some was to run away, while others chose to revolt against their owners as a path of resistance. This book includes stories of the slave revolts that were attempted. Clearly, the deep sense of injustice was strong for those who attempted to either run away or revolt, because those who failed were severely punished. The reaction to the resistance and revolts of the slaves was to adjudicate even more repressive laws and controls over African Americans. Usually these measures were directed at slaves, but there were often repercussions for all Blacks.

This book includes a chronology of events from 1441 to 1888, along with resources and a glossary of terms. As with many of the books on this subject, pictures speak louder than words and leave a powerful impression on the reader.

Genre: Nonfiction/Informational

Hansen, Joyce, and Gary McGowan. *Breaking Ground, Breaking Silence:The Story of New York's African Burial Ground.* New York: Henry Holt, 1998.

We hope that the story we have told and the efforts of the women and men who continue to reclaim this lost history will challenge young people to seriously consider archaeological research as an exciting and rewarding career. The important work of understanding our collective past continues, and needs young men and women who are empathetic to the cultures and people they study—who understand that what we learn about the past helps us to understand who we are now.[18]

It is not hard to come away from a glimpse into the story of slavery in America convinced, if you live in the North, that slavery was a southern phenomenon. This book gives the reader an extraordinary portrait of slavery in early New England as it records the rediscovery of the country's oldest known cemetery for people of African descent. It shares information about archaeology as it tells the story of this discovery and the exploration of the African Burial Ground located in New York City. The brutality of life as a slave is made real in these discoveries.

Each burial site told the unique story of the person buried there. At one site, the archaeologists found the remains of an adult female and determined that she had died from a musket ball that was lodged in her chest. They asked themselves,

> Why was she shot? Perhaps she'd tried to run away, as many enslaved New Yorkers attempted to do. However, runaway slaves would not be shot and killed—they were valuable property. A difficult person would be sold off so that the owner did not take a financial loss. If she had committed a crime under the colonial laws she would have been either hanged or burned at the stake. Perhaps she was shot during the attempted slave revolt of 1712.[19]

The book goes on to describe the slave revolt of 1712 and the restrictive laws that followed. One such law forbade Blacks, Indians, and mulattoes from owning land. The consequence of this law was that Black men and women who had acquired property could no longer will that property to their own families: "the new law effectively kept their children from inheriting the land. And unless their offspring had received manumission papers (certificates of freedom), they could possibly be re-enslaved as well."[20]

As children read these stories, they will surely want to join the archaeologists in their questions. Did the cowrie shells and amber beads discovered with one woman's body have significance regarding her identity in her African heritage? Could she have been a healer or the daughter of royalty?

> Perhaps she had been honored by other blacks, both slave and free, because she was a direct link to their past. People like her could replenish memories of a fading African past and disappearing African traditions. Her presence may have been a constant reminder of what had been lost to slavery.[21]

The remains found in these graves reveal much about the lives of those buried there. They show hard work and poor medical care. They show injury and violence. But they also speak of the ideals that these individuals valued and the belongings that their loved ones wished to send with them. These remains and the items buried with them give voice to the men, women, and children who were silenced and oppressed even at death:

> Whether they were slave or free, people of African descent could not be buried within the city limits. African New Yorkers were allowed to bury their dead on a site near the land of the black farmers on the outside of the city. . . . It was a separate place, apart from the city, undesirable land that had not been consecrated or blessed by the church . . . a place for outcasts and a dumping ground for the refuse from the nearby pottery kilns.[22]

Their voices from the grave make up powerful voices of a people who, in spite of overwhelming opposition, maintained their ancestral culture.

Genre: Nonfiction/Informational

Award: Coretta Scott King Author Honor

McKissack, Patricia C., and Fredrick L. McKissack. *Hard Labor: The First African Americans, 1619.* Illustrated by Joseph Daniel Fiedler. New York: Aladdin, 2004.

> One of the significant contributions the first Africans made was to help eliminate the threat of starvation. In an official document, the governor of Virginia ordered rice to be planted in 1648 "on the advice of our Negroes." He was told that the conditions for growing rice in Virginia were the same as in "their country." Rice became a profitable export, and a staple commodity in the colonial diet, thanks to African captives.[23]

This book, part of the Milestone Books series, gives a brief history of slavery as not originating in America and not being a racial phenomenon. Sharing the early history of exploration and settlement, the McKissacks highlight the early contributions and accomplishments of Africans who came to the New World as indentured servants, free men and women, and slaves. They describe indentured servitude as often harsh but offering the prospect of eventual freedom. Indentured servitude was contractual, and the book tells of servants who won a court case for their freedom by claiming that they were being held beyond their term of service.

During these early years of colonization, "it was possible for an indentured servant to become successful regardless of race."[24] With land, hard work, and ingenuity, African Americans could prosper. When a White settler and a Black settler were walking on the street, one could not assume which was the indentured servant, which was the landowner, or which might be a slave. But that was not to continue, and the face of slavery was to change. Gradually, as competition increased in the production of agricultural products, the rationalization for slavery and who should be slaves began to emerge. The McKissacks trace this change to religious leaders preaching that Blacks were deserving of servitude, and to slave dealers characterizing African slaves as wild and uncivilized. Playing on prejudice, as "racist attitudes became more acceptable, laws were changed to reflect those beliefs."[25]

The story of three indentured servants who escaped from a farm on which they worked is a dramatic illustration of how race became the determinant of fate in the colonies. Two of the servants were White, and the third was Black. When captured, all three were severely punished, but the court, in sentencing the two White servants, added one year to their servitude to the farmer from whom they had escaped and sentenced them to three additional years of servitude to the colony. But the Black servant, John Punch, was sentenced to "serve his said master or his assigns for the time of his natural life."[26] John Punch was sentenced to slavery because of his color.

In an incident in 1663, White and Black indentured servants planned a revolt but were unsuccessful. The threat was enough to prompt a series of repressive laws aimed only at the Black servants. These laws effectively drove a wedge between the White and Black servants. People who at one time shared the harsh times, the hopes of future freedom, and the status of indentured servitude were now viewed differently by the courts. New laws would have a powerful and oppressive impact on the lives of African Americans for hundreds of years to come. Children of slave mothers would be born slaves. "Blacks could no longer own White slaves, and interracial marriages were forbidden."[27] Gradually, the prosperity of the early successful Black colonists would be diminished through the false accusations and unethical transactions that the courts allowed when the defendant was Black.

Genre: Nonfiction/Informational

MIDDLE GRADES

Haskins, James, and Kathleen Benson. *Bound for America: The Forced Migration of Africans to the New World*. Illustrated by Floyd Cooper. New York: Lothrop, Lee & Shepard, 1999.

> Africans were not as susceptible to disease as the native Indians, they were available in abundance, and the profits to be made from the African slave trade were enormous.[28]

Written by the same authors as *African Beginnings* and with the same impeccable research, in many ways *Bound for America* is the next logical book to read. With a brief history of slavery in the world, the authors describe the torturous journey as kidnapped prisoners were marched to the coast for their eventual voyage to the New World.

> By the 1700's slaves were being captured as far as a thousand miles inland, and the march back to the coast might take sixty, seventy, or even eighty days. En route, the slaves might be forced to carry loads as heavy as sixty pounds for up to fifteen miles a day.[29]

These details are hard to read and the illustrations are very true to the text, but an honest look at this history may ensure that we learn from it and remember it. In this book, the authors have presented difficult material in concise and understandable terms.

A chronology is included of milestones in the history of slavery from 1441 to 1860.

Genre: Nonfiction/Informational

Grant, R. G. *The African-American Slave Trade*. Hauppauge, NY: Barron's Educational Series, 2002.

> But however well treated they might be, all slaves knew they could be sold at any time—and sale always threatened them with separation from family and friends and an abrupt end to decent treatment.[30]

Vivid and intense and best considered for middle school and beyond, *The African-American Slave Trade*, part of the Lives in Crisis series, is particularly graphic, largely because of the authentic pictures that support the text. The photographs, art reproductions, and artifacts from early years represent well the realities of the time.

Again, the reader is given much detailed information about all aspects of the slave trade. Often people think that the slave traders and the slave owners were the only ones who prospered because of slavery, but Grant points out that "the bankers and the insurers who handled the financial side of the business, manufacturers who profited from shipping their products to Africa or the plantations, and monarchs and politicians who backed the trade and took their cut"[31] all prospered as well. In fact, "consumers benefited from slavery each time they drank a cup of sweetened coffee."[32]

In describing the voyage across the Atlantic, Grant points out that many slaves attempted to take their own lives. Some found an opportunity to jump from the ship with no hope of survival. Slaves who attempted to commit suicide with a hunger strike were severely punished, and the crew watched to make sure that slaves ate their rations. The conditions were very harsh, and if anyone showed resistance, punishments were brutal or even fatal as a threat to others who might think of escape.

In spite of the inhuman treatment on board the ship, the slave ship captains had a vested interest in seeing as many slaves as possible arrive at their destination. However, one factor the captain was powerless to control was disease such as smallpox or dysentery. "At the first sign of contagious disease the slaves affected would be thrown overboard and left to drown."[33] According to Grant, it is estimated that an average of one in eight slaves died making the crossing.

Genre: Nonfiction/Informational

CONCLUSION

During the second half of the seventeenth century, a terrible transformation, the enslavement of people solely on the basis of race, occurred in the lives of African Americans living in North America. These newcomers still numbered only a few thousand, but the bitter reversals they experienced—first subtle, then drastic—would shape the lives of all those who followed them, generation after generation.[34]

Historian Peter Wood describes the latter half of the 1600s as a time of terrible transition. Laws were enacted that continued to narrow the definition of who could be a slave until ultimately the definition was one of race. Where at first Christian converts could not be enslaved, laws were changed to eliminate that condition: "Within a generation, the English definition of who could be made a slave had shifted from someone who was not a Christian to someone who was not European in appearance."[35] In fact, in 1680, Reverend Morgan Godwyn wrote that the "two words, Negro and Slave," had now "by custom grown Homogeneous and Convertible."[36] In other words, the terms "Negro" and "Slave" had become synonymous.

According to recorded history, the first years of the settlement of America were troubled times. The magnitude of the difficulties encountered by the first settlers in the New World colonies was enormous. Life was not easy for anyone. But very early in this history, African Americans began to have their fate decided by the color of their skin and not the industriousness, courage, and creativity that they shared with others. Men, women, and children from the continent of Africa were kidnapped and transported to the New World to be sold as slaves, and free Blacks ran the risk of losing their precious and hard-earned gains because, although they were free, they became swept up in the racial division that was to become a dominant feature of early American history.

NOTES

1. Meltzer, *Slavery*, 211.
2. Haskins and Benson, *Bound for America*, 45.
3. Haskins and Benson, *Building a New Land*, 5.
4. Haskins, *Black Stars*, 12.
5. Haskins and Benson, *Building a New Land*, 6.
6. Hamilton, *Many Thousand Gone*, 5. Hamilton's work spans the period from the early colonial times to the Emancipation Proclamation and will be referred to throughout the chapters that relate to this timeframe.
7. Haskins, *Black Stars*, 12.
8. Wood, *Strange New Land*, 39.
9. McGill, *Molly Bannaky*.
10. McGill, *Molly Bannaky*.
11. Palmer, *The First Passage*, 24.
12. Two biographies of Benjamin Banneker are included in chapter 3.
13. Hamilton, *Many Thousand Gone*, 5.
14. Raven, *Circle Unbroken*.

15. Haskins and Benson, *Building a New Land*, 1.
16. Haskins and Benson, *Building a New Land*, 21.
17. Haskins and Benson, *Building a New Land*, 21.
18. Hansen and McGowan, *Breaking Ground*, xii.
19. Hansen and McGowan, *Breaking Ground*, 48–9.
20. Hansen and McGowan, *Breaking Ground*, 52.
21. Hansen and McGowan, *Breaking Ground*, 42.
22. Hansen and McGowan, *Breaking Ground*, 33–34.
23. McKissack and McKissack, *Hard Labor*, 39.
24. McKissack and McKissack, *Hard Labor*, 45
25. McKissack and McKissack, *Hard Labor*, 48.
26. McKissack and McKissack, *Hard Labor*, 51.
27. McKissack and McKissack, *Hard Labor*, 52.
28. Haskins and Benson, *Bound for America*, 14.
29. Haskins and Benson, *Bound for America*, 20.
30. Grant, *African-American Slave Trade*, 38.
31. Grant, *African-American Slave Trade*, 7.
32. Grant, *African-American Slave Trade*, 7.
33. Grant, *African-American Slave Trade*, 28.
34. Wood, *Strange New Land*, 23.
35. Wood, *Strange New Land*, 32.
36. Wood, *Strange New Land*, 32.

BIBLIOGRAPHY OF BOOKS FOR CHILDREN

Grant, R. G. *The African-American Slave Trade*. Hauppauge, NY: Barron's Educational Series, 2002.

Hamilton, Virginia. *Many Thousand Gone: African Americans from Slavery to Freedom*. Illustrated by Leo Dillon and Diane Dillon. New York: Knopf, 1993.

Hansen, Joyce, and Gary McGowan. *Breaking Ground, Breaking Silence: The Story of New York's African Burial Ground*. New York: Henry Holt, 1998.

Haskins, James, and Kathleen Benson. *Bound for America: The Forced Migration of Africans to the New World*. Illustrated by Floyd Cooper. New York: Lothrop, Lee & Shepard, 1999.

———. *Building a New Land: African Americans in Colonial America*. Illustrated by James E. Ransome. New York: HarperCollins, Amistad, 2001.

McGill, Alice. *Molly Bannaky*. Illustrated by Chris K. Soentpiet. Boston: Houghton Mifflin, 1999.

McKissack, Patricia C., and Fredrick L. McKissack. *Hard Labor: The First African Americans, 1619*. Illustrated by Joseph Daniel Fiedler. New York: Aladdin, 2004.

Raven, Margot Theis. *Circle Unbroken*. Illustrated by E. B. Lewis. New York: Farrar, Straus and Giroux, 2004.

BIBLIOGRAPHY OF REFERENCE WORKS

Haskins, James, ed. *Black Stars of Colonial and Revolutionary Times: African Americans Who Lived Their Dreams*. Hoboken, NJ: Wiley, 2002.
Meltzer, Milton. *Slavery: A World History*. New York: Da Capo, 1993.
Palmer, Colin A. *The Young Oxford History of African Americans*. Vol. 1, *The First Passage: Blacks in the Americas, 1502–1617*. New York: Oxford University Press, 1995.
Wood, Peter H. *Strange New Land: Africans in Colonial America*. New York: Oxford University Press, 2003.

• 3 •

African Americans and the
Beginning of a New Nation

In the mid-1700's the largest stream of immigration was that of black slaves. By 1700 the black population in the colonies had grown to nearly half a million. . . . The transatlantic passage was terrible, costing untold thousands of lives from revolts, suicides, and above all, disease on shipboard.[1]

$\mathcal{T}$he nightmarish voyage of the *Venus* offers sobering evidence of the fate of many of the Africans whom French slave traders packed off to Louisiana. Of the 450 slaves loaded aboard the *Venus* in Africa in April 1729, only 363 reached the Mississippi River. Another forty-three succumbed before they disembarked in New Orleans. According to officials, the remaining slaves were so disease ridden that "more than two-thirds of those who were sold at auction into the hands of the inhabitants . . . died soon afterward. If a slave arrived young, the harsh realities of physical exhaustion, malnutrition, and rampant disease aged them quickly."[2]

There is no way to reconcile the institution of slavery. Tragedy and sadness are inherent in the stories of slavery, prompting us to want to move past these stories as soon as possible: to not feel the pain and suffering that such extraordinary violence to the human spirit can mean. But to do that would make invisible in our history the exceptional courage and resilience of these Americans; to do so would negate their contributions to the nation; to do so would escape the obligation to look at their lives filled with injustice and lost promise so that there will never be another injustice like that again.

The time that slavery existed was so significant in our history that to try to move past it hurriedly, or to not acknowledge the enormity of

27

over two hundred and fifty years of history, would mislead and misinform. During two hundred and fifty years, at least a dozen generations could be born—twelve generations of families of slaves, many of whom lost each other, as they were sold apart and separated forever.

This chapter looks at slavery around the time leading up to the Revolutionary War and moving into the early 1800s. You can imagine African American slaves working on farms and plantations and in the homes of the masters, experiencing life as chattel, not considered human, yet listening to colonists protesting the unfairness of England and their "taxation without representation." The fruits of their labor were not their own, these rebellious colonists complained. "We will not be slaves to England" was a common cry. One is left to wonder how these same people could hold slaves themselves. How could the founders of our country, the fighters of our revolution for freedom, those who declared freedom an inalienable right, own another human being?

The books in this chapter highlight this period of history and perhaps answer some of these questions for interested students. By this time, slavery was well established. Names from this time have become synonymous with freedom, liberty, and courage: Thomas Jefferson, George Washington, Benjamin Franklin, and John Adams, to name but a few. Unfortunately, some of our famous historical figures not only owned slaves but did not free them either in their lifetimes or at their deaths. In his will, Washington did allow that, when his wife Martha died, his slaves would be free, and Jefferson, who had fathered children with his slave Sally Hemings, "freed nine of his 'faithful retainers' and left the others in slavery after his death."[3]

During this time, the Revolutionary War was fought and the Declaration of Independence written. Soon, the new nation held a convention to create the Constitution, which established the government of the United States and stated Americans' basic rights and freedoms. During the convention, the delegates from the thirteen states revealed the country's regional differences and disagreements. One of the principal disagreements was about the continuation of slavery in the new nation. There were many delegates "in both the North and the South who wanted to do away with human bondage."[4] But in the end, the delegates decided "that it was more important to form a nation than to end slavery."[5] This decision meant the continuation of slavery for nearly eighty more years—perhaps four generations.

Through the process of contentious debates, compromises were reached with the slave states to keep them in the union. One compromise was that the importation of slaves, human beings kidnapped on the continent of Africa, would be allowed to continue until 1808. Sadly, it should be noted that even after that time, slavery was allowed to exist in states designated as "slave states" and, in spite of the limit imposed by the Constitution, the slave trade continued illegally well after 1808.

Another compromise was in the apportionment of taxes and representation in the House of Representatives. "In the heated debates over representation in the Congress, the question arose as to how slaves should be counted."[6] It was agreed that each slave would be counted as three-fifths of a person. A human being counted as three-fifths a human being! This counting did not mean that the concerns or needs of slaves would be included, even in some small margin, in the representation in Congress.

Another proposal had to do with return of property. As John Hope Franklin notes, "It is significant that there was almost no opposition to the proposal that states give up fugitive slaves to their owners."[7] He points out that these terms had been included in Indian treaties, so they would likely not have been considered new. He also notes, "When the provision came before the convention for consideration, it was late, August 28, and the delegates were already impatient to return to their homes. Too, the slave owners had already won such sweeping constitutional recognition of slavery that the question of fugitive slaves was an anticlimax to the great debates.[8]".

The following books tell the stories of the experiences of African Americans in the early 1700s to the early 1800s, when the slave trade was a thriving institution, the country went to war to establish its independence from England, and deep divisions surfaced about what it means to have liberty and justice for all.

EARLY ELEMENTARY

Brennan, Linda Crotta. *The Black Regiment of the American Revolution.* Illustrated by Cheryl Kirk Noll. West Rockport, ME: Moon Mountain, 2004.

The plan for the Black Regiment was placed before the Rhode Island legislature. Many of the state's lawmakers and wealthiest citizens were slave traders and slave owners. They were against the idea of arming slaves. They worried that enlisting slaves in the army would brew trouble with the slaves left behind. But no one had any better ideas for finding the soldiers Rhode Island needed.[9]

Telling the story of the creation of the Black Regiment from Rhode Island serves to inform students about many aspects of the African American soldier in the Continental Army, including the reluctance to arm Black soldiers, the outstanding courage and commitment of African Americans to the cause of national freedom, and the sad returns that Black soldiers received for their service. Probably one of the most troubling problems these veterans encountered was that even if they gained their freedom, their wives and children did not, and many heroes of the Revolutionary War were forced to work at poorly paying, back-breaking jobs to pay for the freedom of their loved ones.

Genre: Nonfiction/Informational

Ferris, Jeri. *What Are You Figuring Now? A Story about Benjamin Banneker.* Illustrated by Amy Johnson. Minneapolis, MN: Millbrook, 1998.

In 1753, two years after he had borrowed the gold watch, Benjamin put all the pieces together. He remembered just how each one had fit into the next one in the watch. When he was finished, they fit perfectly, like the pieces of a puzzle. He built a case, put the gears and wheels and pins inside just so, and added a bell made of iron. Benjamin had made his *own* clock.[10]

This accomplishment is one of the amazing stories about Benjamin Banneker. After having been loaned a watch, he drew each piece and memorized how the pieces went together. After working all day on his farm, he gathered the materials he had purchased for the project and put them together to make a clock.

Wonderful as a read-aloud in early elementary or later as an independent read for older students, this book tells this story and others about Benjamin Banneker and is a great addition to the story of his grandparents in *Molly Bannaky*[11] and Andrea Pinkney's biography of Banneker.[12] These stories give the reader a unique opportunity to see the connections between three generations. Banneker, the grandson of a freed slave and a grandmother who came to this country as an indentured servant, grew up with encouragement and the opportunity to learn, and learn he did. His story is one of genius and accomplishment as a surveyor and astronomer, and as with many other biographies, it acquaints the reader with the historical events he encountered.

Genre: Biography

Hamilton, Virginia. *Many Thousand Gone: African-Americans from Slavery to Freedom*. Illustrated by Leo Dillon and Diane Dillon. New York: Knopf, 1993.

> The underground road was neither a road nor underground. It was any number of houses, caves, hay mounds, root cellars, attics, high branches of trees, chimneys, hidden rooms, and empty barns—any place a running-away could hide. It was also all the paths and trails leading to such places.[13]

The "underground road" would later be called the Underground Railroad, as Hamilton explains in this book that tells so many stories from different parts of American history. This book was cited in chapter 2 but is also included here because of its treatment of the Revolutionary War period. Court cases, revolts, and issues around slavery and our national borders are included. A very interesting piece that Hamilton includes is a newspaper notice posted by William Brown about a runaway slave who had successfully disappeared for twenty years, and then "on the evening of March 5, 1770, the escaped slave, whose name was Crispus Attucks, turned up on Dock Square in Boston."[14] The rest, of course, is history.

Genre: Nonfiction/Informational

Harper, Judith E. *African Americans and the Revolutionary War*. Chanhassen, MN: Child's World, 2001.

> In the spring of 1775, the villages and towns of Massachusetts were buzzing with activity. The American colonists were fed up with British rule. They wanted freedom from British tyranny. White and black men formed militias. They prepared to fight the British. These soldiers were called minutemen because they promised to fight at a minute's notice. Early on the morning of April 19, the British marched toward the town of Concord. They planned to seize the patriots' military supplies. The minutemen rushed to defend their property.[15]

This is a story that most people are familiar with from history, but this mention of Black men as part of the militia in those early days of the conflict is often overlooked in many accounts in history books.

Harper's book, which is appropriate for younger readers, is illustrated with period art that includes depictions of events and portraits of people at the time of the Revolutionary War. It offers biographical background of individuals, along with reflections on the historical events in which they took part. Many of the people included may not be well known in history books, but without them the Revolutionary War would have been a different story and perhaps had a different end.

Students may be surprised that African Americans, particularly slaves looking for their freedom, fought on both sides of the war. In the South, many slaves ran away from plantations to fight for the British because of their promise of freedom. This was very dangerous. "If the slaves were caught and returned to their owners, they were severely punished. Sometimes they were put to death."[16] For the slaves who fought for the American forces, the greater surprise might be that although these Americans fought with courage and dedication, "a number of slave owners forced their slaves to return to slavery."[17] Throughout this book, Harper highlights what may be new and unfamiliar vocabulary for a reader, and she includes a glossary at the conclusion of the text.

Genre: Nonfiction/Informational

Lasky, Kathryn. A *Voice of Her Own: The Story of Phillis Wheatley, Slave Poet*. Illustrated by Paul Lee. Cambridge, MA: Candlewick, 2003.

> At first there was just blackness. Complete blackness. Then the blackness dissolved into darkness, and the world in the creaking hold of the slave ship slid with shadows. The air reeked. The little girl could pick out shapes—shapes of men, women, and children; most from Senegambia, on the west coast of Africa.[18]

Phillis Wheatley's story is one of the most amazing from this era. Kidnapped from her family in Africa, she was brought to America on a slave ship as a child of seven and purchased as a slave. Her life as a house slave in Boston, Massachusetts, was very different from that of the slaves who toiled in the fields of southern plantations. In spite of the cultural and sometimes legal prohibition to teaching slaves to read, she was taught to read and excelled at academic accomplishments, most notably as a poet.

Before Phillis was allowed to publish any of her poems, she was tested by a group of eighteen men who were leaders in Boston. They asked her questions, "perhaps to conjugate Greek verbs, or maybe to recite a poem by the famous English poet John Milton, whom she admired."[19] Although they concluded that she was indeed intelligent and the author of the poems she wished to publish, she still could not find a publisher. Published in England when she could not be published here, she became a world-renowned poet.

Although her story is not typical, it is a profound statement that no matter how "well treated" a slave might appear, the condition of slavery is always one of being owned. The story also makes one wonder how many brilliant poets, artists, scientists, and scholars were never discovered or recognized because of their forced servitude or their loss to the sea in the dangerous voyage to America. This book, through the sharing of Wheatley's life, also chronicles the events that led up to the Revolutionary War.

Genre: Biography

Pinkney, Andrea Davis. *Dear Benjamin Banneker*. Illustrated by Brian Pinkney. San Diego, CA: Harcourt Brace, Voyager, 1998.

> No slave master ever ruled over Benjamin Banneker as he was growing up in Maryland along the Patapsco River. He was as free as the sky was wide, free to count the slugs that made their home on his parents' tobacco farm, free to read, and to wonder: *Why do the stars change their place in the sky from night to night? What makes the moon shine full, then, weeks later, disappear? How does the sun know to rise just before the day?*[20]

This book tells the story of Benjamin Banneker, who grew up to answer the many questions that his creative mind asked as a child and went on as an adult to become a leading surveyor and astronomer. It wasn't easy for a young man, working to make a success of his tobacco farm during the day, to find time to study after a hard day's work—but learning was Banneker's passion. It was also his passion to address the grievous disparity between what he was hearing in the years prior to the American Revolution and the conditions he knew other Black people were living in as slaves. This book gives an excellent account of both Banneker's striving to become one of the most acclaimed scientists of his day and his letter to Thomas Jefferson, in which he confronted him on what Banneker believed was Jefferson's hypocritical stance on slavery as one of the authors of the Declaration of Independence and as an owner of slaves.

Genre: Biography

Pringle, Laurence. *American Slave, American Hero: York of the Lewis and Clark Expedition*. Illustrated by Cornelius Van Wright and Ying-Hwa Hu. Honesdale, PA: Calkins Creek, 2006.

> In late October the explorers halted for the winter. York and the other men labored for several days, felling trees and building a small fort near the villages of two Indian tribes, the Mandan and the Hidatsa. One Hidatsa chief wet his finger and, expecting paint to wash off, rubbed York's skin. Once again, York was hailed as "big medicine" and was admired and honored by the Mandan and Hidatsa people.[21]

This book about York, who was William Clark's slave, is a good companion book to Blumberg's award-winning account of York's life, particularly the coverage of his participation in the Corps of Discovery, the group that embarked on the Lewis and Clark Expedition. The reading level and the concepts in this book are appropriate for early elementary but also could be used in the later elementary classroom for differentiated instruction with more challenged readers. The watercolor illustrations go very nicely with the text.

Pringle explains in his notes why he decided to write a book about York. After he wrote a book about the expedition from the perspective of Seaman, Lewis's dog, he noticed that few books had been written about York and several of these had inaccuracies. One reason that Pringle's book is such a good companion to Blumberg's is that, although they wrote for different reading levels, both authors have worked to create well-researched books about this man who was a major contributor to the success of the Lewis and Clark Expedition.

Genre: Biography

Weidt, Maryann N. *Revolutionary Poet: A Story about Phillis Wheatley*. Illustrated by Mary O'Keefe Young. Minneapolis, MN: Carolrhoda, 1997.

> Though the day was hot and humid, the dark skinned child stood on the Boston dock and shivered. For clothing, she wore a piece of dirty carpet. She spoke no English. She did not know where she was, but she knew she had traveled many days on a ship so crowded with people that many of them had died. Some had died of hunger, for on the ship there was only rice to eat and little water to drink. Some died of disease. Some, if they found the chance, threw themselves overboard and drowned.[22]

This biography is written as a chapter book. Although it has fewer illustrations than Lasky's book, it has more details, both about Wheatley's life and the events of the Revolutionary War era. As a read-aloud for early elementary grade students or an independent read for third graders and up, this is an important story to share.

Genre: Biography

LATER ELEMENTARY

Blumberg, Rhoda. *York's Adventures with Lewis and Clark: An African-American's Part in the Great Expedition.* New York: HarperCollins, 2004.

> Imagine a boy of twelve or thirteen being the slave of a fourteen-year-old master! That took place on a plantation in Caroline County, Virginia, in 1784, when an enslaved Black boy was assigned to be Master William Clark's personal "body servant." Like many other slaves, this boy didn't have the legal right to a last name. Family names were for whites only. He was just York, called "that Negro York" or "that boy York."[23]

This book is very comprehensive in that it tells many details of the amazing story of York, the personal slave of William Clark during the Lewis and Clark Expedition. It is well written, and the author is clear that although York may have been considered fortunate to be living with the Clarks, his condition as a slave would always be unpredictable and humiliating: that he would own nothing and be looked upon as a piece of property that "could be bought and sold at his owner's will."[24] There was always the possibility that a master's wealth and status might change and that any of their slaves might end up being sold. "There might be a direct sale to another master, or he could be placed on an auction block, where every part of his body would be inspected and where bidders known to be brutal could buy him."[25]

Blumberg's book chronicles in detail the many and varied adventures that the Lewis and Clark Expedition encountered. It is interesting to note the numerous ways York improved the chances for the expedition to succeed. From all accounts, York was an exceptionally valuable member of the expedition. At the completion of the expedition, however, York was the only member not compensated with a salary or a reward of double wages and a parcel of land. As a slave he was not eligible.

Not only does this story provide an extraordinary record of the expedition and one of its most significant participants, but it also tells the story of a wealthy White fourteen-year-old boy becoming master of a twelve-year-old Black slave with whom he used to play. The story is profound.

Genre: Nonfiction/Informational/Biography

Award: Orbus Pictus Award for Outstanding Nonfiction for Children

Cox, Clinton. *Come All You Brave Soldiers: Blacks in the Revolutionary War.* New York: Scholastic, 1999.

> And less than a week after the surrender [at Yorktown], Washington established a guardhouse and ordered officers to place all black men and women in them until they could prove they were not slaves. He also ordered that advertisements for slaves be placed in newspapers so their owners could claim them (the same newspapers he and Jefferson sometimes used to advertise for their own escaped slaves).[26]

Cox's well-researched book about African Americans who fought in the Revolutionary War serves as a reminder that this time in America's history was fraught with contradictions for African Americans. The story of Black participation in the Revolutionary War brings with it an honesty that creates a fuller understanding of this time. Read as a chapter book from cover to cover, this book gives an extensive picture of the events of the war and is no less the story of American history as it introduces new heroes and sheds new light on old ones.

Genre: Nonfiction/Informational

Davis, Burke. *Black Heroes of the American Revolution.* San Diego, CA: Harcourt Brace, Odyssey, 1976.

> By the time he had grown to manhood, Crispus was a slave, the property of William Brown of Framingham, Massachusetts. But even as a slave, young Attucks was unusually independent. He became well known in his home town as a trader of horses and cattle, shrewd enough to deal with free white men. But though he kept for himself the money he made, Attucks was unable to buy his freedom from his master—and he was fiercely determined to be free.[27]

How interesting that Crispus Attucks, who eventually ran away to freedom, would be the first person to die in the war for independence and whose blood, according to Thomas Jefferson, "nourished the tree of liberty."[28]

This book provides another opportunity to share with students not only the story of the American Revolution but also a larger picture of the African American heroes who made a difference. As Davis points out, these "invisible" patriots listened to the words of freedom and liberty in a new country and risked all to achieve it. Students will listen to the tales of these brave patriots and remember their stories, many of which are not included in our history books. These and the many similar stories leave one wondering why they have not been woven into what we have come to know about American history. The answers will bring a greater experience to us all.

Genre: Nonfiction/Informational/Biography

Greenfield, Eloise. *How They Got Over: African Americans and the Call of the Sea*. Illustrated by Jan Spivey Gilchrist. New York: HarperCollins, Amistad, 2003.

> Thomas Forten's grandfather had been kidnapped in Africa and brought to America on a slave ship. Thomas' father, also held as a slave, had been allowed by the slaveholder to work nights, at the end of each long day of forced labor, and earn money. Most of his earnings had to be turned over to the slaveholder, but a small part of it belonged to Thomas, and he finally saved enough to buy freedom for himself and his wife.[29]

Although this book highlights the history of African Americans called to a life on the sea from the mid-1700s to the present, it is included in this era for the stories of Paul Cuffee and James Forten. Both were sons of former slaves and became successful in establishing careers on the sea. During their lifetimes they actually came to know one another, and although they disagreed on Cuffee's contention that Blacks should return to Africa, both worked for the freedom of others who were not able to reach their potential because of the injustices that dominated the lives of most African Americans. These two men's lives were marked with courage, intelligence, skill, and generosity.

Genre: Nonfiction/Informational/Biography

Haskins, James. *Black Stars of Colonial and Revolutionary Times: African-Americans Who Lived Their Dreams*. Hoboken, NJ: Wiley, 2002.

> Sampson chafed against the restriction of life in that Massachusetts town when such exciting events were taking place elsewhere. At some point, she determined to volunteer for the Continental army. Sampson was above average in height for a woman. Years of hard work for the Thomas family had made her strong. She purchased fabric and sewed a man's suit for herself. Then she walked to Billingham, Massachusetts. Using the alias Robert Shurtleff . . . she enlisted in the Continental army. [30]

Haskins's account of African Americans during this time includes many names we see mentioned often—like Paul Cuffee, Crispus Attucks, and Phillis Wheatley—and others who may be found only here, such as Deborah Sampson and "Free Frank" McWorter.

Sampson's story is fascinating. When she was shot in the battle at Yorktown, her gender identity was discovered by the operating physician, who allowed her to recuperate in his own home. Afterward, she never tried to hide her experiences disguised as a male soldier in the Revolutionary War. She went on to have a family and give lectures about her experiences. In her later years, Paul Revere wrote a letter that supported her petition for a military pension.

Genre: Nonfiction/Informational/Biography

Klots, Steve. *Richard Allen: Religious Leader and Social Activist*. New York: Chelsea House, 1991.

> In February 1786, Richard Allen came home to Philadelphia, where he had spent the first part of his childhood. Born into slavery 26 years earlier, he had been removed from Philadelphia at the age of 7, when his family had been sold to a farmer in Delaware. Now a young Methodist preacher, Allen was returning to the city of his youth at the invitation of the white elder in the local Methodist church. [31]

Richard Allen is generally regarded as one of America's first major Black leaders, someone who influenced major events of the period. Born into slavery, Allen eventually was able to buy his freedom and move to Philadelphia. Having discovered his faith, he followed his desire to preach and, as an excellent orator, became a Methodist minister. He worked tirelessly to strengthen the Black community and went on to establish the African Methodist Episcopal Church, still an important part of many Black communities today.

Genre: Biography

McCully, Emily Arnold. *The Escape of Oney Judge: Martha Washington's Slave Finds Freedom*. New York: Farrar, Straus and Giroux, 2007.

> One day, Mrs. Washington said, "Oney, you've become like another of our children."
> Oney bent her head to show thanks. Then she blurted, "Mrs. Washington, please may I learn to read?"
> Mrs. Washington laughed. "No child, you may not. There is no need for you to learn."
> Oney was crushed, but she hid the hurt.[32]

Judge's story is much like Phillis Wheatley's in that she was treated relatively well as a slave, but nonetheless her life was limited beyond belief. Slaves were never safe from the possibility of being sold, and the decisions and opportunities that we take for granted were not allowed to slaves. Mc-Cully captures some of the interesting nuances of Judge's life when she includes the fact that Washington, being well aware of the time constraints for having slaves in Philadelphia, rotated his slaves back to Virginia. Also, Judge, because she was owned by Martha Washington, was not expected to be freed after her owner's death. It is also interesting that the Washingtons, who championed the cause of freedom from the British, would be so persistent in trying to capture Judge and return her to slavery.

Genre: Biography

Richmond, Merle. *Phillis Wheatley*. Philadelphia: Chelsea House, 1988.

> Wheatley came from an unknown village in West Africa. She was buried in an unmarked grave in America. She spent her life struggling first for recognition and then for mere survival, and she died alone. Nevertheless, she left her mark on American history.[33]

This version of Wheatley's story is of higher reading level than Weidt's. More and more details are introduced, and there is more elaboration and clarification for the events previously introduced. Many more details of the times in which she lived are included. For instance,

> At the time of Phillis Wheatley's arrival in Boston, there were about 230,000 blacks—most of them slaves—in the colonies. Only about

16,000 of these captive Africans and their descendants lived in New England; the rest worked on the South's rice, cotton, and tobacco plantations. The southern states had special laws called slave codes, which forbade blacks to own property, to defend themselves against abuse by their masters, or to testify in court against a white. Among their other provisions, the codes made it a crime to teach a black person how to read or write. It was not a crime, however, for an owner to kill a slave while punishing him.[34]

This version of Wheatley's life along with the two previously annotated could easily be used for differentiated instruction in the fourth, fifth, or sixth grade, with readers reading at their own instructional level yet able to share in conversations as a whole. They can also span the grades between early to later elementary.

Genre: Biography

MIDDLE GRADES

Collier, James Lincoln, and Christopher Collier. *War Comes to Willy Freeman*. New York: Dell, 1983.

What I remembered most was the way the sun flashed and flashed on the bayonets. The British soldiers marched past our cabin in their red jackets, raising dust from the road, and the bayonets flashed and flashed, now this one, now the next one, as they turned just so in the morning sun.[35]

Well-written historical fiction has a way of remaining important in the field. Since it is written about a time that has already gone by, it does not get dated in the same way that contemporary fiction might. New details may emerge regarding events of history that might impact on a story, but for the most part, well-documented work such as this can stay vital.

This is a story about young Wilhemina Freeman, who has been freed by virtue of the fact that her father fought with the patriots in the Revolutionary War. She finds herself in jeopardy when her father dies at the hands of the Redcoats and she goes on a mission to find her mother, who was taken as a prisoner to New York by British soldiers. Disguised as a boy named Willy, she eventually finds her mother, who has been returned to slavery, but encounters hardship and grief as she is unable to prevent her mother's death. Wilhemina's frustration and anger toward her mother's owner lands her in court, where the suspense builds as a decision is made that will affect her life forever.

Many of the people and places in this story are real and are well documented, while some are fictitious. The author provides that information at the conclusion of the book.

Genre: Historical Fiction

Feelings, Tom. *The Middle Passage*. New York: Dial, 1995.

> My struggle to tell this African story, to create this artwork as well as live creatively under any conditions and survive, as my ancestors did, embodies my particular heritage in this world. As the blues, jazz, and the spirituals teach, one must embrace all of life, both its pain and joy, creatively. Knowing this, I, *we*, may be disappointed, but never destroyed.[36]

This book is a silent read. Other than its introduction, the book chronicles the passage of kidnapped men, women, and children from the continent of Africa to the New World entirely through its illustrations. The pictures are intense and graphic, honest and riveting. Feelings took over twenty years to complete these illustrations. The book is considered for mature readers, and a careful review is suggested before it is shared.

Genre: Nonfiction/Informational

Awards: Coretta Scott King Illustrator Award; Jane Addams Children's Book Special Commendation Award

Lester, Julius. *Day of Tears: A Novel in Dialogue*. New York: Hyperion Books for Children, Jump at the Sun, 2005.

> I want to tell them how sorry I am to have to do this. But I don't know if it would matter to them. I see them standing on the auction block and I wonder what they're thinking, what they're feeling. Some of them cry, but most don't show any emotion. Their faces are as blank as tree bark.[37]

On March 2 and 3, 1859, in Savannah, Georgia, the largest slave auction in American history took place. The slaves were the property of Pierce Butler, who had lost most of his inherited fortune through the stock market and gambling. In order to pay off his debts, he sold what property he had left, between 429 and 436 slaves. They were taken to Savannah in railroad cars and placed in horse stalls for the auction. It rained over the course of the two days, and the sale itself became known as the weeping time.

Lester creatively brings the voices of the participants to life with words that reflect the characters themselves. While the incredible life of a slave is a challenge to describe fully, Lester has fairly well transcended that limitation with this piece of historical fiction. The characters we meet in this book are so real as to make this a powerful story of the fears, realities, hopes, and courage of the slaves who would have lived through this sale. Lester's profound understanding of slavery helps the reader learn the complex realities that every slave endured.

> I can still hear the rain. It was so loud we had to almost shout when we had something to say to each other. But wasn't much to say that morning. Or maybe there was a lot to say, but we didn't know the words. Or maybe we was afraid that if we spoke our feelings, nothing but screams would come from our mouths. The rain was so hard and so loud it was like it was doing the grieving for us.[38]

Genre: Historical Fiction
Award: Coretta Scott King Author Award

Lester, Julius. *The Old African.* Illustrated by Jerry Pinkney. New York: Dial, 2005.

> The boy's wrists were tied so that his arms hugged the trunk of the large oak tree. His face was pressed against it as if it were the bosom of the mother he had never known. His back glistened red with blood.[39]

Lester's story begins with a young boy being brutally, nearly fatally whipped for attempting to run away. In the group of slaves who witnessed the beating is an old man: the Old African, who has not spoken since his arrival from Africa and who has a mystical power to transcend the events that are happening. He can also provide this power to those around him, which he does with the other slaves who are witnessing this violence. The Old African is able to use his powers to silence the overseer and rescue the boy. Eventually, he leads the slaves on the plantation to the ocean, where they walk to the other side.

Lester's story follows a legend of slaves walking into the Atlantic Ocean to return to Africa. In Lester's text and Pinkney's illustrations, the slaves succeed. They are welcomed as they arrive on the shore—and the Old African begins to speak again.

Genre: Fantasy

McKissack, Patricia C., and Fredrick L. McKissack. *Rebels against Slavery: American Slave Revolts*. New York: Scholastic, 1996.

> Slavery is as old as recorded history and so are slave rebellions. Whenever and wherever slavery has existed there has been resistance to it, ranging from individual acts of defiance to well-organized, armed revolts. One historian summarized it even more simply: "The cause of slave revolts is slavery."[40]

This conclusion—that slavery causes slave revolts—is certainly understandable when one realizes that "chattel slavery, as it was practiced in the Americas, was a brutal system that reduced human beings to property with no more rights than livestock or household furnishings."[41]

In this book, the McKissacks provide accounts of slaves who revolted in an attempt to gain their freedom. In many of these cases, there were armed confrontations and loss of life. The McKissacks explain that their research in this area and the stories they share are not intended to celebrate violence although violence plays a serious part in many of them. The consequences for those people who revolted were particularly brutal and were intended to forever frighten anyone who might be considering this path to freedom. Despite such incredible danger, however, many slaves rebelled against their enslavement by running away, while others rebelled with attacks on those they held responsible for their untenable bondage.

Genre: Nonfiction/Informational

Award: Coretta Scott King Author Honor

McKissack, Patricia C., and Fredrick L. McKissack. *Black Hands, White Sails: The Story of African-American Whalers*. New York: Scholastic, 1999.

> Later on, when he spoke, Douglass kept his audiences on the edge of their seats with the story of the slow progress of his train ride. Mile by mile, they followed the train as it crossed into Delaware, which was still a slave state. Douglass had to be very careful. At Wilmington, Delaware, he took a steamship up the Delaware River to Philadelphia. There his sailor's protection papers were checked again,

but not closely. From Philadelphia, Frederick took another train and arrived in New York on Tuesday, September 4, 1838. Freedom![42]

Few people are familiar with the fact that Black sailors made up about 25 percent of the sailors who worked on the whaling ships during the golden age of whaling in the years between 1800 and 1860. Indeed, according to the McKissacks, for a period after the Civil War, African Americans comprised over half of this country's whaling crews.[43] Also, the role of the sailor's protection papers in the flight of some slaves seeking freedom has seldom been talked about. These were the papers that provided Frederick Douglass the possibility for the suspenseful passage to freedom described above.

While slave ships carried their human cargo of kidnapped Africans to power the agricultural enterprises in the New World, whaling ships "carried Africans, too, but as valued crew members."[44] The McKissacks weave the history of early whaling into the context of other historical events of the time. From Frederick Douglass's escape from slavery dressed as a sailor with borrowed sailor's protection papers, to the successful Black whaling captains sailing out of Nantucket and New Bedford, to the many men who took on this grueling and dangerous job while being discriminated against, this book shows the best in research and illuminates the resilience and strong desire of our ancestors of color to be productive and successful in early America in spite of unbelievable hardship.

Genre: Nonfiction/Informational

Award: Coretta Scott King Author Honor

McKissack, Patricia C., and Arlene Zarembka. *To Establish Justice: Citizenship and the Constitution.* New York: Knopf, 2004.

> The conflict over extending equal rights guarantees, and even the meaning of the term, continues to this day. The courts are repeatedly asked to make decisions about what equal rights are and who is entitled to these guaranteed protections. During your lifetime, and the lifetimes of the generations to come, the three citizenship questions will be debated, and the answers will keep changing.[45]

This book looks at the struggles by marginalized groups for justice in America, moving from when the Constitution was originally written, through the events that shaped it and changed it, to the present. It serves as a helpful reference, too, as one looks for ways to understand how the Constitution, a statement of liberty, came to be written. This understanding is critical to recognizing how, even after a war for independence, our country continued the bondage of human beings in slavery. The story of the impact of the Constitution over the years of our history with regard to the justice that it promises is important to an understanding of why we are still working toward that promise.

Genre: Nonfiction/Informational

Myers, Walter Dean. *Toussaint L'Ouverture: The Fight for Haiti's Freedom.* Illustrated by Jacob Lawrence. New York: Simon and Schuster Books for Young Readers, 1996.

Several of the books cited here that include stories of slave revolts also mention a slave named Toussaint L'Ouverture, who joined the slave uprising in Saint Dominique and fought the French for the freedom of the slaves in Haiti. L'Ouverture proved to be very successful in battle, and although he died in a French prison before the end of the conflict, the French colonial government was finally defeated in 1803, and L'Ouverture became an inspiration to other slaves. In America, attempts were made to quiet news of his successes, but he became a popular and revered hero nevertheless. This book's illustrations—paintings by Jacob Lawrence—are works of art.

Genre: Nonfiction/Informational/Biography

Nelson, Marilyn. *Fortune's Bones: The Manumission Requiem.* Notes and annotations by Pamela Espeland. Asheville, NC: Front Street, 2004.

> You are not your body,
> You are not your bones.
> What's essential about you
> Is what can't be owned.[46]

In 1996, the Mattatuck Museum in Connecticut decided that they needed to do something about a skeleton they owned. Historians conducted the needed research to discover that the skeleton was that of a slave named Fortune, who along with his family, all owned by Dr. Preserved Porter, were among the last slaves in Waterbury, Connecticut.

Upon Fortune's death, Potter worked methodically to preserve the slave's skeleton so that he could study the anatomy.

Nelson notes that Fortune was freed from slavery only by his death, and she has composed this series of poems to honor this man and his life. She states in an author's note that she wrote this book soon after September 11, 2001, and that she wants this book to be both solemn and a celebration of the life that once existed. As the author indicates in the title, the book is a requiem: the poems follow the order of a traditional funeral mass. Photographs and other illustrations, along with explanatory notes, illuminate the reading of these poems and the reader's understanding of the life of this Connecticut slave in the late 1700s.

Genre: Poetry/Biography

Award: Coretta Scott King Author Honor

Rinaldi, Ann. *Taking Liberty: The Story of Oney Judge, George Washington's Runaway Slave.* New York: Simon Pulse, 2002.

This work of historical fiction tells the story of the real Oney Judge, who grew up as a slave in the household of George and Martha Washington. As a house servant, she received better treatment than slaves who worked in the fields, and based on the available documentation, there is every reason to believe that Judge was in many ways considered by the Washingtons to be part of the family. Nevertheless, she was a slave, and no amount of privilege within the ownership of another could be equal to freedom. By the time she makes her escape at the end of the story, the reader has a clear picture of the emotional conflicts that surrounded the real Oney Judge's decision, the offer she made to return, and the limitations that Washington imposed on himself to negotiate with her regarding her freedom.

Genre: Historical Fiction/Biography

CONCLUSION

Although many Blacks fought for the British, who had promised slaves their freedom in return for their help, approximately 5,000 Black soldiers fought in the Revolutionary War as patriots. One veteran, Oliver Cromwell, received his discharge papers, signed by Washington in 1783, after having served more than six years in the New Jersey Battalion. He left having received the Badge of Merit for his service—"he had enlisted for the duration of the war, at a time when thousands of white Americans refused to enlist at all and when others marched away from the army's camp at the end of their short terms regardless of the country's danger."[47] Sadly at his death in 1853, there was no one to raise a marker to remember his service and his bravery as a twenty-year-old volunteer farm boy who had "endured all the sufferings of defeat and retreat and the winters at Valley Forge and Morristown to take part in the last act at Yorktown."[48] But through these stories of the heroism of Black patriots, Cromwell and the other gallant soldiers of the American Revolution are more likely to be remembered forever in American history.

Harriet Beecher Stowe wrote of Black men who fought so valiantly in the Revolution almost a century after it ended:

> We are to reflect upon them as far more magnanimous . . . [inasmuch as they served] a nation which did not acknowledge them as citizens and equals, and in whose interests and prosperity they had less at stake. It was not for their own land they fought, not even for a land which had adopted them, but for a land which had enslaved them and whose laws, even in freedom, oftener oppressed then protected. Bravery, under such circumstances, has a peculiar beauty and merit.[49]

In 1816 three southerners, including Frances Scott Key, the author of "The Star Spangled Banner," founded the American Colonization Society with the intent of resettling free Blacks in a new colony in Africa that they named Liberia. Its capital was named Monrovia after President James Monroe. Richard Allen was among a group of Revolutionary veterans, free Blacks, and clergy to protest this move. They created a resolution that read in part, "we will never separate ourselves voluntarily from the slave population in this country; they are our brethren by the ties of consanguinity, of suffering, and of wrong."[50] Clearly, the growing role of African Americans in this country's history was becoming more firmly established. Chapter 4 considers the importance of two such individuals and the movements toward escape from slavery and the abolition of slavery.

NOTES

1. Meltzer, *American Revolutionaries*, 29.
2. Berlin, *Many Thousand Gone*, 83.
3. Meltzer, *Slavery*, 121.
4. Myers, *Now Is Your Time*, 67.
5. Myers, *Now Is Your Time*, 66. Walter Dean Myers is a renowned author of children's literature and has written many stories for young readers. Most of his work has been in fiction, but his accuracy in his historical fiction and contemporary stories is reflected in the careful and thoroughly researched depiction of history that he shares in this work.
6. Franklin, *From Slavery to Freedom*, 93.
7. Franklin, *From Slavery to Freedom*, 95.
8. Franklin, *From Slavery to Freedom*.
9. Brennan, *Black Regiment*, 4.
10. Ferris, *What Are You Figuring Now*, 27.
11. See McGill's *Molly Bannaky* in chapter 2.
12. Pinkney, *Dear Benjamin Banneker*.
13. Hamilton, *Many Thousand Gone*, 33.
14. Hamilton, *Many Thousand Gone*, 21.
15. Harper, *African-Americans and the Revolutionary War*, 12.
16. Harper, *African-Americans and the Revolutionary War*, 29.
17. Harper, *African-Americans and the Revolutionary War*, 30.
18. Lasky, *A Voice of Her Own*.
19. Lasky, *A Voice of Her Own*.
20. Pinkney, *Dear Benjamin Banneker*.
21. Pringle, *American Slave*, 21.
22. Weidt, *Revolutionary Poet*, 7.
23. Blumberg, *York's Adventures*, 1.
24. Blumberg, *York's Adventures*, 5.
25. Blumberg, *York's Adventures*, 6
26. Cox, *Come All You Brave Soldiers*, 160.
27. Davis, *Black Heroes*, 31.
28. Davis, *Black Heroes*, 31.
29. Greenfield, *How They Got Over*, 13–14.
30. Haskins, *Black Stars*, 71.
31. Klots, *Richard Allen*, 11.
32. McCully, *Escape of Oney Judge*.
33. Richmond, *Phillis Wheatley*, 104.
34. Richmond, *Phillis Wheatley*.
35. Collier, *War Comes to Willy Freeman*, 1.

36. Feelings, *Middle Passage.*
37. Lester, *Day of Tears,* 18–19. Lester identifies different speakers in a dialogue throughout the book, and this speaker is identified as the "master."
38. Lester, *Day of Tears,* 15. Lester identifies this speaker as "Emma as an old slave women."
39. Lester, *The Old African.*
40. McKissack and McKissack, *Rebels against Slavery,* 1.
41. McKissack and McKissack, *Rebels against Slavery.*
42. McKissack and McKissack, *Black Hands, White Sails,* 42.
43. McKissack and McKissack, *Black Hands, White Sails,* x.
44. McKissack and McKissack, *Black Hands, White Sails,* xi
45. McKissack and Zarembka, *To Establish Justice,* introduction.
46. Nelson, *Fortune's Bones.*
47. Davis, *Black Heroes,* 4.
48. Davis, *Black Heroes,* 5.
49. Davis, *Black Heroes,* 75.
50. Buckley, *American Patriots,* 53.

BIBLIOGRAPHY OF BOOKS FOR CHILDREN

Blumberg, Rhoda. *York's Adventures with Lewis and Clark: An African-American's Part in the Great Expedition.* New York: HarperCollins, 2004.

Brennan, Linda Crotta. *The Black Regiment of the American Revolution.* Illustrated by Cheryl Kirk Noll. West Rockport, ME: Moon Mountain, 2004.

Collier, James Lincoln, and Christopher Collier. *War Comes to Willy Freeman.* New York: Dell, 1983.

Cox, Clinton. *Come All You Brave Soldiers: Blacks in the Revolutionary War.* New York: Scholastic, 1999.

Davis, Burke. *Black Heroes of the American Revolution.* San Diego, CA: Harcourt Brace, Odyssey, 1976.

Feelings, Tom. *The Middle Passage.* New York: Dial, 1995.

Ferris, Jeri. *What Are You Figuring Now? A Story about Benjamin Banneker.* Illustrated by Amy Johnson. Minneapolis, MN: Millbrook, 1998.

Greenfield, Eloise. *How They Got Over: African Americans and the Call of the Sea.* Illustrated by Jan Spivey Gilchrist. New York: HarperCollins, Amistad, 2003.

Hamilton, Virginia. *Many Thousand Gone: African-Americans from Slavery to Freedom.* Illustrated by Leo Dillon and Diane Dillon. New York: Knopf, 1993.

Harper, Judith E. *African Americans and the Revolutionary War.* Chanhassen, MN: Child's World, 2001.

Haskins, James. *Black Stars of Colonial and Revolutionary Times: African-Americans Who Lived Their Dreams*. Hoboken, NJ: Wiley, 2002.

Klots, Steve. *Richard Allen: Religious Leader and Social Activist*. New York: Chelsea House, 1991.

Lasky, Kathryn. *A Voice of Her Own: The Story of Phillis Wheatley, Slave Poet*. Illustrated by Paul Lee. Cambridge, MA: Candlewick, 2003.

Lester, Julius. *Day of Tears: A Novel in Dialogue*. New York: Hyperion Books for Children, Jump at the Sun, 2005.

———. *The Old African*. Illustrated by Jerry Pinkney. New York: Dial, 2005.

McCully, Emily Arnold. *The Escape of Oney Judge: Martha Washington's Slave Finds Freedom*. New York: Farrar, Straus and Giroux, 2007.

McKissack, Patricia C., and Fredrick L. McKissack. *Black Hands, White Sails: The Story of African-American Whalers*. New York: Scholastic, 1999.

———. *Rebels against Slavery: American Slave Revolts*. New York: Scholastic, 1996.

McKissack, Patricia C., and Arlene Zarembka. *To Establish Justice: Citizenship and the Constitution*. New York: Knopf, 2004.

Myers, Walter Dean. *Toussaint L'Ouverture: The Fight for Haiti's Freedom*. Illustrated by Jacob Lawrence. New York: Simon and Schuster Books for Young Readers, 1996.

Nelson, Marilyn. *Fortune's Bones: The Manumission Requiem*. Notes and annotations by Pamela Espeland. Asheville, NC: Front Street, 2004.

Pinkney, Andrea Davis. *Dear Benjamin Banneker*. Illustrated by Brian Pinkney. San Francisco: Harcourt Brace, Voyager, 1998.

Pringle, Laurence. *American Slave, American Hero: York of the Lewis and Clark Expedition*. Illustrated by Cornelius Van Wright and Ying-Hwa Hu. Honesdale, PA: Calkins Creek, 2006.

Richmond, Merle. *Phillis Wheatley*. Philadelphia, PA: Chelsea House, 1988.

Rinaldi, Ann. *Taking Liberty: The Story of Oney Judge, George Washington's Runaway Slave*. New York: Simon Pulse, 2002.

Weidt, Maryann N. *Revolutionary Poet: A Story about Phillis Wheatley*. Illustrated by Mary O'Keefe Young. Minneapolis, MN: Carolrhoda, 1997.

BIBLIOGRAPHY OF REFERENCE WORKS

Berlin, Ira. *Many Thousand Gone: The First Two Centuries of Slavery in North America*. Cambridge, MA: Belknap, 1998.

Buckley, Gail. *American Patriots: The Story of Blacks in the Military from the Revolution to Desert Storm*. New York: Random House, 2001.

Franklin, John Hope. *From Slavery to Freedom: A History of African Americans.* 8th ed. New York: Knopf, 2000.

Meltzer, Milton. *The American Revolutionaries: A History in Their Own Words, 1750–1800.* New York: HarperTrophy, 1993.

———. *Slavery: A World History.* New York: Da Capo, 1993.

Myers, Walter Dean. *Now Is Your Time: The African-American Struggle for Freedom.* New York: HarperTrophy, 1991.

• 4 •

Harriet Tubman, the Underground Railroad, and the Voice of Frederick Douglass

$\mathcal{O}$ver time, slavery changed. Between early colonization, the Revolutionary War, and the circumstances leading to the Civil War, the events that shaped the nation also shaped the institution of slavery. Slaves had seen the country fight for freedom from British rule, but even those slaves who had participated in the fight had not received freedom, and now slaves found that the laws that restricted their lives were becoming even stricter.

Fears that those who were enslaved would revolt led slave owners to pressure for legislation that would severely restrict education, mobility, and even the physical security of slaves who were able to get to free states. Teaching slaves to read and the assembly of slaves for any purpose were illegal in many states. The Fugitive Slave Act, which allowed slave owners to hunt their escaped slaves even in the northern free states, was now a reality, threatening not only escaped slaves, but also free men and women who might be captured, accused, and enslaved. Over the decades of slavery, owners tried through brutal oppression to create a sense of hopelessness, but the spirit of resistance led many to risk all in their attempt to gain freedom, and more and more slaves rebelled by running away.

There was also a growing number of free Black and White allies who refused to support the practice of slavery. Over time, these individuals developed a network of resistance that came to be known as the Underground Railroad, with conductors and stops along the way. The stops formed a secret trail of safe homes for runaway slaves that would lead them to northern free states and even into Canada. Maps of these safe homes often were passed from person to person in song or sewn into the patterns of quilts by knowing slaves.

One slave who received great notoriety and became a legend in her own time is Harriet Tubman. After her own escape from slavery, she returned time and time again to lead others to freedom. Even with a reward on her head, "dead or alive," Tubman accomplished her work in spite of incredible odds, eventually leading over three hundred people north to freedom. She also became a soldier in the Civil War, where her selfless courage was again put to the test.

Another person who emerged as a leader during this time was Frederick Douglass. Also an escaped slave, he devoted his life to the freedom of all slaves and equality and justice for African Americans. Tubman and Douglass were very different in their approaches to these ends, however. While Tubman returned to the South in disguise and led slaves to freedom, Douglass ignited the passions of abolitionists with his eloquent writing and powerful oratory. His words remain as strong today as they did when they were first spoken, with clarity and honesty, about the equality of the human race.

The books in this chapter focus on the Underground Railroad and two people who carved out a place forever in the history of this nation: Harriet Tubman and Frederick Douglass.

EARLY ELEMENTARY

Hopkinson, Deborah. *Sweet Clara and the Freedom Quilt*. Illustrated by James E. Ransome. New York: Knopf, 1993.

> We went north, following the trail of the freedom quilt. All the things people told me about, all the tiny stitches I took, now I could see real things.[1]

This fictional story is based on the many stories about the use of quilts as maps for slaves to find a path to freedom. Separated from her mother and sent to work as a field hand, Clara is raised by Aunt Rachel. Although not her "for-real, blood aunt," Aunt Rachel cares for Clara, and when it is clear that Clara will not survive as a field hand, Aunt Rachel teaches her to sew. Clara does so well that she is moved to the Big House. When Clara hears about the Underground Railroad and slaves escaping across the Ohio River and further into Canada, she talks to the many people who have traveled in the area and designs a quilt that

provides the directions in its patterns. When she runs away, she leaves the quilt with Aunt Rachel for others to follow.
Genre: Historical Fiction

Hopkinson, Deborah. *Under the Quilt of Night*. Illustrated by James E. Ransome. New York: Atheneum Books for Young Readers, 2002.

Hopkinson has created a narrative poem that tells the story of a slave family escaping to freedom. In this story, a quilt is used by a woman in a safe house along the Underground Railroad to signal that it is safe to come to the house. As in the title of the book, the quilt is also a metaphor for the darkness making the stars and nighttime sky their blanket. Briefly the family stays with the host family, gets clothes and food, and continues their journey.
Genre: Historical Fiction

Lawrence, Jacob. *Harriet and the Promised Land*. New York: Aladdin Paperbacks, 1997.

This book about Harriet Tubman is unique in its blend of illustrations and text. Illustrated with paintings by a world-renowned painter who also wrote the text, it is a work of art. Why would this artist decide to write and illustrate a children's book? In his introduction he shares that he has always been interested in American history, and having heard stories about Tubman when he was a young child, he never forgot the remarkable life of the slave woman who, after gaining her own freedom, returned time and again to free others.
Genre: Biography

Miller, William. *Frederick Douglass: The Last Day of Slavery*. Illustrated by Cedric Lucas. New York: Lee and Low, 1995.

> She walked all night to hold him.
>   Frederick remembered her face for the rest of his life: dark skin and warm eyes, a mouth that broke into a loving smile.[2]

Imagine being the mother of a very young child and having to walk all night after working from dawn to dusk to hold the child you love, then having to put him back with his grandmother and leave him to return to another full day of hard labor. When I read the first line on this page, I reread it over and over and just felt the pain of it.

Miller tells the story of Douglass's life as a child and young man. Born into slavery and separated from his mother as a very young child, he questioned the condition of slavery in which he found himself and the treatment of other African Americans who were forced to work under brutal circumstances. This brutality of slavery is shown in several of the incidents that the author describes on the plantation and as Douglass fights to defend himself when being beaten by a slave breaker. The book ends with Douglass dreaming of escape.

We know that Douglass did eventually escape to become a forceful abolitionist and a brilliant orator. His extraordinary writing continues to provide readers with an important historical perspective and truths well worth including in lessons today.

Genre: Biography

Nelson, Vaunda Micheaux. *Almost to Freedom*. Illustrated by Colin Bootman. New York: Scholastic, 2003.

> Lindy takes Miz Rachel's hand, and we sneak out behind our shack and run into the night. I know *I* ain't runnin', but it feels like I am. Feels like I'm flyin'. Branches slap us along the way like they scoldin', warnin' us to go back. But Miz Rachel don't pay no mind. Just keeps runnin'.[3]

This story is told from the perspective of Lindy's handmade rag doll and is about Lindy, a young girl, and her mother, Miz Rachel, traveling on the Underground Railroad and escaping slavery. After she is beaten for asking the Massa's son how to spell her name, Lindy and her mother begin to plan their escape. As they make their way through the darkness, they meet with Lindy's father, who had previously escaped, at the river's edge, and from there they find the boatman who is to take them across the river.

Once across the river, the family finds shelter in homes that are part of the Underground Railroad. When the doll is accidentally left in a basement hideout on the family's hurried departure from their stay at a safe house, the doll grieves. Finally, another family with a little girl travels through, and the child finds comfort in the doll.

This story was inspired by the author's visit to the Museum of International Folk Art in Santa Fe, New Mexico. There she saw a sample of a rag doll with the notation that some had been found in one of the homes on the Underground Railroad, which prompted her to wonder, "If only those dolls could talk."

Genre: Historical Fiction

Award: Coretta Scott King Illustrator Honor

Rappaport, Doreen. *Escape from Slavery: Five Journeys to Freedom*. New York: HarperCollins, 1991.

> Like all slaves, she lived with the gnawing reality that at any moment she could be sold and uprooted from her loved ones. But Eliza's owners had always been so kind to her that she had lulled herself into forgetting reality. Their kindness had vanished with their need for money. Within a few days, Eliza would be separated from her two-year-old daughter, Caroline.[4]

This story, which focuses on Eliza's perilous escape from slavery with her daughter, begins the five true stories that Rappaport shares in this book. Abruptly made aware of her vulnerability in her master's home, where she is considered a piece of property, Eliza risks everything to escape with her daughter. Escape was always dangerous, and Rappaport skillfully has the reader moving from one ice floe to another with Eliza as she crosses the Ohio River in her quest for freedom.

The remaining stories are also captivating as they tell of the many ingenious ways that slaves found to escape. The stories reveal the creativity, resourcefulness, and courage of slaves in their individual revolts against slavery. These stories also help students understand the many ways the Underground Railroad worked to help slaves along their journey.

Genre: Biography

Rappaport, Doreen. *Freedom River*. Illustrated by Bryan Collier. New York: Hyperion Books for Children, Jump at the Sun, 2000.

> Crawl, crawl. The floor creaked slightly as he inched toward the child. Three feet more. Shrofe tossed restlessly in his sleep. Two feet. One foot. John scooped up the baby and threw her pillow at the candle. The room went dark. The pistol clanked to the floor. Shrofe awakened with a start.[5]

This biography is about John Parker, who was born in 1827 to a slave mother and a white father, which meant he was born a slave. Hired out as a child and as an adolescent, he continued to be very defiant even though, after his escape, he was captured and sold repeatedly. Finally, he purchased his own freedom by prearrangement with a new master. As a freeman living in Ohio, he is believed to have helped hundreds of slaves escape. This particular story from his life comes from his efforts on behalf of a couple whose infant was being held hostage by slave owners to prevent the couple from attempting to escape.

Rappaport's text is intense and masterfully crafted. The illustrations by Collier contribute what is best described as a spiritual rendition of the story. This combined effort is a tribute to the people who risked their lives for their and their children's freedom and to all of those brave people who were there to help.

Genre: Biography

Award: Coretta Scott King Illustrator Honor

Ringgold, Faith. *Aunt Harriet's Underground Railroad in the Sky*. New York: Crown, Dragonfly, 1992.

> Every one hundred years that old train will follow the same route I traveled on the Underground Railroad so that we will never forget the cost of freedom. Sometimes the train is a farmer's wagon. Sometimes it is a hearse covered with flowers—inside, a live slave hides in a coffin. You missed this train, Cassie. But you can follow, always one stop behind. When we reach freedom in Canada, you will be reunited with Be Be.[6]

As with other Ringgold stories, the author has Cassie and her little brother Be Be able to fly. In this book, as they are flying one day, they encounter an old train in the sky. The conductor standing in the doorway is Harriet Tubman, who is announcing some northern states and Canada as destinations. In his excitement, Be Be boards the train, and Cassie can't convince him to get off. When Cassie becomes frightened about his leaving on the train, Tubman tells her about slavery and reassures her that Be Be will be fine and that she can join him in Canada if she follows the North Star. Tubman cautions Cassie about how to stay safe in her travels, and Cassie receives whispered directions from her along the way. Finally Cassie rejoins Be Be in Canada, and both children have learned a great deal about slavery and the Underground Railroad.

Like other books by Ringgold, this book is a fantasy that has woven into it a great deal of informational text in a very creative mix. At the same time that we are enthralled with the magical images of these children flying and moving back to another time, we are sharing the information Cassie and her brother Be Be are learning about Harriet Tubman, the Underground Railroad, and slavery itself. Children who read this book get a powerful understanding of this part of American history.

Genre: Historical Fantasy

Award: Jane Addams Children's Picture Book Award

Schroeder, Alan. *Minty: A Story of Young Harriet Tubman*. Illustrated by Jerry Pinkney. New York: Puffin, 1996.

> That evening, Minty told her father that she was going to run away. "I mean it this time," she said.
>
> "Oh, I believe you. Only problem is, you don't know where you're runnin' to." Old Ben rose from his chair. "Come outside, Minty. There's somethin' I want to show you." Silently they walked toward the barn. Old Ben lit his pipe, then pointed up at the sky. "Do you see that star?" he asked. "The bright one? That's the North Star, Minty. And so you see all those stars next to it?" With his finger, he traced the outline of the Big Dipper. "That's the Drinking Gourd," he said.[7]

Although this is a fictional account of Harriet Tubman as a child growing up on the Brodas plantation in the 1820s, it is consistent with many things we know about her. She was frequently punished for behaving in ways that her owners felt were difficult, and she longed for her freedom. Several other books that are mentioned in this chapter furnish many more details from the life of this incredible person.

Genre: Historical Fiction/Biography

Award: Coretta Scott King Illustrator Award

Weatherford, Carole Boston. *Moses: When Harriet Tubman Led Her People to Freedom*. Illustrated by Kadir Nelson. New York: Hyperion Books for Children, 2006.

> She creeps through the woods.
> Her heart flutters. Hush: hoofbeats!
> Please, Lord, don't let them catch me and take me back
> to face master's whip. Don't let my journey end here.
> In the underbrush, Harriet sinks into a deep sleep.
> God cradles her.
> When she wakes, the men on horseback have passed.
> And day breaks.
> Thank You, Lord, for watching over me.[8]

Sometimes you walk into a bookstore and see a book cover that draws you across the room; *Moses* has just such a cover. It has a very spiritual essence that clearly reflects the tone of Weatherford's depiction of Harriet Tubman. On page after page of this biography for young readers, Tubman again and again calls on her faith to guide and protect her.

In many descriptions of Tubman, her faith is mentioned, and her belief that she was protected by and following the will of her God must have contributed to her extraordinary confidence to return to the South, where there was a large reward for her capture, to eventually lead over three hundred slaves to freedom. This would be a good biography to place with others so children can compare the different focus that each author brings to the work.

Genre: Biography

Awards: Coretta Scott King Illustrator Award; Caldecott Honor

Winter, Jeanette. *Follow the Drinking Gourd.* New York: Knopf, Dragon-fly, 1988.

> At night they walked again,
> singing Joe's song
> and looking for the signs
> that marked the trail.
> *The riverbank makes a very good road,*
> *The dead trees will show you the way,*
> *Left foot, peg foot, traveling on,*
> *Follow the drinking gourd.*[9]

This book tells the story of a legendary character who went around teaching slaves a song that had the directions to freedom in its lyrics. Working on different plantations, he would teach the song until slaves had the message, and then he would move on. The song describes the path to freedom as leading to the river, and between two hills to the shore of another river, and then a boat ride to the other side and to the safe houses of the Underground Railroad.

The story takes us along with a family who follows the course and meets with fearful situations along the way: the master's hounds that trail them, the hunger, the hunters who chase them, all the time with the Big Dipper, the Drinking Gourd, in front of them. Finally, after moving from safe house to safe house, they find their way to Canada.

Genre: Historical Fiction/Music

LATER ELEMENTARY

Allen, Thomas B. *Harriet Tubman, Secret Agent: How Daring Slaves and Free Blacks Spied for the Union during the Civil War.* Washington, DC: National Geographic, 2006.

> Slaves uncovered information that only they could get. They had lived their lives as invisible people. That quality of invisibility, which Harriet Tubman knew well, became the basis for using ex-slaves as spies for the Union.[10]

Not much information exists about many of the Civil War spies, as both sides destroyed their documents in order to protect those involved. In this book, Allen pulls together a good deal of what is known about the Union's use of African Americans as spies during that time. Allen uses Harriet Tubman as a line of continuity throughout the text, but the information provided in this small but very informative volume goes far beyond one person's involvement. Illustrations at the beginning introduce the reader to many of the major figures of the time.

Genre: Nonfiction/Informational/Biography

Bial, Raymond. *The Underground Railroad.* New York: Houghton Mifflin, 1995.

> Certainly, tens of thousands of slaves, aided by more than 3,200 railroad "workers," escaped to the northern states and Canada, and today scores of little towns from Maine to Iowa have their secrets about the railroad. It is usually a story talked about at the café or a footnote in a local history book about a runaway who was hidden in an old barn at the edge of town; the child who slipped under a bed when the slave catcher knocked on the door; the husband and wife who held their breath in the attic while the sheriff searched for them downstairs; or the house up the street with a tunnel through which fugitives were smuggled out late at night.[11]

Bial points out early in this book that it is difficult to know the full extent of the people who were involved in the Underground Railroad, because it was forced to operate in secrecy. From the stories that have been told and the artifacts that do exist, Bial has provided readers with photographs, historic pictures, and text that chronicle this amazing piece of history. He asks the reader to imagine wading across the Ohio River, running through the woods in bare feet, and coming upon a safe house in the night.

This book has connections with several of the stories mentioned in this chapter. There is a picture of a doll that is an example of one that Levi Coffin made, with women gathered in her home, to provide comfort to runaway slave children.[12] Bial also tells the story of John Parker, who helped hundreds of slaves escape to freedom, and his incredible effort to reunite an infant with her parents in order to escape.[13]

Genre: Nonfiction/Informational

Burchard, Peter. *Frederick Douglass: For the Great Family of Man.* New York: Atheneum, 2003.

> Less than a year before he died, Douglass went back to his birthplace. His grandmother's cabin was no longer standing. When a reporter asked him why he had returned, he said, "I came to drink water from the old-fashioned well that I drank from many years ago, to see the few old friends that are left of the many I once had, to stand on the old soil once more before I am called away by the great master, and to thank Him for His many blessings to me during my checkered life."[14]

This well-researched volume chronicles the life of one of the greatest, if not the greatest, orators of the nineteenth century. An escaped slave who spent his life working for the freedom of slaves along with the rights of all people, his place in history cannot be endorsed too enthusiastically.

Burchard does an excellent job providing young readers with a thorough look at the events of Douglass's life. Coupling this volume with one in which Douglass's speeches are included would be a wonderful opportunity to visit some of the issues he so eloquently addressed and relate them to his lived experiences. It is particularly interesting to learn about how other public figures of this time, such as those who are mentioned in this chapter, interacted with Douglass.

Genre: Biography

Davis, Ossie. *Escape to Freedom: A Play about Young Frederick Douglass.* New York: Puffin, 1976.

> [My mother] did not live with me, but was hired out by my master to a man who lived about twelve miles down the road, which she had to walk, at night, after she was through working, in order to see me at all. She couldn't stay long, being a field hand—the penalty for not

> showing up in the fields at sunrise was a severe whipping. It was whispered that my master was my father, but my mother, in the few times I ever got to see her, never told me one way or another.[15]

This play was first performed in New York at the Performing Arts Repertory Theater in 1976. It opens with Douglass's early years, starting with his birth in Talbot County, Maryland, in 1817 or 1818, and it ends with the suspenseful moments as he escapes to freedom with borrowed seaman's papers. During the last moments of the play, characters speak to Douglass's later accomplishments, which could be a great beginning to inquiry projects for students.
Genre: Biography
Award: Jane Addams Children's Book Honor

Ferris, Jeri. *Go Free or Die*. Illustrated by Karen Ritz. Minneapolis, MN: Carolrhoda, 1988.

> Harriet made her last trip South in 1861, and then she became a scout, nurse, spy, and cook for the Union army during the Civil War. The Emancipation Proclamation of 1863 freed slaves of the southern states as soon as the Union army took those states. Harriet's dream of freedom for her people came true with the passage of the Thirteenth Amendment in 1865, which absolutely outlawed slavery in all parts of the United States.[16]

This story, written at the same reading level as *The Story of Harriet Tubman, Conductor of the Underground Railroad*, shares many of the details of other books on this subject, but it also introduces some new ones. In one story told here, Tubman is sitting at a train station where her reward poster is displayed. She hears a couple of men talking about her and wondering if she is the sought-after criminal. They dismiss the possibility when she takes a book from under her arm and opens it, since the poster describes her as illiterate. Her fear, since it is true that she could not read, is whether she is holding the book right side up. A mistake like that could mean her capture.
Genre: Biography

Hansen, Joyce, and Gary McGowan. *Freedom Roads: Searching for the Underground Railroad*. Illustrated by James E. Ransome. Chicago: Cricket, 2003.

> A century from now, when students and scholars want to know what life was like in the twentieth and twenty-first centuries, they will have many wonderful resources to help them re-create our history.

Besides books, newspapers, magazines, and government documents, they will have film, video, audio recordings, and photographs.[17]

Not only do Hansen and McGowan tell the story of the Underground Railroad, but they give the reader the background for their
searches and the media they use to gather information and data. They
also show how they synthesize information to create an accurate portrait
of the time and events they are studying. This would be a great opportunity for students to develop an understanding of the process of inquiry
used by these researchers at the same time they are being informed about
this remarkable part of our history.

Genre: Nonfiction/Informational

Haskins, James. *Get on Board: The Story of the Underground Railroad.* New
York: Scholastic, 1993.

> There is a story in Underground Railroad lore that in 1831 a slave
> named Tice Davids ran away from his master in Kentucky. With the
> master in hot pursuit, Davids made his way to the Ohio River, which
> formed the border between the slave state of Kentucky and the free
> state of Ohio. The master saw Davids plunge into the river and, as
> he searched frantically for a boat, kept his eyes on his slave. When he
> set off after his slave in a boat, he went directly toward him. When
> Davids reached the opposite shore near the town of Ripley, Ohio, his
> master was just minutes behind him. But then Tice Davids vanished
> from sight.[18]

Thus begins Haskins's book focused on the Underground Railroad.
In his usual well-crafted approach to sharing history with young readers,
he has again provided a well-researched nonfiction text. Haskins takes
the reader from the folklore of the name of the Underground Railroad
to the distinctive language that was used: the people who worked on it
were called conductors and stationmasters; the people who took it were
referred to as parcels or passengers; the places they went through were
called depots and stations.

Haskins highlights some of the people who became associated with
the Underground Railroad and the dangers slaves placed themselves in by
escaping. He explains how the Fugitive Slave Act not only affected escaped
slaves but also threatened all African Americans because all were in danger
of being identified as escaped slaves and had to prove otherwise if accused.

Genre: Nonfiction/Informational

McCurdy, Michael, ed. *Escape from Slavery:The Boyhood of Frederick Douglass in His Own Words*. New York: Knopf, 1994.

> Very little communication ever took place between us. Death soon ended what little we could have while she lived, and with it her hardships and suffering. She died when I was about seven years old, on one of my master's farms, near Lee's Mill. I was not allowed to be present during her illness, at her death, or burial.[19]

Douglass and his mother were separated when he was "but an infant." When she was able, she would walk the twelve miles after her work to be with him. She would soothe him to sleep but would need to leave and be back in the field at sunrise or be harshly punished. Certainly, had she lived, she would have been enormously proud of his accomplishments. Mother and son never had that opportunity.

Douglass's story of his childhood is available to us because he escaped and was able to record the events of his life and provide significant insights into the events that shaped our nation. His passion for the freedom of all people and his work for human rights marked the rest of his life.

Genre: Autobiography

McGovern, Ann. *"Wanted Dead or Alive":The True Story of Harriet Tubman*. New York: Scholastic, 1965.

> In the little slave cabins they whisper her name and hope she will come soon. In the big plantation houses, the masters wonder, "Who is this person they call Moses?"[20]

This story is an incredible one, full of courage and selfless caring. Born into slavery, Tubman sustained injuries from beatings so severe at seven years old that she carried the scars on her neck throughout her life. Later, again not cooperating with an overseer, she was struck by a heavy iron weight and almost died. She suffered from this injury for the rest of her life, as it caused her to fall asleep unpredictably.

This book shares Tubman's escape from slavery and her assistance to others in their escape on the Underground Railroad. Her ability to lead so many slaves to freedom, including her seventy-year-old parents, in spite of the bounty on her head, made her an icon among the heroes of the pre–Civil War years. Her work during the war, also included in this book, is less widely known, and the fact that she lived to ninety is often not mentioned.

Genre: Biography

McMullan, Kate. *The Story of Harriet Tubman, Conductor of the Underground Railroad*. Illustrated by Steven James Petruccio. New York: Yearling, 1991.

> Harriet looked out at the audience. "Yes, ladies," she began, "I was the conductor of the Underground Railroad for eight years, and I can say what most conductors can't say. I never ran my train off the track and I never lost a passenger."[21]

This book tells pretty much the same story as McGovern's "*Wanted Dead or Alive*" but is written with more detail and is more of a chapter book. The variety of books mentioned in this chapter can make up a very good range of texts for differentiated reading or a comparison of the stories and details for a critical read.

Genre: Biography

Simon, Barbara Brooks. *Escape to Freedom: The Underground Railroad Adventures of Callie and William*. Washington, DC: National Geographic, 2004.

> Over time, the idea of slavery began to trouble some Americans. Many who were troubled were Quakers, members of the Society of Friends, a religious group. Quakers did not believe in slavery. Some began to help slaves escape. Gradually, an informal network of trails and safe houses grew to help slaves run away to freedom. The network was called the Underground Railroad.[22]

Simon provides a mix of information to explain the movements of Callie Taylor and William Ballard as they escape to freedom. Although they are fictionalized characters, their stories represent many untold stories. Their stories and that of Martha Taylor, Callie's grandmother who stays back on the plantation, are included as first-person notes that provide updates on what is happening in the text.

Genre: Nonfiction/Informational

CONCLUSION

The books cited in chapters 2 through 4 give the history of most of the years during which slavery existed in America. These are the stories that have survived in spite of the exclusion of the experiences of African

Americans from much of our nation's written history. We may never know the stories of many African Americans who were involved in important moments of history because they were not included in the recorded history volumes. It is also true that unless we are intentional in our efforts, we may perpetuate this exclusion.

It is safe to say that from the early 1600s to the mid-1800s, Black men and women were in nearly every colony, in every state, in every part of this country. When you look at a history book for colonial times, the Revolutionary War, and Civil War years, look for a person of color, because without authentic representation, the picture is not complete.

Chapter 5 covers the years that led up to the Civil War and the years during which the Civil War was fought. Slavery began to take on a different look as Tubman challenged slave owners, the Underground Railroad actively conducted slaves to freedom, and Douglass put pressure on the nation to live up to its promise of equal birth.

NOTES

1. Hopkinson, *Sweet Clara.*
2. Miller, *Frederick Douglass.*
3. Nelson, *Almost to Freedom.*
4. Rappaport, *Escape from Slavery,* 3.
5. Rappaport, *Freedom River.*
6. Ringgold, *Aunt Harriet's Underground Railroad.*
7. Schroeder, *Minty.*
8. Weatherford, *Moses.*
9. Winter, *Follow the Drinking Gourd.*
10. Allen, *Harriet Tubman,* 95.
11. Bial, *Underground Railroad,* 3.
12. See Micheaux, *Almost to Freedom.*
13. See Rappaport, *Freedom River.*
14. Burchard, *Frederick Douglass,* 197.
15. Davis, *Escape to Freedom,* 6.
16. Ferris, *Go Free or Die,* 62–63.
17. Hansen and McGowan, *Freedom Roads,* viii.
18. Haskins, *Get on Board,* 1.
19. McCurdy, *Escape from Slavery,* 4–5.
20. McGovern, *"Wanted Dead or Alive."*

21. McMullan, *Story of Harriet Tubman*, 99.

22. Simon, *Escape to Freedom*, 4.

BIBLIOGRAPHY OF BOOKS FOR CHILDREN

Allen, Thomas B. *Harriet Tubman, Secret Agent: How Daring Slaves and Free Blacks Spied for the Union during the Civil War.* Washington, DC: National Geographic, 2006.

Bial, Raymond. *The Underground Railroad.* New York: Houghton Mifflin, 1995.

Burchard, Peter. *Frederick Douglass: For the Great Family of Man.* New York: Atheneum, 2003.

Davis, Ossie. *Escape to Freedom: A Play about Young Frederick Douglass.* New York: Puffin, 1976.

Ferris, Jeri. *Go Free or Die.* Illustrated by Karen Ritz. Minneapolis, MN: Carolrhoda, 1988.

Hansen, Joyce, and Gary McGowan. *Freedom Roads: Searching for the Underground Railroad.* Illustrated by James E. Ransome. Chicago: Cricket, 2003.

Haskins, James. *Get on Board: The Story of the Underground Railroad.* New York: Scholastic, 1993.

Hopkinson, Deborah. *Sweet Clara and the Freedom Quilt.* Illustrated by James E. Ransome, New York: Knopf, 1993.

———. *Under the Quilt of Night.* Illustrated by James E. Ransome. New York: Atheneum Books for Young Readers, 2002.

Lawrence, Jacob. *Harriet and the Promised Land.* New York: Aladdin Paperbacks, 1997.

McCurdy, Michael, ed. *Escape from Slavery: The Boyhood of Frederick Douglass in His Own Words.* New York: Knopf, 1994.

McGovern, Ann. *"Wanted Dead or Alive": The True Story of Harriet Tubman.* New York: Scholastic, 1965.

McMullan, Kate. *The Story of Harriet Tubman, Conductor of the Underground Railroad.* Illustrated by Steven James Petruccio. New York: Yearling, 1991.

Miller, William. *Frederick Douglass: The Last Day of Slavery.* Illustrated by Cedric Lucas. New York: Lee and Low, 1995.

Nelson, Vaunda Micheaux. *Almost to Freedom.* Illustrated by Colin Bootman. New York: Scholastic, 2003.

Rappaport, Doreen. *Escape from Slavery: Five Journeys to Freedom.* New York: HarperCollins, 1991.

———. *Freedom River.* Illustrated by Bryan Collier. New York: Hyperion Books for Children, Jump at the Sun, 2000.

Ringgold, Faith. *Aunt Harriet's Underground Railroad in the Sky*. New York: Crown, Dragonfly, 1992.

Schroeder, Alan. *Minty: A Story of Young Harriet Tubman*. Illustrated by Jerry Pinkney. New York: Puffin, 1996.

Simon, Barbara Brooks. *Escape to Freedom: The Underground Railroad Adventures of Callie and William*. Washington, DC: National Geographic, 2004.

Weatherford, Carole Boston. *Moses: When Harriet Tubman Led Her People to Freedom*. Illustrated by Kadir Nelson. New York: Hyperion Books for Children, 2006.

Winter, Jeanette. *Follow the Drinking Gourd*. New York: Knopf, Dragonfly, 1988.

· 5 ·

The Civil War Era

$\mathcal{M}$ilton Meltzer, in *They Came in Chains: The Story of the Slave Ships*, defines human migration as "the movement of people from one place to another, with the intent of settling down in a new country or region."[1] Certainly that has been the case for the millions of people from every part of the world who have come to and settled in America. "But all these people *wished* to change their lives, *wished* to leave home, *wished* to build a new life in what they hoped would be a better place."[2] The largest and most difficult migration to reconcile was very different: "It was a *forced* migration. Between the fifteenth and the nineteenth centuries perhaps 20 million African men, women, and children were captured, bought, or kidnapped by European and American slave traders and sold to labor on the plantations and in the mines of the Americas."[3]

This chapter focuses on the years leading up to the Civil War as well as the years of fighting between the northern states and the southern states that wanted to secede from the Union. By this time, some states had outlawed slavery, and no more slaves were being legally transported on the Middle Passage from Africa: the time permitted for continuing to transport slaves from Africa had expired in 1808. Nevertheless, by the 1860s there were 4 million slaves in the United States.[4] Generation after generation of children born into slavery grew up and had families that had no right to stay together and marriages that could not be legitimized. Slaves who may have kept some semblance of their name of origin from years before by now probably had the name of their slave owner—or no last name at all.

While Blacks fought on both sides of the Revolutionary War, neither side in the Civil War eagerly welcomed them as soldiers. Certainly, they did fight in both the Union and Confederate armies, but especially in the South, they were almost always relegated to support positions rather than armed as soldiers. A good deal of debate still remains regarding how many free Blacks and slaves fought for the Confederacy.

In the years leading up to the war, the dispute over whether slavery should continue became more vocal and was sometimes violent. Although it is often thought that the Civil War started because of slavery, the cause was actually the decision of the southern states to secede from the union of states, or "the Union," as the United States was often called. The role that slavery played evolved over the course of the first years of the war, and by 1863 Lincoln had issued the Emancipation Proclamation that freed the slaves in the Confederate States. It would be two more years before the proclamation would take effect and several additional months—until June 19, 1865, now celebrated as "Juneteenth"—when the last slaves were told of their freedom.

In 1835 the movement to abolish slavery in America was growing stronger. In fact, America was not alone in questioning the practice of slavery:

> Great Britain, which had freed a handful of slaves in the British Isles proper in 1770, abolished slavery entirely in 1833 by emancipating the West Indies, offering twenty million pounds in compensation to slave owners, and with no bloodshed. Not only were British slaves free, but blacks in Canada could vote. American slavery now stood alone in Christendom, a "peculiar institution."[5]

With the growing pressure to end slavery, southern states were able to convince Congress to pass a "gag rule" to prohibit the publication of abolitionist literature. President Andrew Jackson asked Congress to implement severe penalties for circulation through the mail of incendiary publications. With this gag rule, "antislavery petitions could neither be read, discussed, nor acted upon by that body."[6] The gag rule was eventually withdrawn in 1845 due largely to the efforts of John Quincy Adams.

The slave revolts that had taken place in the years around the Revolutionary War had prompted a number of laws that imposed greater and greater restrictions on the movement, assembly, and education of slaves. When the Fugitive Slave Act gave slave owners the right to go into Free States to capture their runaway slaves, even free Blacks were threatened: if they were accused of being runaway slaves and could not prove otherwise, they could be enslaved.

The books discussed in this chapter chronicle this very complex time. Some are stories of slavery and resistance, and some are about a nation preparing for and finally fighting a war that divided the nation, families, and races. There are stories of justice and injustice, bravery and cruelty, hope and sadness. This was a unique time when the country fought against itself.

EARLY ELEMENTARY

Bearden, Romare. *Li'l Dan the Drummer Boy: A Civil War Story*. New York: Simon and Schuster Books for Young Readers, 2003.

Fortunately, twenty years after Bearden wrote and illustrated this story, it is offered to readers. Fortunately, too, Harvard scholar Henry Louis Gates Jr. offers a foreword that shares his acquaintance with Bearden and how he was introduced to his work on this book when he was invited to Bearden's studio years ago. The story of Li'l Dan is a story that, according to Gates, "percolated" in Bearden's mind and reflects not only his great talents as an artist but also his thoughtful look at history.

The story takes place before one of the concluding battles of the Civil War. Slaves are being freed as Union troops march through the South. Li'l Dan, who lost his parents years before, follows the Black Union soldiers in Company E as they march past his home. He takes with him his handmade drum that he has learned to play, imitating the sounds around him. His playing comes in handy at just the right time at the end of the story. This book obviously belongs in the Civil War chapter, but it also has a relationship with the Harlem Renaissance (discussed in chapter 9), the period when Bearden gained fame as an artist.

Genre: Historical Fiction

Polacco, Patricia. *Pink and Say*. New York: Philomel, 1994.

> "Master Aylee had a library full of books right here," he said. "He taught me to read even though it was against the law."
>
> "He must have been a good man," I said.
>
> "More bad than good, Say. Sometimes I think he just liked bein' read to. There was this book of poetry, Say, that was this thick. Every night I'd read out loud to him from that book.

> "I blessed this house because of all those beautiful books . . . but
> I cursed it, too for what it stood for."
>   We walked a bit further.
>   "To be born a slave is a heap o' trouble, Say. But after Aylee taught
> me to read, even though he owned my person, I knew that nobody,
> ever, could really own me."[7]

This book begins as many of Polacco's stories do: she tells her readers that this is a true story told through the generations of her family, and
she is retelling it as it was told to her. The plot opens with Say, a young
white Union soldier who has been shot, lying injured in a field. He is
discovered by Pinkus Aylee, a young Black Union soldier, and taken to
his rescuer's home close by. There he recuperates, and as the two talk
about going back to the army, Say shares his fears and the admission that
he was shot when he was running away from the battle.

Although I have shared this story with early elementary students, it is
not without the realities that war brings, and in this case, Pinkus's mother
is killed by marauders. Both young soldiers are captured and end up in An-
dersonville, the Confederate stockade for captured Union soldiers, where
only one of them survives. I need to warn you that I have never read this
book without crying at the end—and I have read it many, many times.

Genre: Historical Fiction/Biography

Rappaport, Doreen. *Freedom Ship.* Illustrated by Curtis James. New
York: Hyperion Books for Children, 2006.

> Someone is tapping me on the shoulder. "Samuel, git up." . . .
>   "Samuel, put on ya clothes real silent-like," Mama says.
>   "Why?" I ask, in between yawns.
>   "No questions now. Just do as I say."[8]

Rappaport gives the reader a story based on a true event during the
Civil War when an ingenious sailor figured out a way to fool the Confederate soldiers who were guarding the harbor. The sailor escapes with
not only the boat that he usually works on but also the cannons that are
on board. Even with everything planned to the last detail, Robert Small,
with his family and friends on board, moves carefully in the water, hoping that everything he has planned will work perfectly. Fortunately, it
does, and their greatest threat comes when they are in Union territory
and have to identify themselves as friendly, since Small has to fly the
Confederate flag as the boat leaves the harbor.

Rappaport, in a note at the end of the book, tells more of the details about Robert Small (also known as Robert Smalls) and notes that along with this amazing exploit, he distinguished himself with many accomplishments during his long lifetime. Students may find it interesting to compare several books and biographical sketches about his life.

Genre: Historical Fiction/Biography

Vaughan, Marcia K. *Up the Learning Tree*. Illustrated by Derek Blanks. New York: Lee and Low, 2003.

> Before Pap got sold away, he told me book learning would help us escape slavery. That's why white folks don't allow slaves to read.
> There must be something powerful in books, and I want to know what it is.[9]

One of the responsibilities of young slave Henry Bell is to walk his master, Simon, to school each day. Henry begins to hide in a nearby sycamore tree in order to listen to the lessons. He practices his letters by carving them into the branches of the tree. When Simon must stay home, Henry carries his lessons to and from the teacher to correct. The teacher is sympathetic toward Henry and supports his learning until the two are caught.

Genre: Historical Fiction

Woodson, Jacqueline. *Show Way*. Illustrated by Hudson Talbott. New York: Putnam's, 2005.

> At night, Big Mama told the children stories.
> Stories she'd tell in a whisper about
> children growing up and getting themselves free.
> And the children leaned in.
> And listened real hard.[10]

This is the story of a family, of generations that began to be recorded by Woodson, beginning with the great-grandmother of her own great-grandmother, Soonie. In a poem that sings in the reading like a song, Woodson shares her lineage from daughter to daughter using a common thread, the quilts that originally led slaves to freedom. The story moves through the years of slavery until the end of the Civil War, when Soonie was born. Soonie's granddaughters witnessed the civil rights years. Woodson's story comes full cycle to the present with the birth of her own daughter, Toshi Georgiana. The illustrations combine dreamlike images in watercolor with collages made from newspapers and pictures from history. The combination of text and illustration is powerful.

Woodson gives young readers a story that will help them understand the concept that slavery was not something that impacted Americans for only one or two generations. It was a reality for many generations, and in that time people who were family were too frequently separated and killed and names of ancestors lost.

Genre: Historical Fiction/Biography
Award: Newbery Honor

LATER ELEMENTARY

Bolden, Tonya. *Maritcha: A Nineteenth-Century American Girl*. New York: Abrams, 2004.

> Too, many white New Yorkers, poor to wealthy, had come to hate the war because they felt it was less about keeping the North and the South one nation and more about ending slavery. And many of them had no quarrel with slavery. Many had grown rich from doing business with slaveholders—buying their raw materials, reaped from slave labor, for manufacture of goods; selling them luxury items, and making money from loans to them. Poor whites saw abolition as a threat to their livelihoods: more free blacks would mean stiffer competition for jobs.[11]

Bolden has done an amazing job of bringing Maritcha Rémond Lyons's memoir and all of the artifacts and documentation that surround her life together for young readers to examine and learn from. This is made all the more important because events that might be referred to in other contexts, like the reaction to the draft for the Civil War, can be seen through the experiences of this family whose house was attacked by mobs over the course of several days because of the violent response from angry White rioters.

Lyons's struggle to be allowed to complete high school and her career as a teacher and assistant principal in New York make for fascinating reading. This book, a wonderful find, will make an important contribution to the work of young researchers.

Genre: Nonfiction/Informational/Biography
Award: Coretta Scott King Author Honor

Brooks, Victor. *African Americans in the Civil War*. Philadelphia: Chelsea House, 2000.

> Old men and women who had lived their lives in slavery tottered up to the African-American soldiers and exclaimed, "Thank God that I have lived to see this day!"[12]

This thin volume covers the Civil War from the first gathering of troops in 1861 through Lee's surrender in 1865. What makes this book unique is its focus on the role that African Americans played in both the Union and Confederate armies. Although many of these individuals, particularly in the South, were used in service positions, this book emphasizes the role of those who actually served as soldiers. This book would serve well as a companion to a more general book on the soldiers of the Civil War.

Genre: Nonfiction/Informational

Brown, Susan Taylor. *Robert Smalls Sails to Freedom*. Illustrated by Felicia Marshall. Minneapolis, MN: Millbrook, 2006.

> When Robert was 17, he married a slave named Hannah. He still worked for Mr. McKee. But Robert was allowed to keep a little money for himself. Still, Robert was not happy. He and his wife still belonged to white owners. Even his new baby, Elizabeth Lydia, belonged to Hannah's master. They could each be sold to different owners at any time. Then they might lose each other forever. Robert hated that. He wanted to keep his family safe.[13]

This is a very powerful story for early readers. Smalls's commitment to freedom for himself, his family, and several other slaves who wished to make their escape with him leads to an ingenious and successful escape plan that is a spellbinder. His success as a sailor in the Union navy after his escape and his life of accomplishment make his story an important example of our nation's brilliant patriots. Because of his work as a legislator after the war, Smalls might be a good topic for an inquiry project as one discusses the later years of Reconstruction.

Genre: Biography

DeAngelis, Gina. *The Massachusetts 54th: African American Soldiers of the Union*. Mankato, MN: Bridgestone, 2003.

> In the summer of 1861, General John Fremont freed slaves in Missouri and Kansas. He then enlisted them in the Union Army. Union

leaders did not approve of these actions, and Lincoln removed Fremont from his command.[14]

This book comes from the Let Freedom Ring series and provides the reader with a well-organized and understandable book about the formation of the Massachusetts 54th, the events that led up to its creation, and the remarkable role it played in the Union victory. Drawings, photos, and pictures of artifacts help the reader create greater understandings from the text.

Genre: Nonfiction/Informational

Hamilton, Virginia. *Anthony Burns: The Defeat and Triumph of a Fugitive Slave*. New York: Knopf, 1988.

> The prisoner was definitely the slave Anthony Burns. He had admitted as much when he had first faced the colonel. It was a simple matter, then, of going through the proceeding according to law. Colonel Suttle had provided an affidavit of ownership, and Commissioner Loring had issued a warrant for Burns' arrest. There would be a hearing as soon as possible, it was hoped—all strictly according to provisions of the Fugitive Slave Act.[15]

Hamilton uses extensive research and thoughtful and creative connecting to make Anthony Burns's experiences come to life. After young Burns escaped slavery in Virginia, he made his way to Boston, Massachusetts, where he was captured. Because of the Fugitive Slave Act, runaway slaves were no longer safe when they reached the North; it was now legal for slave owners to reclaim their slaves and transport their "property" back to the South. This would have happened to Burns if abolitionists had not heard about the case and argued for his release. Although sentiments were strong for many in the North to disallow the law, it was a federal mandate and Burns found himself a slave again.

Transported back to the South, Burns was harshly imprisoned and sold again. At the time of his sale, the auctioneer pledged not to allow anyone from the North to bid, angry that they would intend to free him. Fortunately, by chance, his supporters in Boston were able to find out his whereabouts and were also able to purchase his freedom from his new owner.

This remarkable story is particularly interesting because it shows the intensity of the reaction to the efforts of the abolitionists by the southern slaveholders. Their reaction, of course, was directed at Burns after he was sent back to the South, and his life was in jeopardy by a mob mentality of outrage and revenge. This would be an excellent read for inquiry into the Fugitive Slave Act and to get an understanding of the intensity of the debate that raged between abolitionists and slaver owners and, most of all, how a young man was the victim of first slavery and then of a law that would take away his freedom and, for a time, his hope of a new life.

Genre: Biography

Award: Jane Addams Books for Older Children Award

Jurmain, Suzanne. *The Forbidden Schoolhouse: The True and Dramatic Story of Prudence Crandall and Her Students.* New York: Houghton Mifflin, 2005.

> She saw that "the prejudice of the whites against color was deep." For the first time in her life, as she explained in a newspaper article, Prudence began to wonder if she could do something—anything—that "might . . . serve the people of color."[16]

This is a true story. Prudence Crandall was a young White teacher at a White girls' school in Canterbury, Connecticut, in 1831. Slavery was still legal, and Nat Turner had just led a revolt that had terrified White southerners. In Connecticut, there were few African Americans and far fewer slaves. Crandall wasn't an abolitionist, but she had been raised a Quaker, so she had been taught that slavery was wrong. It was when her Black housekeeper introduced her to the *Liberator*, an abolitionist newspaper, that she began to develop a passion to contribute to a change in the treatment of African Americans. She admitted a young Black woman to her school, which created a stir in the town. She then decided to admit only Black women to her school, and that was the beginning of a hateful and violent response from town members that finally resulted in her having to close her school in spite of the help of strong allies.

It is interesting that this story was happening at the same time that slavery was very much a part of the American southern landscape. It is also a story of northern prejudice and violence against any advancement of African Americans. At the end of her life, Crandall did have some small recognition for her personal dedication to this effort.

Genre: Nonfiction/Informational/Biography

Award: Orbis Pictus Award for Outstanding Nonfiction for Children Honor

McKissack, Patricia C. Amistad: *The Story of a Slave Ship*. Illustrated by Sanna Stanley. New York: Grosset and Dunlap, 2005.

> On board the *Amistad*, the officers asked the Spanish sailors what had happened. The sailors said the *Amistad* was a slave ship. They told how Joseph Cinque and fifty-three other slaves had killed the captain and taken over the ship. The sailors were hostages. All that was true. But the two Spanish sailors claimed that the Africans had been born in Cuba. That was a lie.[17]

You might ask, "Why would the sailors have lied about where these slaves were from?" Since the year was 1839, it was well beyond the date of 1808 that the Constitution had set as an end to the kidnapping and transporting of slaves from Africa. Thus, the ship was acting illegally, and that argument would become the basis of the slaves' defense in a legal case that would eventually lead to the Supreme Court of the United States.

Writing for the young reader, McKissack explains the background of the leader of the slave revolt onboard the *Amistad*. Born into the Mende tribe, Sengbe Pieh was a prosperous farmer and leader in his village. Kidnapped one day as he walked alone, he was forced onto a slave ship and taken first to Cuba, where his name was changed to Joseph Cinque. There, he and the other slaves were sold and put on the *Amistad*, but once the *Amistad* set sail, they were able to take over the ship. Prevented from reaching Africa, they spent two years in legal wrangling before their case closed in their favor. This is a good example of how a case moved through the judicial system, even in 1839.

Genre: Nonfiction/Informational

McKissack, Patricia C., and Fredrick L. McKissack. *Christmas in the Big House, Christmas in the Quarters*. Illustrated by John Thompson. New York: Scholastic, 1994.

> At last the master hands out passes to the slaves he's allowing to spend the holiday week with a family member on a nearby plantation. Shout hallelujah! A husband's gon' get to visit his wife. Clap your hands and jump for joy! A daughter's gon' get to visit her mammy. It's reunion time for families sold away from their loved ones. They'll be together again . . . if only for a little while.[18]

Slaves and their owners both celebrated Christmas, but in very different ways. This book details those differences as it shares with the reader what Christmas might have looked like on a plantation in 1859. The similarities of joy and togetherness are tempered by the very real differences of ownership, separation from family, backbreaking work, and absolute poverty. Although slaves might have experienced happiness at Christmas, it was also the time when they would learn of their fate for the upcoming year, which could include being sold away from family. Extensive notes make this a useful book, and the lively text helps readers feel as if they are truly part of Christmas on this plantation six years before the end of slavery.

Genre: Nonfiction/Informational

Awards: Coretta Scott King Author Award; Orbis Pictus Award for Outstanding Nonfiction Author Honor

McKissack, Patricia C., and Fredrick L. McKissack. *Sojourner Truth: Ain't I a Woman?* New York: Scholastic, 1992.

> "What is your last name?" the woman asked.
>
> Sojourner didn't know what to say. All her life she'd been Hardenbergh's Belle, Dumont's Belle, always her master's names. Then the thought came beautifully complete. "The only master I have now is God and His name is Truth." So she gave herself the last name Truth.
>
> "Sojourner Truth is my name," she answered, adding, "because from this day I will walk in the light of His truth."[19]

Consistent with their other work, the McKissacks provide their readers with comprehensive, well-researched background to tell a story from history. In this case, they share the story of Sojourner Truth from her early years through her years in freedom working as an abolitionist and women's rights advocate. Portions of her writing that are shared regarding post–Civil War Reconstruction and the women's rights movements of the late 1800s and early 1900s can be helpful in understanding this history.

One can't come away from reading about Truth without recognizing that she is one of the strongest orators in American history. Her ability to speak clearly and deliberately about complex and contentious issues will hopefully serve to keep her words alive forever.

Genre: Biography

Award: Coretta Scott King Author Honor

Myers, Walter Dean. Amistad: *A Long Road to Freedom*. New York: Puffin, 1997.

> Slavery was not ended, but the efforts of many people—the abolitionists; the people of New Haven, Farmington, and New York; as well as students and teachers for Yale—brought the plight of all people of African descent into sharp focus. The real conflict between those natural rights of which Thomas Jefferson speaks in the Declaration of Independence and the positive laws that allowed people to be enslaved was not settled until the end of the Civil War. But the victory of those who struggled so that the *Amistad* captives could go free brought more and more people into that struggle to secure freedom for all.[20]

This book provides a detailed description of the events that took place onboard the *Amistad* as well as the years that followed. This is an important story as it chronicles a case where the judicial system eventually arrived at a just decision. Unfortunately, the men who had been kidnapped and fought for their freedom were forced to fight for their freedom again in a country that stands for freedom.

Genre: Nonfiction/Informational

Rappaport, Doreen. *No More! Stories and Songs of Slave Resistance*. Illustrated by Shane W. Evans. Cambridge, MA: Candlewick, 2002.

> Free blacks and slaves had fought with distinction in the American Revolution and the War of 1812. They were eager to fight with the Union now. Frederick Douglass urged President Lincoln to enlist free blacks. Douglass was shocked and angered when Lincoln rejected the idea. The President feared that the border states would leave the Union if blacks were allowed to fight. Most white Northerners weren't eager to fight alongside black men, whom they considered inferior. In fact, most Northern soldiers were not fighting to end slavery. They were fighting to bring the Southern states back into the Union.[21]

In this book of song, poetry, and narrative, Rappaport covers the history of the African American experience from the beginning years of slavery to the end of slavery with the Thirteenth Amendment to the Constitution. This is a very honest telling of stories of individuals whose lives were touched by slavery and, with Evans's illustrations depicting each story with brilliant artistry, makes for a powerful picture book. In the introduction, Rappaport describes a poem by Harriet Wheatley that gave her an insight into slavery. The poem is of a daughter describing her father as a man who was not a slave: although he was in bondage, he saw beyond what those around him could see. The excellence in research that supports Rappaport's work is typical of her many offerings that include Black history.

Genre: Nonfiction/Informational/Music

Rockwell, Anne. *Only Passing Through: The Story of Sojourner Truth.* Illustrated by R. Gregory Christie. New York: Dell Dragonfly, 2000.

> Strangers stared while the auctioneer poked and pointed at the girl with his stick—showing how tall and strong she was. He promised that since she was only about nine years old and already so tall, she'd soon be able to do the work of any man.[22]

It was 1806 in Kingston, New York. That day, Isabella Baumfree, who years later would rename herself Sojourner Truth, was sold after the auctioneer offered to include a flock of sheep in the deal. Purchased by an English-speaking owner and speaking only Dutch herself, she did not know what he was asking her to do, and she was whipped so often and so harshly that she carried the scars for life.

After finally being purchased by a man she trusted, he betrayed her by reneging on his promise to set her free, which meant that she would remain a slave for one more year, since New York had outlawed slavery effective at the end of that year. Frustrated and angry, she ran away and took refuge at the home of an abolitionist couple who immediately confronted her owner, purchased her, and set her free, explaining that they did not believe in slavery. Sojourner Truth became an outspoken abolitionist herself, and when she found that her son had been sold out of state to someone in Alabama, which was then against the law in New York, she went to court and got him returned. With her intelligence and courage, her physical stature, and her beautiful voice, she lived the rest of her life delivering the message of freedom.

Genre: Biography
Award: Coretta Scott King Illustrator Honor

Tingle, Tim. *Crossing Bok Chitto: A Choctaw Tale of Friendship and Freedom.* Illustrated by Jeanne Rorex Bridges. El Paso, TX: Cinco Puntos, 2006.

> There is a river called Bok Chitto that cuts through Mississippi. In the days before the War Between the States, in the days before the

Trail of Tears, Bok Chitto was a boundary. On one side of the river lived the Choctaws, a nation of Indian people. On the other side lived the plantation owners and their slaves. If a slave escaped and made his way across Bok Chitto, the slave was free. The slave owner could not follow. That was the law.[23]

There are many historical instances of Black Americans and Native Americans forming alliances. Many escaped slaves found refuge among Native American communities. This story, retold from the folklore of the Choctaw nation, tells of a friendship and an escape, of a family soon to be torn apart by the sale of the mother, and of how the courage of two young friends saves the escaping slave family from the guards, dogs, and guns by their use of a secret stone path across the Bok Chitto River.

Genre: Historical Fiction

MIDDLE GRADES

Fleischman, Paul. *Bull Run*. New York: HarperCollins, 1993.

To be a Negro living in the midst of whites, unknown to them, is to be a ghost spying on the living. Oftentimes I felt I must have joined the Southern army by mistake. The soldiers mercilessly abused a stuttering black cook in our company and tormented the collie dog he'd brought with him. Most of them said they were fighting against secession, not against slavery. Some declared they'd rather shoot Negroes than the Rebels. My ears burned at such words.[24]

Fleischman tells this story through the voices of sixteen very different characters, eight from the North and eight from the South. Each shares his or her own experience of the beginnings of the Civil War, from those going to fight to those who see the battles as mere amusement. In this manner, the reader gets a varied view of how those living through this time may have experienced these events.

Genre: Historical Fiction

Fox, Paula. *The Slave Dancer*. New York: Bantam Doubleday Dell Books for Young Readers, 1973.

At first, I made a promise to myself: I would do nothing that was connected ever so faintly with the importing and sale and use of slaves. But I soon discovered that everything I considered bore, some-where along the way, the imprint of black hands.[25]

This book is a classic. In 1840, Jessie, a young White boy, is kid-napped from New Orleans by the captain of a slave ship. His role is to play his fife for newly captured slaves, who will be forced to dance in or-der to keep their muscles in shape. The ship sails to Africa, then heads back with the cargo of slaves. When the slave ship is almost caught in its illegal activity, since this capture of slaves is happening long after the 1808 deadline ending the importation of slaves from Africa, most of the slaves are thrown overboard in a scene that is horrifying to imagine. A storm ensues, and only Jessie and one young slave survive. Both of their lives are forever changed. This book remains as vivid and important to-day as when it was first published.

Genre: Historical Fiction

Hansen, Joyce. *Which Way Freedom?* New York: Avon, 1986.

> Buka patted Obi's knee with his wrinkled hand. "You born a man, not a slave—that the thing to remember. You got to learn which way freedom be. It here first," he said, touching his own creased forehead. "In you own mind."[26]

As the Civil War begins, Obi realizes that he needs to escape. If he remains, he will not only be a slave, he will be a slave fighting for the Confederate Army. He and two others make a daring escape, with Obi hoping to find his mother, from whom he was taken as a young child. Instead he finds himself first a slave soldier, then a free soldier. This book gives a clear sense of the temporary and fragile nature of relationships among slaves and among Civil War soldiers, all of them facing danger on a daily basis.

Genre: Historical Fiction

Lester, Julius. *From Slave Ship to Freedom Road*. Illustrated by Rod Brown. New York: Puffin, 1998.

> I think often of those ancestors of mine whose names I do not know, whose names I will never know, those ancestors who saw people thrown into the sea like promises casually made and easily broken. It was primarily the youngest and strongest who survived the Middle Passage, that three-month-long ocean voyage from the western

shores of Africa to the so-called New World. My ancestors might have been young when the slave ship left, but when it docked, they were haunted by memories of kinsmen tossed into the sea like promises never meant to be kept, and of gulls crying like mourners. They could still hear the wind wailing at the sight of black bodies bobbing in blue water like bottles carrying notes nobody would ever read.[27]

This is a picture book that asks the reader to think deeply about the events and history of slavery. It is personal as Lester, reflecting on his own exploration into the history of his ancestors, finds himself "begging, pleading, imploring you [the reader] not to be passive, but to invest your soul and imagine yourself into the images."[28] Throughout the book, Lester prompts the reader to answer questions. Sometimes they are directed at Whites, sometimes at Blacks, and sometimes at both. The reader is asked to look at Brown's paintings, stark and real, and answer him.

This book was written thirty years after *To Be a Slave* (below), and again Lester has given voice to the voiceless: the men, women, and children lost to the ocean depths and the days enslaved. Lester conveys well the violence, terror, and inhumanity that was slavery.

Genre: Nonfiction/Informational

Lester, Julius. *To Be a Slave.* Illustrated by Tom Feelings. New York: Puffin, 1968.

To be a slave. To be owned by another person, as a car, house, or table is owned. To live as a piece of property that could be sold—a child sold from its mother, a wife from her husband. To be considered not human, but a "thing" that plowed the fields, cut the wood, cooked the food, nursed another's child; a "thing" whose sole function was determined by the one who owned you.

To be a slave. To know, despite the suffering and deprivation, that you were human. To know joy, laughter, sorrow, and tears and yet be considered only the equal of a table.

To be a slave was to be a human being under conditions in which that humanity was denied. They were not slaves. They were people. Their condition was slavery.[29]

This award-winning classic holds its importance over time. Lester's research allows his readers to hear the voices of the past. The stories from the lives of slaves speak to many different experiences: some carry the memories of slaves they had known, some recount the stories they had heard from someone who had been captured in Africa. Many of the stories that are shared reveal the day-to-day lives of work, preparation of meals, and community, along with the horror of witnessing or being the victim of harsh punishment. There are stories of lives filled with dreams of freedom and acts of resistance. Whatever they chose to share, their voices are powerful. Lester's introductions to each chapter help the reader contextualize the stories shared.

Genre: Nonfiction/Informational

Award: Newbery Honor

Lyons, Mary E. *Letters from a Slave Girl: The Story of Harriet Jacobs*. New York: Simon Pulse, 1992.

Told in the form of letters, this book is based on the true story of Harriet Jacobs, her passion for freedom, and the hardships she met in her pursuit of this freedom. In these letters, Jacobs writes about the pre–Civil War years, when she escapes and becomes a fugitive hidden seven years in a small crawlspace close to her old home. Even from her hiding place, she can hear and sometimes sees the events unfolding around her, and she describes the increasing fear among slave owners that their slaves will revolt and attack them. She shares with her readers the horrors that surround these fears, which take over after any revolt of slaves against their owners. The lives of slaves become even more dangerous, and for Jacobs, conditions are so intolerable that she is willing to live for seven years in a space not much larger than two coffins until she can finally escape to real freedom.

Genre: Biography

Award: Jane Addams Children's Book Honor

Pinkney, Andrea Davis. *Silent Thunder: A Civil War Story*. New York: Hyperion, Jump at the Sun, 1999.

> Clem was hugging himself. He was rocking with the heat of his own words. "Oh, freedom, you so sweet. I gots to get to you. *Gots* to! . . . *Will* find you, freedom—*will*. Any, any way I can. Won't stop till I do. Comin' to you, freedom—soon. Getting' me *free*.[30]

This work of historical fiction is based on real events and places, and the characters are based on photographs that drew the author in.

Silent thunder, young Rosco tells us in the book, is a kind of strong desire that one can feel deep inside. Each of the characters in this book has a silent thunder, including the ever-present desire for freedom and the desire to learn to read.

Set in 1862, this book portrays well the reality of life as a slave during the Civil War and at the very edge of emancipation. Rosco and his little sister, Summer, live with their mother at the Parnell plantation. During the course of the book, the silent thunder of each of the children swells and causes both moments of concern and moments of bravery.

Genre: Historical Fiction

CONCLUSION

With the end of the Civil War came the end of slavery. But what were slaves to do? They had freedom but they had no home, no money, and no job:

> After a lifetime of slavery they received no recompense for past labor, just as the slave-holders received no recompense for their loss, through emancipation, of some two billion dollars in human property. The South was in shambles, its major cities gutted and shelled, its farms neglected, crops ungathered, banks closed, Confederate money worthless and about one-third of its male citizens killed or wounded.
>
> For both Black and White men there was a prospect of desolation and starvation but the immediate future looked bleaker for the Negroes. To cope with this situation, in March 1865, Congress set up the Freedmen's Bureau under the Army.[31]

The war was over and slaves were free, but the country was not at peace with itself. The divisions that had prompted the war were still very much present. The freedom of the slaves, so important to humanity, did not have the emancipating impact it could have had if provisions had been made for a transition of property and the means for self-sufficiency. While the Freedmen's Bureau attempted to meet the needs of the newly freed slaves, resources were never equal to the task. Chapter 6 presents the years that followed the end of the Civil War, the complex and difficult time called Reconstruction.

NOTES

1. Meltzer, *They Came in Chains*, 7.
2. Meltzer, *They Came in Chains*, 7.
3. Meltzer, *They Came in Chains*, 7–9.
4. Buckley, *American Patriots*, 57.
5. Buckley, *American Patriots*, 63.
6. Buckley, *American Patriots*, 62.
7. Polacco, *Pink and Say*.
8. Rappaport, *Freedom Ship*.
9. Vaughan, *Up the Learning Tree*.
10. Woodson, *Show Way*.
11. Bolden, *Maritcha*, 24.
12. Brooks, *African Americans*, 59.
13. Brown, *Robert Smalls*, 16.
14. DeAngelis, *Massachusetts 54th*, 12.
15. Hamilton, *Anthony Burns*, 36.
16. Jurmain, *Forbidden Schoolhouse*, 7.
17. McKissack, *Amistad*, 22.
18. McKissack and McKissack, *Christmas in the Big House*, 19.
19. McKissack and McKissack, *Sojourner Truth*, 77.
20. Myers, *Amistad*, 89.
21. Rappaport, *No More!* n.p.
22. Rockwell, *Only Passing Through*.
23. Tingle, *Crossing Bok Chitto*.
24. Fleischman, *Bull Run*, 39.
25. Fox, *Slave Dancer*, 151.
26. Hansen, *Which Way Freedom?* 76.
27. Lester, *From Slave Ship to Freedom Road*, 6.
28. Lester, *From Slave Ship to Freedom Road*, author's note.
29. Lester, *To Be a Slave*, 28.
30. Pinkney, *Silent Thunder*, 176.
31. Hughes and Meltzer, *Pictorial History*, 188.

BIBLIOGRAPHY OF BOOKS FOR CHILDREN

Bearden, Romare. *Li'l Dan the Drummer Boy: A Civil War Story*. New York: Simon and Schuster Books for Young Readers, 2003.

Bolden, Tonya. *Maritcha: A Nineteenth-Century American Girl.* New York: Abrams, 2004.

Brooks, Victor. *African Americans in the Civil War.* Philadelphia: Chelsea House, 2000.

Brown, Susan Taylor. *Robert Smalls Sails to Freedom.* Illustrated by Felicia Marshall. Minneapolis, MN: Millbrook, 2006.

DeAngelis, Gina. *The Massachusetts 54th: African American Soldiers of the Union.* Mankato, MN: Bridgestone, 2003.

Fleischman, Paul. *Bull Run.* New York: HarperCollins, 1993.

Fox, Paula. *The Slave Dancer.* New York: Bantam Doubleday Dell Books for Young Readers, 1973.

Hamilton, Virginia. *Anthony Burns: The Defeat and Triumph of a Fugitive Slave.* New York: Knopf, 1988.

Hansen, Joyce. *Which Way Freedom?* New York: Avon, 1986.

Jurmain, Suzanne. *The Forbidden Schoolhouse: The True and Dramatic Story of Prudence Crandall and Her Students.* New York: Houghton Mifflin, 2005.

Lester, Julius. *From Slave Ship to Freedom Road.* Illustrated by Rod Brown. New York: Puffin, 1998.

———. *To Be a Slave.* Illustrated by Tom Feelings. New York: Puffin, 1968.

Lyons, Mary E. *Letters From a Slave Girl: The Story of Harriet Jacobs.* New York: Simon Pulse, 1992.

McKissack, Patricia C. *Amistad: The Story of a Slave Ship.* Illustrated by Sanna Stanley. New York: Grosset and Dunlap, 2005.

McKissack, Patricia C. and Fredrick L. McKissack. *Christmas in the Big House, Christmas in the Quarters.* Illustrated by John Thompson. New York: Scholastic, 1994.

———. *Sojourner Truth: Ain't I a Woman?* New York: Scholastic, 1992.

Myers, Walter Dean. *Amistad: A Long Road to Freedom.* New York: Puffin, 1997.

Pinkney, Andrea Davis. *Silent Thunder: A Civil War Story.* New York: Hyperion, Jump at the Sun, 1999.

Polacco, Patricia. *Pink and Say.* New York: Philomel, 1994.

Rappaport, Doreen. *Freedom Ship.* Illustrated by Curtis James. New York: Hyperion Books for Children, 2006.

Rappaport, Doreen. *No More! Stories and Songs of Slave Resistance.* Illustrated by Shane W. Evans. Cambridge, MA: Candlewick, 2002.

Rockwell, Anne. *Only Passing Through: The Story of Sojourner Truth.* Illustrated by R. Gregory Christie. New York: Dell Dragonfly, 2000.

Tingle, Tim. *Crossing Bok Chitto: A Choctaw Tale of Friendship and Freedom.* Illustrated by Jeanne Rorex Bridges. El Paso, TX: Cinco Puntos, 2006.

Vaughan, Marcia K. *Up the Learning Tree.* Illustrated by Derek Blanks. New York: Lee and Low, 2003.

Woodson, Jacqueline. *Show Way*. Illustrated by Hudson Talbott. New York: Putnam's, 2005.

BIBLIOGRAPHY OF REFERENCE WORKS

Buckley, Gail. *American Patriots: The Story of Blacks in the Military From the Revo-
lution to Desert Storm*. New York: Random House, 2001.
Hughes, Langston, and Milton Meltzer. *A Pictorial History of the Negro in Amer-
ica*, new rev. ed. New York: Crown, 1963.
Meltzer, Milton. *They Came in Chains: The Story of the Slave Ships*. New York:
Benchmark, 2000.

· 6 ·

Hope and Reconstruction
after the Civil War

As the early winter months of 1865 came on, the Confederacy fell
apart. Union armies had control of important sections of the South.
Many of its cities lay in ruins. Fields, crops, and homes were destroyed. A third of its white men were dead or wounded. And
many—black and white alike—were hungry and homeless.

On March 4, 1865, President Lincoln took again the oath of office, appealing to America "to do all which may achieve a just and
lasting peace." On April 9, General Lee surrendered to General Grant
at Appomattox Courthouse. The Confederate government evapo-
rated. On April 14, while watching a play at Ford's Theatre in Washington, Lincoln was shot by John Wilkes Booth. He died the next
morning without regaining consciousness. His vice president, Andrew Johnson of Tennessee, became president.[1]

Surely there has been no other time in the history of the United States
when the nation was as stretched to deal with the incredibly complex needs
of so many citizens. The four-year Civil War had left the North and the
South with far fewer men. It is estimated that 620,000 men died from battle and disease, and those who survived were not necessarily whole: "in
1866, the year after war's end, Mississippi spent one-fifth of its revenue on
artificial arms and legs for returning veterans."[2] The landscape in parts of
the South was devastated. Survivors of the war spoke of burned barns,
chimneys standing without houses around them and roofless, windowless,
doorless houses on farmland that "had no cattle, hogs, sheep, or horses or
anything else."[3] In this landscape, 4 million newly freed slaves found themselves homeless and penniless in an angry land. But, for African Americans
who had been enslaved, there was unspeakable joy and relief. For, in spite
of the incredibly difficult situation they found themselves in, they were free.

It is hard to know what would have happened differently if Lincoln had lived. With his death, the plans that he had envisioned for peace after the Civil War were in the hands of the new president, Andrew Johnson. A Freedmen's Bureau had already been created for the purpose of meeting some of the immediate needs of freed slaves.

> The Bureau was to "distribute clothing, food, and fuel to destitute freedmen and oversee 'all subjects' related to their condition in the South. Despite its unprecedented responsibilities and powers, the Bureau was clearly envisioned as a temporary expedient, for not only was its life span limited to one year, but incredibly, no budget was appropriated—it would have to draw funds and staff from the War Department."[4]

Most of the freedmen had never been allowed an education and were most eager to have schools for their children and themselves. The Freedmen's Bureau helped facilitate the establishment of schools, and even though "most schools for blacks had poor facilities, inadequate supplies, and insufficient teachers . . . African Americans attended them in larger and larger numbers."[5] In fact, it is reported that their thirst for knowledge was so great that "when a Freedmen's Bureau agent told a group of 3,000 they were to have schools, he reported that 'their joy knew no bounds.' . . . When school opened, parents often sat in classrooms with children. As soon as they could read and write, the new learners taught others."[6]

The first two years of Reconstruction were called Presidential Reconstruction. During those years, the divisions that had driven the country to war had not disappeared, and as different factions clashed, President Johnson appeared to side with ex-Confederates, whom he pardoned liberally. He also vetoed a bill to make the Freedmen's Bureau permanent. "Aroused by the refusal of most southern states to ratify the Fourteenth Amendment protecting Negro citizenship, by the revival of the Black Codes of slavery days and by growing violence against the Negro,"[7] in 1867, congress approved its own Reconstruction Act. This act, which led to a period known as Congressional Reconstruction, provided military occupation of the South for the protection of the newfound rights of African Americans. It also stipulated that new constitutions for states be drawn up and that the Fourteenth Amendment be ratified by states before they sought admission to the Union.[8] During Congressional Reconstruction, "many blacks got a chance to go to school, to vote, and to hold public office."[9]

Black representation in government began to be realized as many well-educated, politically minded African Americans were allowed to come in from the sidelines and participate in government. Many outstanding political figures emerged during this era and became elected or appointed representatives. Almost simultaneously, reaction from angry Whites grew, and violence from organized gangs such as the Ku Klux Klan, the White Brotherhood, and the White Camellia terrorized local lawmakers and voters. Courts in the South began the practice of sentencing Blacks to terms of servitude that replicated the position many had just been freed from.

The election of President Rutherford B. Hayes marked the end of Reconstruction. In 1877 the president ordered federal troops removed from the South. With the "illegal terror and state laws limiting Negro suffrage . . . the South again became the 'solid South' "[10] Throughout the Presidential Reconstruction and Congressional Reconstruction periods, there were definitely gains made. There were also incredible forces at work against the freed slaves and the free-born Blacks, denying them the freedoms that the Constitution now promised. Some freed slaves had been given the right to settle on land, only to find that it would be taken back by repatriated southern plantation owners. Schools would be built, and then angry mobs would burn them to the ground. The right to vote would be attained, and Black citizens would have to risk their lives to actually vote.[11]

The books described in this chapter present aspects of what some people might have experienced in this complex and troubled time. Some of the books cover more than one time period but are included here because they can help students better understand the complicated period of Reconstruction.

EARLY ELEMENTARY

Bradby, Marie. *More Than Anything Else*. Illustrated by Chris K. Soentpiet. New York: Scholastic, 1995.

> Before light—while the stars still twinkle—Papa, my brother John, and I leave our cabin and take the main road out of town, headed to work. The road hugs the ridge between the Kanawha River and the mountain. We travel it by lantern. My stomach rumbles, for we had

no morning meal. But it isn't really a meal I want, though I would not turn one down.[12]

This is a fictionalized story of the early life of Booker T. Washington. The story takes place right after the war ends, when former slaves can now go where they choose. As he heads off to work shoveling salt into barrels for transporting it from the saltworks, nine-year-old Washington longs to learn to read. Now that his family is free, learning to read is not against the law, but there are still many obstacles. Who will teach him? When will he have time to learn? Where will he get the books? There are no libraries to access books. With the need to earn money, this child works all day. Without the ability to attend school, where will he find teachers? It may be helpful to have children speculate about these questions to help them understand this period of history.

As it turns out, in the evening when the people in the town get together to tell stories and visit, Washington hears a man reading aloud from a newspaper to a group gathered around him. His dad and brother urge him home, where he tells his mother how much he wants to learn to read. Later, when she provides him with an alphabet book, he finds the man who had been the reader that evening, who teaches him the alphabet in a song and how the letters sound in words. Washington is joyous about his new discovery.

Genre: Historical Fiction/Biography

Hopkinson, Deborah. *A Band of Angels: A Story Inspired by the Jubilee Singers*. Illustrated by Raúl Colón. New York: Atheneum, 1999.

The young narrator of our story loves to hear her Aunt Beth tell the story of great-great-grandmother Ella. As the story goes, Ella was born into slavery. After the Civil War, Ella becomes one of the first students at Fisk University, where she joins the choir. When the choir director decides to raise funds for the school by taking the choir on a tour of the North, Ella is among those who summon the courage to go along. They find themselves turned away from some restaurants and hotels, but they persevere. As they sing the songs they expect their White audiences will want to hear, they face little success. Fearing the closing of Fisk University that they are trying to forestall, one night, Ella breaks out into a slave spiritual at the concert. The audience loves it, and spirituals become the main attraction of the Jubilee Singers.

Hopkinson writes that this book is historical fiction, but it is based on a real person. She notes that the real "great-great-grandmother Ella," Ella Sheppard Moore, was born into slavery. Her father was able to free himself and his daughter, but when he went back to buy his wife, he found that she had been sold away.

Genre: Historical Fiction

Howard, Elizabeth Fitzgerald. *Virgie Goes to School with Us Boys*. Illustrated by E. B. Lewis. New York: Simon and Schuster, 2000.

After the Civil War, religious organizations were often the ones building new schools to serve the needs of children of newly freed slaves. This book tells the story of a girl who finally goes to school in spite of all of the family's reservations. One concern is that the children have a very long walk to get there and need to stay all week. Her older brother C.C. convinces everyone that she should go to school when the school year begins. After all, isn't Virgie free, too?

Genre: Historical Fiction

Award: Coretta Scott King Illustrator Honor

LATER ELEMENTARY

Cooper, Michael L. *Slave Spirituals and the Jubilee Singers*. New York: Clarion, 2001.

> The train carrying the Fisk singers arrived in Cincinnati late on October 6. They knew that before the war the river city had been a major stop for slaves fleeing the South on the secret Underground Railroad. And, like the people who had fled from bondage, the singers arrived in the Ohio city full of dreams. But none of them imagined that they were destined to become internationally known stars who sang for a president, a queen, and a king.[13]

In 1866, Fisk University, then Fisk Free Colored School, was founded by the American Missionary Association. While the school quickly filled with students, funds were not readily available, and the school's very survival was at risk. The choir director, George White, proposed that the Fisk choir go on a singing tour of the northern states to earn money for the school. While it seemed a radical idea, it was a very successful one—not only were they able to earn funds for the school, but the Fisk Jubilee Singers became one of the most famous musical groups of their time. The first half of this book provides the background of slave spirituals before discussing the Jubilee Singers and their great success. Source notes, suggested readings, and lyrics and music for seven spirituals at the end of the book enrich the text.

Genre: Nonfiction/Informational/Music

Greene, Meg. *Into the Land of Freedom: African Americans in Reconstruction.* Minneapolis, MN: Lerner, 2004.

> Among the most powerful scenes to take place across the Reconstruction South were the reunions of slave families. For many African Americans, life under slavery had not simply meant hard work, harsh treatment, and injustice. Slavery had also disrupted family life. Many families had been broken apart when family members were sold, and few entertained realistic hopes of ever seeing their loved ones again. Yet, despite the long odds against success, many former slaves set out in search of the families they had lost.[14]

This search was made more difficult because many slaves had never received an education and could not write. But those who could write did, and others found help from missionaries and teachers. The Freedmen's Bureau had set up camps for slaves who had nowhere to go, and some reunions took place as people found shelter there. Some found their loved ones and were hurt anew by evidence of cruel treatment for children they had lost long before.

Greene's book is well researched and a very good resource for middle school students who would like to study this period of history that is often oversimplified, if covered at all. Her book covers many of the conflicting events of these years and gives important understanding of the hopes and dreams that filled this brief period that soon gave way under the hate and violence of the Jim Crow years.

Genre: Nonfiction/Informational

Hakim, Joy. *Reconstructing America 1865–1890.* New York: Oxford University Press, 2003.

> So when the Union army came into Mississippi and Josh Davis fled, his slaves didn't go with him. They went off in different directions.

But Benjamin Montgomery soon came back to the old plantations at Davis Bend. General Ulysses S. Grant helped him rent the Davis plantations. Montgomery advertised in a black newspaper. . . . He wrote that he intended to "organize a community composed exclusively of colored people." He said he was looking for people of "honesty, industry, sobriety and intelligence." Freedmen and freedwomen flocked to Davis Bend. In 1865, laborers there raised 2,000 bales of cotton and earned a profit of $160,000.[15]

The Davis Bend plantations were the family holdings of Jefferson Davis, the president of the Confederate States of America. The plantations had been run by his older brother, Joseph. This remarkable story of a community of freed Blacks under the leadership of Benjamin Thorton Montgomery and Mary Lewis Montgomery ends sadly when Jefferson Davis, after his release from prison, returns and reclaims the plantation.

Hakim provides a clear and concise history from this complex time period. Just as the Civil War had become a conflict between those who believed in slavery and wanted it to continue and those who wanted to see the end of slavery, Reconstruction became a struggle between those who wanted to see representation of Blacks at all levels of government's elective offices and those who wanted to limit their voting privileges, by force and fear if need be. A strong, consistent policy was needed, but Andrew Johnson vetoed the congressional attempts to create a more solid base for Reconstruction. The Freedmen's Bureau was not made permanent. Even with the Thirteenth, Fourteenth, and Fifteenth Amendments to the Constitution, the lives of freed Blacks were placed back in jeopardy. And, by 1877, when President Rutherford B. Hayes ordered federal troops out of the South, Congressional Reconstruction was essentially over.

Hakim's book follows the years of Reconstruction as the country deals with western expansion, the building of a transcontinental railroad, and the movement to get the vote for women. But, for the Black freed men and women, Reconstruction was largely disappointing:

Frederick Douglass, the abolitionist leader who had been a slave, wrote in 1882 that the slave, "was free from the individual master, but the slave of society. He had neither money, property, nor friends. He was free from the old plantation but he had nothing but the dusty road under his feet."[16]

Genre: Nonfiction/Informational

Hansen, Joyce. *I Thought My Soul Would Rise and Fly: The Diary of Patsy, a Freed Girl*. New York: Scholastic, 1997.

> The Yankee President Lincoln was killed a week ago. James and Cook both seem worried. Cook said, "Maybe we not free then, since the man who free us is dead."[17]

The months after the signing of the Emancipation Proclamation were confusing in terms of the status of newly freed slaves, especially those who were children without parents. In this book, Patsy, a slightly disabled child of about twelve, watches as her fellow slaves become poorly paid house servants and field hands living in a sharecropping situation very similar to slavery. Knowing that they will never be truly free until they leave the plantation, they leave one at a time, while Patsy wonders what will become of her.

When she was a slave, Patsy listened to the lessons of the White children and taught herself to read. She secretly practices her skills, including the writing of the diary that forms this book. As she waits and hopes for the promised teacher to come to teach her and the other Black children, she begins to teach the others to read and becomes their schoolhouse teacher. By the time she is ready to leave, she recognizes her skills and has the self-confidence to move into the unknown.

Hansen provides an epilogue for the curious reader who wants to know what might happen after the book ends. She also provides extensive historical notes describing the factual basis for this piece of historical fiction. Sharecropping, the Freedman's Bureau, the education of newly freed slaves, and the tough decision about whether to stay on the plantation that one has known or to strike out on one's own are all addressed in this book.

Genre: Historical Fiction
Award: Coretta Scott King Author Honor

McKissack, Patricia C., and Fredrick L. McKissack. *Days of Jubilee*. Illustrated by Leo Dillon and Diane Dillon. New York: Scholastic, 2003.

> Frederick Douglass wrote, "When you turned us loose you gave us no acres; you turned us loose to the sky, to the storm, to the whirlwind, and, worst of all, you turned us loose to the wrath of our infuriated masters."[18]

The McKissacks tell the story of the earlier years of Black history through the end of the Civil War. They explain as the book begins that the news of the end of the war and freedom came to different people at different times, so it is hard to identify one time as the day of jubilee; that day would be different for each person who was freed.

Abolitionist Samual Gridley Howe observed the communities developed by fugitive slaves in Canada. In one report, he noted, that it was interesting how differently freed slaves had accomplished the building of a "thriving, successful, industrious, hard-working, and intelligent community."[19] His observations were a significant contradiction to the stereotypes perpetuated by pro-slavery advocates and provided "convincing evidence that if the newly freed men of the South are provided with educational and employment opportunities, they have the ability to become successful and contributing members of society."[20]

This is one of the few children's books that chronicle the Reconstruction period of history. It helps students understand not only this complex period of American history but the next period as well. Whatever gains were made in the years after the Civil War would shortly run into the Jim Crow years, when oppression, violence, and social inequity were the rule.

Genre: Nonfiction/Informational
Award: Coretta Scott King Author Honor

Myers, Walter Dean. *Now Is Your Time: The African-American Struggle for Freedom.* New York: HarperCollins, 1991.

> In the months following the end of the War Between the States, Africans—now African Americans—found themselves to be a free people. The chains had been cast off. They had helped to cast them off with their courage, and their lives. That struggle, the struggle to escape being "owned" by other human beings, had ended. But the struggle to find true equality had just begun.[21]

This book offers a comprehensive account of Black history from the roots in Africa to contemporary times. It can be used throughout the study of Black history and will be an excellent source for inquiry projects that students might have. It is included in this chapter because it discusses the period of Reconstruction with a clarity that helps those who are unfamiliar with this particular time.

Genre: Nonfiction/Informational

Peacock, Judith. *Reconstruction: Rebuilding after the Civil War.* Mankato, MN: Bridgestone, 2003.

> Thousands of whites and African Americans from the North moved to the South during Reconstruction. These people included teachers, lawyers, businessmen, and army officers. White Southerners called them "carpetbaggers." These Northerners sometimes carried their belongings in small suitcases made of carpet. Some carpetbaggers wanted to make money for themselves. Most truly wanted to help rebuild the South.[22]

This book is part of the Let Freedom Ring series. It gives the reader an organized and readable text that chronicles the sequence of events and important details of post–Civil War Reconstruction. Photos and drawings help provide students with a context for the story.

Genre: Nonfiction/Informational

Rappaport, Doreen. *Free at Last: Stories and Songs of Emancipation.* Illustrated by Shane W. Evans. Cambridge, MA: Candlewick, 2004.

> Jane Kemper smiles at the sliver of the moon. Maybe luck is with her on this dark night. Step by step, on tiptoe, she inches her way around William Townsend's house. Her former master has stolen her four children. The man at the Freedmen's Bureau said he would try to help her, but he wasn't sure when, so she has come by herself to get them.[23]

This book looks at where this era begins, as slavery is abolished and hope in the joy of new found freedom whispers the promise of a better life. Unfortunately, former slaves, newly free, soon faced the racism that had allowed for slavery to become the institution that it had been for the past two hundred and fifty years in America.

This book shares, through text, poetry, and song, the stories of the years that passed from 1863 to the present. The stories are stark and honest. They speak of the horrors that Blacks faced as angry Whites, determined to maintain supremacy over Blacks, committed all forms of atrocities. These threats and crimes created a culture that was reminiscent of slavery.

Rappaport features individuals, both well known and not as well known, to chronicle the events of this perilous time. Courage, resilience, and the strength of community and song are present in every story.

Genre: Nonfiction/Informational/Music

Robinet, Harriette Gillem. *Forty Acres and Maybe a Mule*. New York: Aladdin, 1998.

In the last months of the Civil War, thousands of runaway slaves, having no place of their own, followed General William Tecumseh Sherman and his troops for protection. Finding it more and more difficult to manage under those conditions, Sherman issued a field order which gave slaves some of the land confiscated by the northern troops. After the war, in July 1865, the Bureau of Refugees, Freedmen, and Abandoned Lands approved the plan with Circular 13. This book tells a fictional story of the initial years of Reconstruction, when families were able to appropriate land for themselves. There, they would not only be free but could earn a living and have an opportunity to prosper. The family in this story rejoiced at having their own farm. With the Freedmen's Bureau establishing schools for both White and Black children, it seemed that, finally, life-changing opportunities were presenting themselves.

Unfortunately, what was given in July in Circular 13 was taken back in September of that same year by Circular 15, in which Sherman claimed that he only meant his order as a temporary solution to the problem of the homeless slaves who were following his army. With hope in their heart, the family in this story tries to deal with this extraordinarily bad news as best they can.

Genre: Historical Fiction
Award: Scott O'Dell Award

MIDDLE GRADES

Meltzer, Milton. *A History in Their Own Words: The Black Americans*. New York: HarperCollins, 1984.

> Reconstruction has often been called the era of "black rule." How mistaken this is can be seen from a quick look at a few facts. Most black officeholders of the Reconstruction served in local and state governments. Only twenty-two sat in Congress between 1869 and 1901. Two of these represented Mississippi in the Senate; the rest were in the lower house. Most served only one or two terms. With important committee posts closed to them, the twenty-two black members of Congress could have little influence on lawmaking.[24]

Even though this book covers history from 1619 to 1983, Meltzer makes a significant contribution to the study of the Reconstruction years. He dispels myths such as the one that Blacks suddenly controlled government. In fact, unless they were in an area that was controlled by the troops that protected their right to vote, they might not be safe to actualize that right.

Meltzer explains the terms that were coined to describe some of the roles that people played during the Reconstruction years. Northerners who came south were called "carpetbaggers" and were accused of coming to the South empty-handed and filling their bags to their own benefit. Actually, many of these northerners played a large part in establishing schools. As teachers, they were often suspected of "spreading notions of political and social equity."[25] "Scalawags" were southerners who didn't support the Confederacy and, after the war, participated in the Reconstruction efforts. Their position was seen as a betrayal that was difficult for the defeated Confederate South to forgive. As with Meltzer's other books, much of how this is shared with the reader is through the voices of people who lived during this time.

Genre: Nonfiction/Informational

Hansen, Joyce. *Bury Me Not in a Land of Slaves: African-Americans in the Time of Reconstruction.* New York: Grolier, 2000.

> The reactions to freedom were as varied as the freed people themselves. The road they traveled on their journey to freedom depended upon the experiences they'd had during slavery, their physical and emotional state, and their natural abilities and talents. Finding their children and kin, choosing names, solidifying relationships through marriage, and deciding for the first time where they would live and work were important steps. But as the freed people began to carve out places for themselves, they discovered that difficult times lay ahead. They learned, as Frederick Douglass had cautioned, that "the work does not end with the abolition of slavery, but only begins."[26]

Hansen has taken personal narratives and documents from the time to provide important background for understanding this dramatic, complex, and difficult period. Her research for this book offers the reader stories of individuals working through the choices and challenges they faced as well as the context of governmental frameworks that were changing significantly with the end of a war. I would highly recommend that this book be included in school and classroom American history library collections.

Genre: Nonfiction/Informational

Thomas, Velma Maia. *Lest We Forget: The Passage from Africa to Slavery and Emancipation*. New York: Random House, 1997.

> Some may argue, "why bring up such a painful period in our country's history?" Some may feel that they have no apology to make, as neither they nor their forefathers were slaveholders. Others may feel dredging up tales of Africans in chains humiliates the race. When one speaks openly of slavery, the nation tightens.[27]

This fascinating book includes photographs and documents from Thomas's Black Holocaust Exhibit in Atlanta. Thomas tells a personal story along with the historical story. It is three-dimensional and interactive, with informational text that tells of the events that surround the documents. A copy of the Emancipation Proclamation is one of the documents you will find tucked away in a sleeve on the page that describes the issues that surrounded the times and the document itself.

Genre: Nonfiction/Informational

CONCLUSION

During the years that followed the Civil War, the U.S. Constitution was amended three times to include the Thirteenth Amendment, abolishing slavery in 1865; the Fourteenth Amendment, giving citizenship to all persons born in the United States or naturalized, in 1868; and the Fifteenth Amendment, giving the right to vote to citizens regardless of race, color, or previous condition of servitude, in 1870. The vote did not extend to women.

In many areas of the South and the North, these amendments did not in any way ensure the rights of freedom to Black men and women. Particularly in the South, state and local laws were made to frustrate the efforts of African American men attempting to vote. Blacks who attempted to vote were often beaten or their homes were burned. African Americans accused of committing wrongs might be executed by mobs, without a trial. The alleged offenses could be anything from murder to disrespect for a White person. Lynchings created an atmosphere of fear in African American communities. People were afraid to speak up for their rights or to take a stand against injustice.[28]

It soon became clear that with the order to withdraw federal troops from the South, most of the gains made during the years of Reconstruction would be lost.

> During Reconstruction, blacks gained freedom, the right to be educated, and the right to vote. But soon, through violence, fraud, and legal tricks, black people in the South lost virtually all the rights they had gained. Public schools that had been opened to them were closed. Without the right to vote, there was little they could do about it.[29]

The years that follow created another period of acute racial discrimination, segregation, and persecution, which became known as the Jim Crow years.

NOTES

1. Meltzer, *Frederick Douglass*, 149.
2. Hakim, *Reconstructing America*, 12.
3. Hakim, *Reconstructing America*, 13.
4. Foner, *Reconstruction*, 69.
5. Franklin, *From Slavery to Freedom*, 225.
6. Hakim, *Reconstructing America*, 17.
7. Hughes and Meltzer, *Pictorial History*, 197.
8. Hughes and Meltzer, *Pictorial History*, 197.
9. Hakim, *Reconstructing America*, 161.
10. Hughes and Meltzer, *Pictorial History*, 215.
11. Foner, *Reconstruction*, 71.
12. Bradby, *More Than Anything Else.*
13. Cooper, *Slave Spirituals*, 53.
14. Greene, *Into the Land of Freedom*, 34.
15. Hakim, *Reconstructing America*, 42.
16. Hakim, *Reconstructing America*, 160.
17. Hansen, *I Thought My Soul*, 10.
18. McKissack and McKissack, *Days of Jubilee*, 113.
19. McKissack and McKissack, *Days of Jubilee*, 90.
20. McKissack and McKissack, *Days of Jubilee*, 90.

21. Myers, *Now Is Your Time*, 194.
22. Peacock, *Reconstruction*, 26.
23. Rappaport, *Free at Last*, 8.
24. Meltzer, *A History in Their Own Words*, 111.
25. Meltzer, *A History in Their Own Words*, 115.
26. Hansen, *Bury Me Not*, 44.
27. Thomas, *Lest We Forget*, 28.
28. Myers, *Now Is Your Time*, 198.
29. Haskins, *Black Stars*, 103.

BIBLIOGRAPHY OF BOOKS FOR CHILDREN

Bradby, Marie. *More Than Anything Else*. Illustrated by Chris K. Soentpiet. New York: Scholastic, 1995.

Cooper, Michael L. *Slave Spirituals and the Jubilee Singers*. New York: Clarion, 2001.

Greene, Meg. *Into the Land of Freedom: African Americans in Reconstruction*. Minneapolis, MN: Lerner Publications, 2004.

Hakim, Joy. *Reconstructing America 1865–1890*. New York: Oxford University Press, 2003.

Hansen, Joyce. *Bury Me Not in a Land of Slaves: African-Americans in the Time of Reconstruction*. New York: Grolier, 2000.

———. *I Thought My Soul Would Rise and Fly: The Diary of Patsy, a Freed Girl*. New York: Scholastic, 1997.

Hopkinson, Deborah. *A Band of Angels: A Story Inspired by the Jubilee Singers*. Illustrated by Raúl Colón. New York: Atheneum, 1999.

Howard, Elizabeth Fitzgerald. *Virgie Goes to School with Us Boys*. Illustrated by E. B. Lewis. New York: Simon and Schuster, 2000.

McKissack, Patricia C., and Fredrick L. McKissack. *Days of Jubilee*. Illustrated by Leo Dillon and Diane Dillon. New York: Scholastic, 2003.

Meltzer, Milton. *A History in Their Own Words: The Black Americans*. New York: HarperCollins, 1984.

Myers, Walter Dean. *Now Is Your Time: The African-American Struggle for Freedom*. New York: HarperCollins, 1991.

Peacock, Judith. *Reconstruction: Rebuilding after the Civil War*. Mankato, MN: Bridgestone, 2003.

Rappaport, Doreen. *Free at Last: Stories and Songs of Emancipation*. Illustrated by Shane W. Evans. Cambridge, MA: Candlewick, 2004.

Robinet, Harriette Gillem. *Forty Acres and Maybe a Mule*. New York: Aladdin, 1998.

Thomas, Velma Maia. *Lest We Forget: The Passage from Africa to Slavery and Emancipation.* New York: Random House, 1997.

BIBLIOGRAPHY OF REFERENCE WORKS

Franklin, John Hope. *From Slavery to Freedom: A History of African Americans.* New York: Knopf, 2000.

Foner, Eric. *Reconstruction: America's Unfinished Revolution, 1863–1877.* New York: HarperCollins, 1988.

Haskins, James. *Black Stars of Civil War Times.* New York: Jossey-Bass, 2002.

Meltzer, Milton, ed. *Frederick Douglass: In His Own Words.* Illustrated by Stephen Alcorn. San Diego, CA: Harcourt, Brace, 1995.

· 7 ·

A Land of Promise:
Exploring and Settling the West

> Most of the great myths of the American West were born following
> the end of the Civil War in 1865. . . . The history of the era and the
> legends that flowed from it continue to fascinate us, but some of the
> most important participants are strangely missing: the black men and
> women who were an integral part of the "Wild West."[1]

$\mathscr{B}$lack Americans had been in the American West since the early days
of settler exploration. Esteban had pushed the boundaries of the known
territory of the West when he explored what is now Arizona and New
Mexico.[2] York had been an important participant in the Lewis and Clark
Expedition.[3] Edward Rose, a fur trapper, "served as chief of the Crows
in the early 1800's and helped open the Missouri River for exploration
toward the Rocky Mountains."[4] A pass through the Sierra Nevada
Mountains, used by thousands of California-bound travelers, was discovered by, and named after, James Beckwourth, a Black "mountain
man," who took on many roles as a prospector for gold, a trading post
operator, a fur trapper, and a chief of the Crows.[5]

In the two hundred and fifty years of slavery, many runaway slaves
headed north, eventually needing to escape all the way to Canada to ensure their freedom. Others headed south and found refuge with Indian
tribes there; even if their status remained that of a slave, their treatment
was significantly different from what it had been on the plantations. And
some found their way west to the land that was increasingly the focus for
new settlement, and where settlers were faced with resistance from the
Native American populations.

This land was challenging in many ways. Unlike the established states
that had formed from the original colonies along the eastern shore of the

new nation, the West was, for the most part, still considered wild. Runaway slaves, traveling with no resources, often found a new home with the Native Americans who had been living on the land for thousands of years, frequently becoming part of the Native American cultures they encountered. "Many Native Americans welcomed African Americans into their villages. Even as slaves many African Americans became part of a family group, and many intermarried with Native Americans—thus many later became classified as Black Indians."⁶ Later, African Americans arrived as part of the military ordered to protect settlers and contain Native American tribes in their proscribed areas. They eventually confronted people who were also victims because of their race.

Another group of western adventurers took part in the largest migration to California during the Gold Rush of 1849. Some arrived as free men and women and some as slaves. In the midst of all this, the western territories had to grapple with whether they would become slave states as they entered the Union. Whatever condition people arrived in, or whichever way the state decided, African Americans were still likely to find discrimination, hostility, and sometimes violence. Life in the American West presented many obstacles to success.

The trip across the unsettled territory was not inexpensive. It required a wagon and an animal to haul the wagon. It required rations that would sustain the family for the months of travel, not to mention a guide for safety and direction in unfamiliar land. As families who had few resources, many African American ex-slaves traveled west using the trails of those who had gone before as their guide.

African Americans worked in many different occupations: farmers, miners, cooks, traders, unskilled laborers, railroad workers, soldiers, and law enforcement officers. Women found employment as innkeepers, schoolteachers, nurses, and cooks. Some women went west as mail order brides, joining men who had traveled to the West previously and become settled as farmers and ranchers.⁷

Who can think of the "Wild West" without thinking about the cowboy? It was not at all unusual for Black men to find jobs on the range as cattle drivers and cooks. Some perfected their skills in riding and roping and became rodeo riders.

The stories in this chapter cover the experiences of African Americans as they moved west. They tell the story of remarkable people and remarkable times. Of course, many of the stories of the Black experience have been lost, since few were gathered, and of those that were, not many have been preserved. Representations of Black pioneers in our history books has been slow to come. Many books about the Old West, and the settlers and cowboys who were part of it, do not include a single Black person in the crowd. But Black people were there, doing their part in building and settling the land west of the Mississippi.

EARLY ELEMENTARY

Johnson, Dolores. *Seminole Diary: Remembrances of a Slave.* New York: Macmillan, 1994.

> Monday, April 14, 1834
>   They came quiet like cats into our campsite. They were so beautiful even the men; skin the color of walnuts dressed in feathers, beads, and silver. They pulled dried meat out of pouches and offered it to us. They passed us salve to put on our insect bites. They offered us fresh water to drink and to cool our faces.[8]

When Gina and her mother find an old diary in an attic trunk, they read the story of Libby, a slave girl who escaped with her parents and encountered the Seminole Indians. Although they remained slaves, Libby's family lived a very different life as part of their community. At the end of the diary, the family is planning to join the Seminole Indians in their relocation from Florida to what became the Indian Territory on an Oklahoma reservation.

Genre: Historical Fiction

Lester, Julius. *Black Cowboy, Wild Horses: A True Story.* Illustrated by Jerry Pinkney. New York: Penguin Putman, 1998.

> First light, Bob Lemmons rode his horse slowly up the rise. When he reached the top, he stopped at the edge of the bluff. He looked down at the corral where the other cowboys were beginning the morning chores, then turned away and stared at the land stretching as wide as love in every direction. The sky was curved as if it were a lap on which the earth lay napping like a curled cat. High above, a hawk was suspended on cold threads of unseen winds. Far, far away, at what looked to be the edge of the world, land and sky kissed.[9]

This is a wonderful story of a Black cowboy named Bob Lemmons who goes out on his own to track a wild herd of mustangs and lead them back to the ranch. The story is touching, with the death of a colt, and powerful, with the descriptions of how this man became part of the herd and challenged the lead mustang. Pinkney's watercolors capture the story in depictions of the western landscape and animals that interact with the poetic text, making this not only an interesting story but also a work of art.

Genre: Biography

Lowery, Linda. *Aunt Clara Brown: Official Pioneer.* Illustrated by Janice Lee Porter. Minneapolis, MN: Carolrhoda, 1999.

> When pioneers got old, the state of Colorado had paid them in return for all the work they had done settling the land. The money was called a pension. Anyone who settled in Colorado before 1865 was an official pioneer. Clara had arrived in 1859. But when she tried to get her pension, she discovered some strange rules. All official pioneers had to be white. And all official pioneers had to be men.[10]

When Clara Brown was able to buy her freedom, she set out to find her daughter, Eliza Jane, who had been sold as a child of ten. Thinking that the buyer had headed west, Brown determined to go west in search of Eliza. Courageous, industrious, and caring, Brown became successful as a landowner and businesswoman, but the thing she longed to be able to do, which was to find Eliza, remained out of her reach for years. In the meantime, her caring and support for the many people who entered her life created an extended and loving family who were there for her when she needed them.

This is an independent reading book for second and third graders and a wonderful resource for initiating conversations about pioneering and Brown's life. It is also an excellent example of putting personal values into action.

Genre: Biography

Monceaux, Morgan, and Ruth Katcher. *My Heroes, My People: African Americans and Native Americans in the West.* Illustrated by Morgan Monceaux. New York: Farrar, Straus and Giroux, 1999.

> Bass Reaves was one of a number of black marshals hired by Judge Parker, who realized he needed deputies who knew the Territory and

would be trusted by the people who lived there. A former Texas slave, Reaves was tall, well built, and spoke several Indian languages, though he never learned to read. To serve an arrest warrant, he relied on his memory and, sometimes, on the criminal's own ability to read the warrant.[11]

Monceaux and Katcher have researched well this collection of biographical sketches and historical notes. Each person included in this book is captured in a striking portrait by Monceaux: created with paint, oil pastels, markers, and collage, they draw the reader to each individual figure. The details that are included in the text are incredibly interesting and serve to sustain the reader's motivation to find out more and more about these fascinating characters from the past.

Many of the men and women who are mentioned here (including Bill Pickett, Clara Brown, Toussaint L'Ouverture, and Jim Beckwourth) are seen in other works mentioned in this and other chapters of this book. The descriptions found here will enhance any study of these western heroes.

Genre: Nonfiction/Informational

Nolen, Jerdine. *Thunder Rose.* Illustrated by Kadir Nelson. San Diego, CA: Harcourt, 2003.

> Taking in her first breath of life, the infant did not cry out. Rather, she sat up and looked around. She took hold of that lightning, rolled it into a ball, and set it above her shoulder, while the thunder echoed out over the other. They say this just accentuated the fact that the child had the power of thunder and lightning coursing through her veins.[12]

Born on a stormy night, the child, named Rose until she snored a thunderous sound and Thunder was added to her name, immediately showed miraculous powers. Like *John Henry*, this is a story of tall-tale proportions, from Rose's drinking milk as a baby directly from the cow to her, as a twelve-year-old, subduing the largest steer on the ranch, first wrestling it to the ground, then humming in its ear. Tater, the bull, becomes her trusted riding steed. Set on a western ranch, this book creates a rare opportunity to share a tall tale of a girl, a child of color, in the West.

Genre: Tall Tale/Fantasy
Award: Coretta Scott King Illustrator Honor

Pinkney, Andrea D. *Bill Pickett: Rodeo-Ridin' Cowboy.* Illustrated by Brian Pinkney. San Diego, CA: Harcourt, Brace, 1999.

> Cowboys—the men who tamed the Wild West during the late 1800's—are perhaps the most celebrated of all American legends. Nearly thirty-five thousand cowboys drove cattle when the Old West was in its prime. About one in four of these pioneers was African American.[13]

Andrea Pinkney tells the story of Bill Pickett, a celebrated rodeo rider. The son of freed slaves, Pickett grew up on a cattle ranch listening to the cattle-driving exploits of his two cousins who visited in the evening and told their stories. When he saw a bulldog hold a restless cow by biting the cow's lip, Pickett did the same thing and got the same result. The cow stayed still while being branded. This "bulldogging" technique along with his excellent horsemanship made him a star.

Genre: Biography

Randolph, Ryan. *Black Cowboys.* New York: PowerKids, 2003.

> No matter what their race or background, cowboys trusted one another with their lives, because life on the trail was dangerous.[14]

Written in a large font, this chapter book is well organized and presents information in a very readable format for young researchers. Illustrations are well coordinated with the text, and many pages provide windows of "Did You Know?" facts. This book would complement many of the other books that are mentioned in this chapter, as it gives information about some of the cowboys featured and can help readers understand what the life of a cowboy was like.

Genre: Nonfiction/Informational

LATER ELEMENTARY

Cefrey, Holly. *From Slave to Cowboy: The Nat Love Story.* New York: Rosen, 2004.

> Nat Love decided to become a cowboy. At that time, there were many African American cowboys. They did the same work as white cowboys. African American cowboys were also paid the same as

white cowboys. Being a cowboy was one of the few ways for former slaves to earn the same amount of money as whites.[15]

This biography of Nat Love is told in the form of a conversation between Love and an eleven-year-old boy named Nigel Brexal and Nigel's Aunt Barbara. After Love identifies himself as Deadwood Dick, Nigel asks him questions that Love answers with stories from his beginnings as a slave, being freed at the end of the Civil War, to his father's death, his experiences working with horses, and his move west. Love eventually tells Nigel about how he got his nickname, Deadwood Dick, by winning a shooting contest. In the end, Nigel tells Love that he should write his story, and of course he does in his autobiography, *The Life and Adventures of Nat Love*.

Genre: Biography

Haskins, James. *The Geography of Hope: Black Exodus from the South after Reconstruction*. Brookfield, CT: Twenty-first Century Books, 1999.

> Randolph's will stated, "I give and bequeath to all my slaves their freedom—heartily regretting that I have ever been the owner of one." Randolph's will also provided for money to pay his former slaves' transportation to Ohio, as well as the basic necessities, such as clothing, shelter, and tools, to begin their new lives.[16]

When I read this paragraph, I was heartened to think that this had happened. As I read, I very quickly began to think of what might have happened if all slave owners, many of whom were made enormously wealthy with the work of their slaves, had done just what Randolph had done: freed their slaves and provided them with the resources to begin to support themselves in what became known as manumission settlements. But my enthusiasm was soon dimmed as Haskins goes on to say that, after the freed slaves arrived in Ohio, they discovered that Randolph's relatives had taken the will to court and had it overturned, and they had nothing.

The history that Haskins shares in this story and in this book reveals a time of promise when Black Americans had reason to hope that they would be able to pursue the dream of equality. What they found at almost every turn were roadblocks, based on race, to employment and educational opportunities. Haskins's research is thorough and well worth using with upper elementary students, as well as for informing ourselves as classroom teachers.

Genre: Nonfiction/Informational

Hominick, Judy, and Jeanne Spreier. *Best Cowboy in the West: The Story of Nat Love.* New York: Silver Moon, 2001.

> "Aw, a young boy like you! Cattle thieves and rattlesnakes can't scare you? You haven't heard the worst—about stampedes that go on for thirty miles or more and hail the size of apples hammering your head and Indian attacks," the boss said.
> "Sounds just fine to me," Nat said.[17]

Born a slave, young Nat Love was freed with his family after the Civil War and they went on to farm on land that had never been farmed before. While struggling to get the land productive for farming, his father died. At fifteen years of age, Love left his family and the farm and headed west. With an enormous talent for breaking horses, Love not only became a successful cowboy, but in 1907 at the age of twenty-two, he roped a mustang in record time. He is also credited with winning sharpshooter contests.

This story of Nat Love also chronicles life on the range, as Hominick and Spreier write about the day-to-day events on the trail. The story is set in the early days of cattle drives, when the West was still very unsettled. At one point in a cattle drive, a government scout warns the cowboys not to go farther north because a battle is taking place between the U. S. Cavalry under Lieutenant Colonel George Custer and the Sioux warriors under Sitting Bull. This, of course, was the battle at the Little Big Horn River in Montana, where Custer's forces were defeated and over two hundred soldiers, including Custer, lost their lives.

In his early thirties, Love left the cowboy life and began working on the railroad as a porter. He wrote his autobiography in 1907 and continued to travel throughout America, a land that he loved and often described as a wonderful country to explore.

Genre: Biography

Schlissel, Lillian. *Black Frontiers: A History of African American Heroes in the Old West.* New York: Simon and Schuster, 1995.

> It would be wrong to suggest that the frontier was without prejudice. As settlements grew into cities, Jim Crow segregation laws confronted black settlers. But on those lonely, dangerous, and beautiful lands we call the frontier, black pioneers built new lives.[18]

Schlissel's book includes stories from the many different experiences Black Americans had in the American West during the 1800s. There are stories of cowboys, miners, and soldiers; of men and women home-steaders; of rodeo riders; and of men and women who lived with the many different Native American tribes. African Americans settled in Nevada, California, Kansas, Nebraska, and every other region of the western territory.

The photographs provide a great history in the form of depictions of some ordinary people and some who became famous for their ac-complishments.

Genre: Nonfiction/Informational

MIDDLE GRADES

Cox, Clinton. *The Forgotten Heroes: The Story of the Buffalo Soldiers.* New York: Scholastic, 1993.

> Though a war had just been fought that ended slavery, black people found little acceptance and few opportunities in post–Civil War America. Many young black men joined the United States Army in their search for a freedom most had never known. But in becoming part of the army, they helped take freedom away from people who had always known it.[19]

Clinton's book is a very comprehensive and detailed account of the work of the Buffalo Soldiers. This story of the Buffalo Soldiers is also a story of the many problems that surrounded the westward expansion for the Native Americans who were displaced and found themselves with treaties that were violated more often than not. To add to the complex-ity, at the same time that Black soldiers were risking their lives to enforce the laws and carry out the ambitions of the government in taking over the territory of the west, they were being discriminated against. Even though "the Buffalo Soldiers had fought bravely, made large areas safe for white settlement, and saved the lives of countless people, they received little thanks and no respite from the racism that haunted them."[20] The complexity of this story makes for an interesting middle school read with many opportunities for deep discussions.

Genre: Nonfiction/Informational

Katz, William Loren. *Black Indians: A Hidden Heritage.* New York: Aladdin Paperbacks, 1986.

> Black Indians? The very words make most people shake their heads in disbelief or smile at what appears to be a joke, a play on words. No one remembers any such person in a school text, history book, or western novel. None ever appeared.[21]

Although this book is included in this chapter on the West, it also contains many stories of Black Indians in the South, where many escaped slaves from coastal North Carolina and Georgia found a culture of acceptance with the Seminole Indians who lived in Florida. Whether as part of the tribe or as maroon settlements (established by escaped slaves who allied with the Seminoles), a significant relationship existed between African Americans and Indians, and two of the chapters in this book specifically speak to that relationship.

Katz also records the many ways that African Americans and Native Americans of the West accepted one another and lived together, even building families together. That this is not acknowledged more in our history books is, according to Katz, not a case of distortion, but rather one of omission. He notes that if painters, photographers, journalists, or keepers of records had been more inclined to record observations of Black Indians, their presence would not have been so hidden in history. He cites his own growing awareness of the prominence of Black Indians as he was gathering information for his study of Blacks in the West. As he collected data, he began to see that the relationship of African Americans with the many cultures of Indians was a significant part of the story of American settlement of the West. This is truly exceptional research and a fascinating book.

Genre: Nonfiction/Informational

Katz, William Loren. *Black Women of the Old West.* New York: Atheneum Books for Young Readers, 1995.

> A highly unusual westward migration was carried out by mail order brides. In response to the scarcity of women on early frontiers, some young ladies in the East made an extraordinary decision. They agreed to leave home and family, promised to board frontier-bound trains, and marry the men who paid for their tickets.[22]

This collection of stories includes many interesting circumstances that brought Black women to the west. When married Black women in the mining camps saw that the absence of women was creating problems in the community, they contacted eastern churches and newspapers to arrange for mail order brides.

Many of the stories speak of goals and accomplishments, sometimes within the stories of individual women and sometimes by the state they settled in. With all of the different stories and all of the many and varied roles that were played, these women shared a passion for finding a life that offered opportunity and hope. But none of that came easily. It came with courage, determination, wisdom, and faith.

Genre: Nonfiction/Informational

McPherson, James. *Into the West: From Reconstruction to the Final Days of the American Frontier.* New York: Atheneum Books for Young Readers, 2006.

> Johnson vetoed congressional land-reform bills, and ordered most of the confiscated land returned to the original owners upon their return. A majority of the freedmen did not achieve the economic independence which they had hoped. Instead, they had to work for white landowners, who in many cases were their former masters.[23]

Landlessness was one of the greatest disappointments that former slaves were to have upon their emancipation. Even after some slaves had been awarded land that had been confiscated from former plantation owners, the land was quickly taken back, leaving the freed slaves, who had worked the land to bring great prosperity to the slave owners, landless again.

McPherson has written a book about the West. It is not specifically about African Americans in the West, but Black Americans are very much present in the drama of the times. These times were difficult, complex, and filled with uncertainty and conflict, and McPherson includes it all. Native Americans, women, African Americans, European immigrants, pioneers, outlaws, cowboys, and politicians all made up the West.

Genre: Nonfiction/Informational

Stanley, Jerry. *Hurry Freedom: African Americans in Gold Rush California.* New York: Crown, 2000.

> At the age of twelve, Gibbs observed slavery in the South, and the experience stayed with him for the rest of his life. He was driving a

buggy for a lawyer who was traveling from Philadelphia to Maryland, a slave state. Along the roads in Maryland, Gibbs saw Africans in ragged clothes working on plantations. He saw children his age, who would work their entire lives as slaves and then die, never knowing what it was like to be free. He also witnessed a slave auction, where a baby was sold from its mother's arms, and he saw the mother whipped when she wouldn't let go of her child.[24]

This book shares amazing stories from the years of the Gold Rush. It follows the life and achievement of Mifflin Gibbs, who went to California and, with hard work and a great deal of perseverance and ingenuity, eventually prospered. It is a truly remarkable story that brings forth details of life for African Americans at that time and place in our history.

The book includes the arguments that arose over whether California would be brought into the Union as a slave state. Sad to say, many White people wanted California to be a Free State only because they wanted the state to be for White people only and worried that if it were a slave state, a large number of Blacks would be brought into the state as slaves. There was a great deal of prejudice and violence during this time against Blacks, and some were killed for simply trying to make their dreams come true. It is also true that people worked together regardless of race. However, the hate and violence that Gibbs encountered finally prompted him and his business partner, Peter Lester, to go to Canada, where each of them established families and businesses and prospered.

This is a remarkably honest depiction of California in its early years before and in the beginning of its statehood, as well as the lives of African Americans as they tried again to be part of the "American Dream." As it tells the story of Mifflin Gibbs, it also includes the stories of many others who went to California to seek their fortune, and of the events that shaped life in California during the Gold Rush years.

Genre: Nonfiction/Informational
Award: National Book Award Finalist

Sorensen, George Niels. *Iron Riders: Story of the 1890's Fort Missoula Buffalo Soldiers Bicycle Corps*. Missoula, MT: Pictorial Histories, 2000.

There is, in fact, little firsthand information about the Buffalo Soldier Bicycle Corps at all. The available books, articles, personal letters, official orders, and other correspondence come from the White officers involved. Firsthand accounts from individual black soldiers are scarce as few of these men had any education. A great many were unable to read, much less write their own names. Illiteracy was so pervasive in the army that chaplains were assigned to regiments with the principal task of teaching reading and writing. Obviously, when one can neither read nor write one does not send or receive many letters, which often provide a source of revealing insights. This makes telling this story quite a challenge.[25]

This is a story of the experimental use of bicycles in the West. The riders who made this difficult and perilous trip from Missoula, Montana, to St. Louis, Missouri, a distance of 2,000 miles, were African American soldiers in the Bicycle Corps from Fort Missoula. The book explains how this experiment in transportation of troops came to be, and it includes a well-documented account of the trip. Needless to say, the trip was extremely challenging and would never have been successful without the determination of the men who accomplished it. The narration of the trip is punctuated with photos that provide a pictorial record of this experiment.

Genre: Nonfiction/Informational

CONCLUSION

For many students studying the Old West, the thought of Black men or women as cowboys, settlers, soldiers, miners, or law enforcement officers may be a surprise. But many African Americans joined the stream of migrants headed west, so why should their presence and contributions be a surprise? Perhaps the explanation is the absence of images of African Americans in books about the Old West.

As I look at the illustrations in books about the westward expansion, I don't often see people of color. This invisibility contributes to the illusion that only Whites settled the West. And what does "settled the West" mean when it was already occupied? Young people who become familiar with a more complete history that includes the complex demographics of our rich and diverse country will likely want to explore some of these thought-provoking questions.

NOTES

1. Cox, *Forgotten Heroes*, vii.
2. See Palmer in chapter 1.
3. See Blumberg in chapter 2.
4. Cox, *Forgotten Heroes*, vii–viii.
5. Cox, *Forgotten Heroes*, viii.
6. Sylvester, *African Americans and the Old West*, "Oklahoma Territory."
7. Sylvester, *African Americans and the Old West*, "Lure of the Old West."
8. Johnson, *Seminole Diary*.
9. Lester, *Black Cowboy, Wild Horses*.
10. Lowery, *Aunt Clara Brown*, 33–34.
11. Monceaux and Katcher, *My Heroes, My People*, 24.
12. Nolen, *Thunder Rose*.
13. Pinkney, *Bill Pickett*.
14. Randolph, *Black Cowboys*, 11.
15. Cefrey, *From Slave to Cowboy*, 4.
16. Haskins, *Geography of Hope*, 64.
17. Hominick and Spreier, *Best Cowboy*, 27.
18. Schlissel, *Black Frontiers*, 73.
19. Cox, *Forgotten Heroes*, ix.
20. Cox, *Forgotten Heroes*, 112.
21. Katz, *Black Indians*, 3.
22. Katz, *Black Women of the Old West*, 34.
23. McPherson, *Into the West*, 32.
24. Stanley, *Hurry Freedom*, 5.
25. Sorensen, *Iron Riders*, 1.

BIBLIOGRAPHY OF BOOKS FOR CHILDREN

Cefrey, Holly. *From Slave to Cowboy: The Nat Love Story*. New York: Rosen, 2004.

Cox, Clinton. *The Forgotten Heroes: The Story of the Buffalo Soldiers*. New York: Scholastic, 1993.

Haskins, James. *The Geography of Hope: Black Exodus from the South after Reconstruction*. Brookfield, CT: Twenty-first Century Books, 1999.

Hominick, Judy, and Jeanne Spreier. *Best Cowboy in the West: The Story of Nat Love*. New York: Silver Moon, 2001.

Johnson, Dolores. *Seminole Diary: Remembrances of a Slave*. New York: Macmillan, 1994.

Katz, William Loren. *Black Indians: A Hidden Heritage.* New York: Aladdin Paperbacks, 1986.

Katz, William Loren. *Black Women of the Old West.* New York: Atheneum Books for Young Readers, 1995.

Lester, Julius. *Black Cowboy, Wild Horses: A True Story.* Illustrated by Jerry Pinkney. New York: Penguin Putman, 1998.

Lowery, Linda. *Aunt Clara Brown: Official Pioneer.* Illustrated by Janice Lee Porter. Minneapolis, MN: Carolrhoda, 1999.

McPherson, James. *Into the West: From Reconstruction to the Final Days of the American Frontier.* New York: Atheneum Books for Young Readers, 2006.

Monceaux, Morgan, and Ruth Katcher. *My Heroes, My People: African Americans and Native Americans in the West.* Illustrated by Morgan Monceaux. New York: Farrar, Straus and Giroux, 1999.

Nolen, Jerdine. *Thunder Rose.* Illustrated by Kadir Nelson. San Diego, CA: Harcourt, 2003.

Pinkney, Andrea D. *Bill Pickett: Rodeo-Ridin' Cowboy.* Illustrated by Brian Pinkney. San Diego, CA: Harcourt, Brace, 1999.

Randolph, Ryan. *Black Cowboys.* New York: PowerKids, 2003.

Schlissel, Lillian. *Black Frontiers: A History of African American Heroes in the Old West.* New York: Simon and Schuster, 1995.

Sorensen, George Niels. *Iron Riders: Story of the 1890's Fort Missoula Buffalo Soldiers Bicycle Corps,* Missoula, MT: Pictorial Histories, 2000.

Stanley, Jerry. *Hurry Freedom: African Americans in Gold Rush California.* New York: Crown, 2000.

Sylvester, Melvin. *African Americans and the Old West.* www.liu.edu/cwis/cwp/library/african/west/west.htm.

· 8 ·

New Laws, Old Racism:
The Jim Crow Years

What remains certain is that Reconstruction failed, and that for blacks its failure was a disaster whose magnitude cannot be obscured by the genuine accomplishments that did endure. For the nation as a whole, the collapse of Reconstruction was a tragedy that deeply affected the course of its future development. If racism contributed to the undoing of Reconstruction, by the same token Reconstruction's demise and the emergence of blacks as a disenfranchised class of dependent laborers greatly facilitated racism's further spread, until by the early twentieth century it had become more embedded in the nation's culture and politics than at any time since the beginning of the antislavery crusade and perhaps in our entire history.[1]

After the Civil War, Reconstruction provided the nation with an incredible opportunity to begin to change the disposition of this nation away from allowing the domination of one race over another. Slaves were freed, first by the Emancipation Proclamation in the slave states and finally with the Thirteenth Amendment, passed soon after the Civil War, that abolished slavery in the whole nation. The Fourteenth and Fifteenth Amendments passed soon after that, and Black representation began to be seen in local, state, and national elected government offices.

Unfortunately, in many ways, the promise ended with a political deal. When the bitterly contested presidential election of 1876 ended with Samuel Tilden receiving a slight margin in the popular vote but the electoral college vote evenly divided between Tilden and Rutherford B. Hayes, Congress had to break the tie and decide a winner. Secretly, Hayes urged southern senators to vote for him, promising to withdraw federal troops from the South. Once elected, he kept his promise and withdrew the troops.[2] The gains that had been made with Congressional Reconstruction, the work of the Freedmen's Bureau, and the protection and enforcement of troops were soon dismantled by violence and hatred that would paralyze communities with fear and poverty.

Anne Wallace Sharp describes the impact of this political action on the rights of African Americans: "Following the end of Reconstruction, Southern politicians moved quickly to eliminate many of the rights that African Americans had been granted."[3] This period became known as the "Jim Crow years," named after a minstrel show performer, a white vaudeville actor who put black makeup on his face and behaved as a buffoon. Clearly, this played into negative stereotypes that African Americans had faced from racist elements in our nation. The Jim Crow years lasted from the end of the 1800s to the civil rights era in the mid–1960s, a long period during which African Americans were overtly and covertly oppressed, as Sharp describes: "African American dreams of equality and freedom were repeatedly denied during the Jim Crow era as white supremacy reigned."[4]

In *Now Is Your Time: The African-American Struggle for Freedom*, Walter Dean Myers describes how early Jim Crow laws worked to subjugate individuals. "The first laws, passed after the Union Army ended its occupation of the South, were known as the Black Codes, and were designed to keep African Americans in an economic and social position below European Americans."[5] The Black Codes, which were almost identical to the prewar restrictions that had limited the freedom of African Americans, were passed to differentiate the rights of citizens along racial lines. Targeting Black Americans for segregated housing, education, transportation, entertainment, and services, these codes included the establishment of curfews, restrictions on owning land, requirements of evidence of employment, and "punishments for gestures, acts, and behaviors that whites could find insulting."[6]

Tragically, what characterized this time more than anything else were the violence and the enforced segregation. The Ku Klux Klan and other white supremacy organizations, the lynchings, and the second-class citizenship accorded to African Americans took an incredible toll as part of the Black experience during these years. Yet, in the nation's time of need, Black men and women took part in the two world wars that the country faced during these years. African Americans' courage and contributions during these wars took place against a backdrop of segregation and inequality in their own lives in the country they were risking all to protect.

Chapter 6 gave us stories of the years of Reconstruction between 1865 and the later 1800s, when the nation had 4 million newly freed slaves, an assassinated president, and a South in ruins. Chapter 7 provided stories about the many contributions of African Americans to the development of the West. It is worth noting that many of the events and circumstances that we will read about in this chapter were present from the beginning of colonization, had continued to fester in the years of Reconstruction, and were happening simultaneously in the West.

The books discussed in this chapter bring to life the years that followed Reconstruction, which was effectively ended in 1877 with the removal of federal troops from the South, when the force that had been present to protect African Americans from the violence of an angry and defeated South was gone.

EARLY ELEMENTARY

Aliki. *A Weed Is a Flower: The Life of George Washington Carver*. New York: Prentice Hall, 1965.

> The baby born with no hope for the future grew into one of the great scientists of his country. George Washington Carver, with his goodness and devotion, helped not only his own people, but all peoples of the world.[7]

Carver's story is one of a miracle. As an infant survivor of a deadly disease and a violent attack that separated him from his mother forever, he was lucky to be alive. Out of that sadness and horror, the child grew to be a man of many talents. Almost deciding to follow his artistic abilities, he eventually decided to pursue his interest in plants. His discoveries helped poor farmers to move from planting only cotton to farming sweet potatoes and peanuts, both of which he found many uses for. Carver's simple and humble bearing makes him all the more fascinating. Uninterested in money, he often didn't cash the checks he received, and he worked all of his life, until he was over eighty years old.

Genre: Biography

Barasch, Lynne. *Knockin' on Wood: Starring Peg Leg Bates*. New York: Lee and Low, 2004.

> "Black or white, one leg or two, it doesn't matter. Good is good."[8]

Clayton Bates was born in South Carolina in 1912, the son of a sharecropper mother. As a young boy, he danced in the local barbershop, where White men would toss him coins. To escape sharecropping, Clayton, still a child, went to work at a cottonseed mill, but his leg got caught in one of the machines and had to be amputated. As he recovered, he felt music driving his soul, and he convinced his uncle to whittle him a wooden leg on which he could dance. He danced at first for Black audiences but soon found himself a national figure, appearing in Harlem and even on the *Ed Sullivan Show*. Despite his fame, his race kept him from being able to eat or sleep at the restaurants and hotels that served Whites only. He eventually opened his own resort, where he performed and welcomed guests. The mix of this young man's determination and the issues of racism make this a book to consider.

Genre: Biography

Chocolate, Debbi. *The Piano Man*. Illustrated by Eric Velasquez. New York: Walker, 1998.

> My grandfather had silver hair by the time I was born, and he didn't tune pianos anymore. But he did tell me all there was to know about silent movies, medicine shows, vaudeville, and ragtime music.[9]

In this book, Chocolate shares the true story of her grandfather, Sherman L. Robinson, who played piano in a variety of settings: the sound background for silent movies, dance music for the Follies on Broadway, Joplin's ragtime for a medicine show, and even vaudeville. When he married and his daughter was born, he wanted to settle in one place, so he returned to playing for silent movies. When the "talkies" arrived and his music was no longer required, he turned to piano tuning. His granddaughter, the author, has clearly enjoyed the stories of his musical past.

Genre: Biography

Award: Coretta Scott King New Talent (Illustrator)

Coleman, Evelyn. *White Socks Only*. Illustrated by Tyrone Geter. Morton Grove, IL: Whitman, 1996.

> I was slurping up that water mighty fast when this big white man with a black and white bandanna 'round his neck grabbed me off the stool and pushed me to the ground. The white man pointed to the sign and yelled at me, "Can't you read, girl? Why, I'm gon' whup you 'til you can't sit down." His big fingers fumbled and tugged at his belt.[10]

When a little girl asks her grandmother if she can go to town by herself, her grandmother tells her of a time when she was a little girl and went to town by herself. It was during the Jim Crow years, and when she had finished what she had come to town to do, she stopped at a fountain to get a drink. The fountain had a "whites only" sign on it, but the girl thought it meant that you needed to have white socks on to drink at the fountain. Her drink was interrupted by an angry White man who threatened her. An older Black woman came to her defense by drinking from the fountain, too. Other Black people came to where the disturbance was, and more White people also came and began yelling at the girl. Finally, as the man was hitting the child, her neighbor stepped through the crowd, confronted the man, and helped the little girl leave to go home. According to the story, the sign was not at the fountain after that day.

Genre: Historical Fiction

Greenfield, Eloise. *Mary McLeod Bethune.* Illustrated by Jerry Pinkney. New York: HarperCollins, 1977.

> One day, a student became very ill. Because there was no hospital for blacks for many, many miles, Mrs. Bethune rushed her to the nearest white hospital. The doctors agreed to take care of her, but not inside the hospital. They put the patient on the back porch with a screen around her bed.[11]

As Greenfield's biography of the educator details, Mary McLeod Bethune responds to this incident by creating a small two-bed hospital that eventually grows to twenty-two beds. This was typical of Bethune, who accomplished many goals that she had for the African American community. Most notable were her efforts in education and the school she started that, over time, grew from an elementary school to a high school to a junior college and finally to a college. At that point, the all-girls college joined a men's college and became the Bethune-Cookman College, with Bethune as president.

Greenfield shares Bethune's early years and the many challenges she overcame to do her good work. This story provides a window into not only her wonderful accomplishments, and her commitment and faith, but also the strong desire of African Americans to get an education, and the tremendous effort made by the community to support Bethune's work.

Genre: Biography

Harrington, Janice N. *Going North.* Illustrated by Jerome Lagarrigue. New York: Farrar, Straus and Giroux, 2004.

> We're on the road again, moving fast,
> car filled with gasoline,
> Brother wearing a chocolate bar.
> Mama's hand on Daddy's shoulder.
> Long road, but we're moving fast, moving fast.[12]

When our young storyteller finds out that her family is moving north, she is not happy and does not want to go. She does not want to leave Big Mama, but her parents are going to pack up their yellow station wagon and travel to a new home in Lincoln, Nebraska. They have to pack their food for the trip and hope for the best in finding a gas station that will serve African Americans. We are on the ride with them as parents, little brother, and baby sister make their way, feeling like pioneers, leaving the fields of the South and crossing the line to the North.

Genre: Historical Fiction

Holiday, Billie, and Arthur Herzog Jr. *God Bless the Child.* Illustrated by Jerry Pinkney. New York: HarperCollins, Amistad, 2003.

> Mama may have,
> Papa may have,
> But God bless the child
> That's got his own![13]

Certainly this song by Billie Holiday is familiar to many of us. In this beautifully illustrated picture book for young readers, Jerry Pinkney has used words of this song as a text to accompany his visual interpretation of the Great Migration. The book opens with a family living in poverty in the South. As it continues, the family is packed and prepared to move north. By the end, they appear to be settled in Chicago, ready to begin a life with perhaps more promise.

Genre: Picture Book

Award: Coretta Scott King Illustrator Honor

Johnson, Angela. *I Dream of Trains*. Illustrated by Loren Long. New York: Simon and Schuster, 2003.

> But when my time comes for leaving
> I will take a train and
> remember as I roll away
> what Papa said about Casey
> and his soul-speaking whistles
> and my place in the big wide world.[14]

When a young boy is working in the field picking cotton, he hears the train whistle and dreams of trains. He and his father share a fascination with the legend of Casey Jones and his fireman (stoker), Sim Webb, and the tragic accident that took Casey's life. The boy and his father go together to the spot where the accident took place. Season after season, the boy works in the fields but knows that someday he will leave, that someday he will ride a train away.

Genre: Historical Fiction

Krull, Kathleen. *Wilma Unlimited: How Wilma Rudolph Became the World's Fastest Woman*. Illustrated by David Diaz. San Diego: Harcourt, Voyager, 1996.

> Ever since the day she had walked down the aisle at church, Wilma had known the power of concentration. Now, legs pumping, she put her mind to work. In a final, electrifying burst of speed, she pulled ahead. By a fraction of a second, she was the first to blast across the finish line.[15]

Wilma Rudolph won three gold medals at the 1960 Olympics in Rome, despite her childhood battle with polio. This book focuses on Rudolph's childhood, helping the reader to understand her childhood illnesses and physical struggles, before moving to her great athletic achievements. As an African American child growing up in Clarksville, Tennessee, in the 1940s, Rudolph was directly affected by Jim Crow laws. Racial differences had an impact on Rudolph's ability to get the best medical care.

Genre: Biography

Award: Jane Addams Children's Picture Book Award

McKissack, Patricia. *Flossie and the Fox*. Illustrated by Rachel Isadora. New York: Scholastic, 1986.

> "Lil' Flossie skipped on through the piney woods while that Fox fella rushed away lookin' for whatever he needed to prove he was really who he said he was."[16]

This is a retelling of a story Patricia McKissack remembers hearing from her favorite storyteller, her grandfather. It shares a young girl's creativity and cleverness in outsmarting the fox. It is a positive story largely because it is about a bright little girl with a great deal of ingenuity.

Genre: Folktale

Miller, William. *Richard Wright and the Library Card*. New York: Lee and Low, 1997.

> Richard loved the sound of words. He loved the stories his mother told about the farm where she grew up.
> "There was a willow tree by a bend in the river," she explained. "I dreamed all my girl dreams there."
> Richard loved to hear his grandfather tell about the war, how he ran away from his master and fought the rebel army.
> "I was only a boy," his grandfather said proudly, "but I fought as well as any man. I fought in the rain and the mud. I carried the flag at the head of the troops."[17]

This is a fictionalized story of an actual incident in Richard Wright's life. As a child, one of the things Wright wanted to do most was learn to read. One of the problems in becoming the reader he wanted to be was that he could not afford to purchase books. As an African American, he could not get a library card, but he was able to get a card from someone he worked with. When a suspicious librarian accused him of getting books for himself with the card, he pretended that he couldn't read. Out of this incredible struggle for literacy, Wright went on to become one of the outstanding authors of his generation.

Genre: Biography

Nobisso, Josephine. *John Blair and the Great Hinkley Fire.* Illustrated by Ted Rose. Boston: Houghton Mifflin, 2000.

> John Blair faced a terrible scene. Women clutching babies screamed for their other children. Neighbor begged neighbor for news of family members. Men shouted out loved ones' names, only to sob when no response came. Settlers who'd come out of the woods to fight small fires in town sank to their knees, begging, begging John to stop the train so they could fetch their families. John thought of his own wife and sons, and of how all these people were depending on him.[18]

This is a story about a true incident and a true hero. John Blair was the porter on a train run from Duluth to St. Paul. Those on the train had noticed the air heavy with smoke, but fires were not unusual in Minnesota, where forest fires often marked the dry end of summer. Blair worked that day to meet the needs of the passengers, who were growing increasingly concerned as the train began to encounter fire closer to the tracks. At first, the train seemed to pass in and out of danger, but then it suddenly came to a stop. A group of frightened people from a nearby town had escaped the flames, which had become a firestorm, and were asking for help to take them on the train and escape sure death. Many were already injured from their earlier encounter with the fire. A difficult decision was made to let additional passengers aboard and go back to a lake they had passed, since the fire appeared to be worse ahead. Traveling back was dangerous and horrifying, but Blair's cool head and determination to help the people in his charge saved the lives of his terrified passengers.

Work on the railroads was difficult but offered African Americans jobs that they then made their own. One such job was that of porter: throughout the days when passenger trains flourished, most of the men who worked that job were African American. This book complements the other books in this chapter that relate to the jobs African Americans performed on trains: Johnson's *I Dream of Trains* (see above) tells the story of stoker Sim Webb, and Woodson's *Coming On Home Soon* (described below) tells about an African American mother who goes to Chicago to help clean trains during the war.

Genre: Biography

Tobias, Tobi. *Marian Anderson.* Illustrated by Symeon Shimin. New York: Crowell, 1972.

In a small house in Philadelphia a three-year-old girl was singing.
She sat at a little table that she liked to make believe was her piano.
The walls of the room were covered with flowered paper. The child
thought she saw friendly faces in the flowers, looking down at her
as she played and sang. The child's name was Marian Anderson.
When she grew up, she became one of the world's best-loved
singers.[19]

This biography of Anderson deserves to be included here because, in spite of its age, it is well written and nicely illustrated with
pencil and watercolor wash. The text, readable for students in the second or third grade, gives a comprehensive look at this woman's incredible career.
     Genre: Biography

LATER ELEMENTARY

Adair, Gene. *George Washington Carver: Botanist*. New York: Chelsea
House, 1989.

> An ecologist before the word became fashionable, Carver taught that
> everything in nature was interrelated. [20]

This biography is far more detailed than Aliki's is for younger readers. It provides more information from Carver's formative years but also
gives the reader some insights into his Tuskegee Institute years and his
work with Booker T. Washington. It is also interesting to read the more
detailed descriptions of Carver's many innovative discoveries that eventually made him and his work famous.
     Genre: Biography

Curtis, Christopher Paul. *Bud, Not Buddy*. New York: Delacorte, 1999.

> I remember what happened to my best friend, Bugs, when a cock-
> roach crawled in his ear one night at the Home. Four grown folks
> had held Bugs down whilst they tried to pull it out with a pair of
> tweezers but the only thing they did was pull the roach's back legs
> off. When they were digging around in Bug's ears with the tweezers
> you'd've thought they were pulling his legs off, not some cockroach's,
> I'd never heard a kid scream that loud.[21]

Bud is not having an easy time. He's a good kid, and what he really wants, after the death of his mother, is to find his father. With the clues he has, he goes on his search, and Curtis takes the reader along.

This book won the Newbery Medal along with the Coretta Scott King Award and many other awards given for writing, and the awards are well deserved. It is hard to pick up this book without finding a passage worth reading. The story of Bud has a degree of suspense that holds the reader to the plot. It also has a look at a period of history when unions were new and union organization was meeting with some hostility, when it wasn't safe for Black people to be in some White residential areas, and when jazz was king. Curtis's humor and seriousness work together to make for a great read.

Genre: Historical Fiction

Awards: Coretta Scott King Author Award; Newbery Medal Winner

English, Karen. *Francie*. New York: Farrar, Straus and Giroux, 1999.

It wasn't until I was in bed that I cried so hard I though I'd make myself sick. I could hear Mama out on the porch. The slow creaking of the swing sounded sad and hopeless.[22]

Twelve-year-old Francie lives in Noble, Alabama, with her mother and her brother, Prez; her father has gone north to Chicago to work as a Pullman porter and he hopes to send for them soon. In this time before the gains of the civil rights movement, Francie experiences racism in every facet of her life, but she maintains enough innocence and determination to stay hopeful. Even young Prez faces racial violence as they wait for their chance to move north. English develops her main characters well, and readers both witness and feel the struggles and hopes of Francie and her family.

Genre: Historical Fiction

Award: Coretta Scott King Author Honor

Grimes, Nikki. *Talkin' about Bessie: The Story of Aviator Elizabeth Coleman*. Illustrated by E. B. Lewis. New York: Scholastic, 2002.

Bessie Coleman was born in Atlanta, Texas, at a time when segregation—with its Jim Crow laws and racist organizations like the Ku Klux Klan—was a way of life in the South, and lynchings of African-American men were commonplace. So-called separate-but-equal schools did little to prepare African-American children to compete in the world of business and academics, because many whites considered African Americans to be mentally inferior and descendants of African slaves were only expected to be field hands or factory workers.[23]

Being born in Texas during the Jim Crow years might have prevented Bessie Coleman from becoming a barnstormer or stunt pilot, but her determination to make something of herself was great. She took lessons to become a pilot in France after she could not find someone to teach her in the United States. Her daring feats as a pilot when she came back from Europe won her acclaim, but it was during a test flight that she lost her life.

Grimes's story is fictionalized but based on fact. It takes place in Chicago after Coleman's death, when mourners have come to grieve. Each person, in turn, talks about Coleman's life in whatever capacity they knew her. The stories are based on the real people who were part of her life, and Grimes has captured the essence of those relationships. The last person to be included is Bessie herself. The watercolor illustrations that are Lewis's trademark create a beautiful companion piece to the brief yet poignant comments of Coleman's family, friends, and acquaintances that Grimes has included in the book.

Genre: Biography

Awards: Coretta Scott King Author Honor; Coretta Scott King Illustrator Award

Hathaway, Barbara. *Missy Violet and Me*. Boston: Houghton Mifflin, 2004.

> All of a sudden, I felt real important. "Gonna work for Missy Violet, work for Missy Violet!" I sang softly under my breath. "Gonna catch a baby, gonna catch a baby!"[24]

When eleven-year-old Viney's baby sister is born, their father cannot afford to pay the midwife, Missy Violet. Instead, they work out an arrangement in which Viney will spend her summer vacation working for Missy Violet, helping her gather herbs, sterilize supplies, visit the sick and elderly, and attend births. Set in the South in the 1930s, this story describes the community at the time as the reader follows Viney through her summer.

Genre: Historical Fiction

Johnson, Dolores. *Onward: A Photobiography of African-American Polar Explorer Matthew Henson.* Washington, DC: National Geographic, 2006.

> The Inuit saw a brother in Matthew Henson not only because of his skin color but because he, of all those in the expedition, chose to learn their language and their way of life. They shared their survival skills with him, and he, in turn, taught Peary and the rest of the crew.[25]

Every classroom has children fascinated by explorers; here is a book to further whet the curiosity of these students. Lieutenant Robert Edwin Peary and Matthew Henson, the son of sharecroppers, began their partnership in 1887, when Peary hired Henson to accompany him as a manservant on a trip to Nicaragua. From that warm trip, their adventures turned to the Arctic, and after many unsuccessful attempts, the two reached the North Pole in 1909. Unfortunately, their accomplishment was questioned, which led to an apparent rift between the two. Also unfortunately, Henson's important role in the endeavor was not recognized with the kind of celebration and honor that Peary earned. This book works to set the story straight. With its black-and-white photographs and quotes from Henson, it will certainly interest upper elementary adventurers.

Genre: Biography

Lasky, Kathryn. *Vision of Beauty: The Story of Sarah Breedlove Walker.* Illustrated by Nneka Bennett. Cambridge, MA: Candlewick, 2000.

> As Madam Walker spoke, every person in the room listened. Even if they had not touched a bollworm with their bare fingers, they knew about bollworms, and if they had not seen the hooded Klansmen burn a church or a school, they could still smell the ashes.[26]

As this biography of the successful businesswoman describes, when Walker spoke to the mainly male audience at the National Negro Business League convention, all listened attentively as she shared her history, one of working in cotton fields at age five as a sharecropper's daughter, and her goal, to use the money she earned from her success to help others. Although she lived only fifty-one years, Walker did a great deal, both financially and as a model, to demonstrate success and philanthropy. From her, young Black women saw that they might be able to become entrepreneurs, and those who had success saw the importance of giving back to the African American community. The pictures in this book might make it possible to share with younger children, but the information will likely be more interesting to those who are a little older.

Genre: Biography

Lawrence, Jacob. *The Great Migration: An American Story*. New York: HarperCollins, 1993.

> Around the time I was born, many African-Americans from the South left home and traveled to cities in the North in search of a better life. My family was part of this great migration.[27]

This is both a personal story and a story of many people. Illustrated with Lawrence's incredible art work, it describes in word and in picture the conditions in the South that prompted Blacks to leave their homes and move north. Lawrence describes the excitement of African Americans to move away from the harshness of living without justice in the courts, the treatment given to sharecroppers, and the everyday dangers that they faced in the South. The migration was not always easy to accomplish, and once in the North, the promise of better housing, jobs, and education soon gave way to the prejudice that also existed there.

Lawrence lived this history and explains to the reader how his paintings, in sequence and detail, came to be. At the conclusion of the book, Walter Dean Myers shares a poem of appreciation for Lawrence's work that speaks to the images in the art and of looking forward with the hope that Lawrence found in the presence of children.

Genre: Nonfiction/Informational

Lester, Julius. *The Blues Singers: Ten Who Rocked the World*. Illustrated by Lisa Cohen. New York: Hyperion Books for Children, Jump at the Sun, 2001.

> So what are the blues? Well, the blues are like having the flu in your feelings. But instead of your nose being stuffed up, it's your heart that feels like it needs blowing.[28]

What a book! Lester begins with an introduction that provides an explanation for the book: he sets up a grandfather teaching his granddaughter about the blues on a summer vacation. This introduction establishes a friendly, comfortable tone in which the grandfather introduces ten great voices of blues music: Bessie Smith, Robert Johnson,

Mahalia Jackson, Muddy Waters, Billie Holiday, B. B. King, Ray Charles, Little Richard, James Brown, and Aretha Franklin. Each singer is introduced by a colorful illustration and quote, then described with three pages of biographical information, written in a child-appropriate tone. A bibliography and suggested listening list at the end provide resources for students who want to know (or hear!) more.

Genre: Biography

McKissack, Patricia C., and Fredrick L. McKissack. *Mary McLeod Bethune: A Great Teacher*, rev. ed. Berkeley, NJ: Enslow, 2001.

> Mrs. Eleanor Roosevelt was the president's wife. She was a friend to Mrs. Bethune. At the time, some people didn't think a black person should be invited to the White House. But the Roosevelts did. Mrs. Bethune was always welcome at the White House and in the Oval Office, too.[29]

This large-font book is open to earlier readers as it chronicles the events of Bethune's life from her birth as the fifteenth child of former slaves. When her father agrees to allow her to go to a newly available school offered after the Civil War, she begins a journey in education that will take her through her own education and on to creating a school for girls that became a prominent college for African American men and women. The photos really help the reader relate to the events that are described in the text. Any study of Bethune's life and work could incorporate this book with the others mentioned here for different reading levels, and students might consider how the stories treat different details from her life.

Genre: Biography

Meltzer, Milton. *Mary McLeod Bethune: Voice of Black Hope*. Illustrated by Stephen Marchesi. New York: Puffin, 1987.

> Violence against blacks exploded often on the nation's front pages. In the first decades of the 1900's terrible race riots broke out. Mobs of furious whites swept through the streets of several cities, beating and killing the blacks they met. And thousands of lynchings took place not only in the South but in many parts of the North.[30]

It was during these tumultuous times that Mary McLeod Bethune worked to make real the promise of a better life with education and health for African Americans. In the years before the civil rights movement, Bethune was pressing for equal rights. When she was called to Washington, D.C., she found a ready ear in Eleanor Roosevelt and often went directly to President Franklin Delano Roosevelt and his wife when she discovered blatant discrimination, such as the Whites-only policy in the White House press corps. She pressed for Black interests, from federal judgeships to funding for housing. She picketed and lobbied in later years, after she had already built a strong school system that lifted many lives to reach their potential and their hopes for a future. She continued to deal with pressing issues until she died of a heart attack in 1955, just one year after the *Brown v. Board of Education* decision of the Supreme Court that ended school segregation.

Genre: Biography

Miller, William. *Joe Louis, My Champion.* Illustrated by Rodney S. Pate. New York: Lee and Low, 2004.

> "Joe Louis is the heavyweight champion of the world!" I cried, and Papa gave me a hug. We were all champions now—every one of us who believed in Joe Louis.[31]

Sammy wants more than anything to be a great boxer like Joe Louis. He even trades help with schoolwork for boxing lessons from his best friend, Ernie Block. On the night of the big fight between Joe Louis and James Braddock, Sammy stands with his family and neighbors at Mister Jake's country store, listening to the play-by-play announcements over the radio. He is transfixed as he thinks about Joe Louis refusing to quit. The next day, Sammy realizes that try as he might, he is never going to be a famous boxer like his hero. He comes to understand that his father, Mister Jake, and Ernie are right: the most important lesson to be learned from Joe Louis is not about boxing, but about being the best you can be at whatever you do.

Genre: Historical Fiction

Miller, William. *Night Golf.* Illustrated by Cedric Lucas. New York: Lee and Low, 1999.

> "I'll do whatever it takes," James said. "I really want to play—I mean caddy."
> The man laughed out loud. "For a second, I though you said you wanted to play golf. Heck, boy. This is a game for white folks only—rich white folks at that."[32]

When young James finds an old rusted golf club and balls in a garbage can, he quickly realizes he has found his sport. Sadly, his father has to tell him that Blacks aren't allowed on the golf course. James checks out the golf course for himself, and he finds that it is true that Blacks can't play, but they can caddy. He takes on the role of caddy and finds a mentor who sees himself as a young man in James. For the rest of the summer, Charlie teaches James to golf on the golf course after dark, and James is finally given a chance to prove himself. In an author's note, Miller lets us know that this is based on the actual experiences of many Black caddies of the 1950s.

Genre: Historical Fiction

Mitchell, Margaree King. *Uncle Jed's Barbershop.* Illustrated by James E. Ransome. New York: Scholastic, 1993.

This is a story about a rural community and a barber named Jedediah Johnson, known as Jed, who travels from farm to farm cutting people's hair. His goal is to have enough money someday to have his own barber shop. When the narrator, his grandniece, becomes very ill and her parents do not have the money for her treatment, Uncle Jed dips into his savings and, without hesitation, provides the needed cash. As the story goes on, there are more obstacles in the way of his achieving his goal, but in the end, he succeeds. He is even more successful in teaching a child to dream and demonstrating that some things are more important than money. Set in the Jim Crow years in the South, this book gives the reader much to think about.

Genre: Historical Fiction

Award: Coretta Scott King Illustrator Honor

Myers, Walter Dean. *Now Is Your Time: The African-American Struggle for Freedom.* New York: HarperCollins, 1991.

> Africans had been brought to America for one reason: to provide cheap labor. The South was still an agricultural society and still needed that cheap labor. But captive labor could be controlled. Now the African Americans, free from bondage, were competing against whites. But new controls were soon imposed in the form of policies, based solely on race, that restricted opportunities for African Americans.[33]

Walter Dean Myers is a prolific author of children's literature, with many award-winning books to his credit. As an informational text, this book is something of a departure from his usual genres of realistic and historical fiction, but it offers the reader an excellent, well-researched history for the young reader. The book actually records history from the very early years of exploration through the civil rights era. It would be appropriate in any chapter so far and could be used in the chapters that are yet to come. It is a wonderful resource—a readable and reliable text.

Genre: Nonfiction/Informational

Award: Coretta Scott King Author Award

Pinkney, Gloria Jean. *Back Home*. Illustrated by Jerry Pinkney. New York: Dial Books for Young Readers, 1992.

> "Hey, Ernestine!" said Uncle June, lifting her satchel. "I knew right off it was you. I do declare," he exclaimed, "if you don't favor my oldest sister Zulah when she was a girl."
> Ernestine felt warm inside. I look like Grandmama! she thought.[34]

The migration of African Americans to the North meant that many families would have relatives still in the South. Trips back to the relatives in the South were not uncommon, and many, such as the one described in this story, provided sweet memories of time spent with loving family on the old family farms. These trips presented many new opportunities and experiences, and in this case, Ernestine, dressed in her mother's old overalls, explores the farm with her cousin Jack, who has a tendency to tease his citified cousin. Their friendship is strong by the end of the summer, and Ernestine looks forward to the possibility of visiting again.

For many families, the trips south presented a challenge, because they were going back to a place where African Americans lived with fear and intimidation much of the time. Pinkney shares a story about the other part of that world, when you were on the farm and with family, away from town and the complexity of racial relations that were most threatening; there was great joy and love in being together and gentle memories for a lifetime.

Genre: Historical Fiction/Memoir

Ryan, Pam Muñoz. *When Marian Sang*. Illustrated by Brian Selznick. New York: Scholastic, 2002.

> In 1939, Howard University in Washington, D.C., booked a concert with Marian Anderson and began looking for an auditorium big enough to hold the audience she attracted. They decided that the

4,000-seat Constitution Hall would be perfect. But the manager of the hall said it wasn't available *and* no other dates were offered because of their *white performers only* policy.[35]

Marian Anderson had an amazing voice from the time she was a young child. In spite of her talent, she was not admitted to a music school in Philadelphia, and she rode in segregated train cars when she traveled to performances. Finally, after Giuseppe Boghetti, a famous master voice teacher, reluctantly allowed her to audition, he recognized her extraordinary talent and became her teacher. As an accomplished artist, Anderson toured Europe and received world acclaim only to return to America and the Jim Crow prohibitions like the one the book describes above. Finally, Eleanor Roosevelt intervened and Anderson was invited to sing at the Lincoln Memorial to an audience of thousands. Gradually, her great talent overcame the prejudice that marked that period and she was asked to perform at the Metropolitan Opera.

Along with being a well-written biography, this is a beautifully illustrated picture book. It is unique in that it is almost exclusively drawn in shades of beige and reddish-brown until Anderson is in the colorful spotlight of the Met.

Genre: Biography

Award: Orbis Pictus Winner

Vander Zee, Ruth. *Mississippi Morning*. Illustrated by Floyd Cooper. Grand Rapids, MI: Eerdmans Books for Young Readers, 2004.

> I'd sweep the wooden floor and listen to my pa. It seemed that somebody was always stopping in at one time or other to talk to him. In fact, one afternoon one of those men walked over to where I was working and said, "You know, James William, most of the important decisions in our part of Mississippi are made right here in the porch of your papa's store."[36]

It is 1933, and William's world is good. As a young White boy in Mississippi, he does his chores, helps his mother out, works in his dad's hardware store, and still has time to wander in the woods around his home. Listening to the men who come into his dad's store, he realizes that his father is influential in the town, and he is proud of him. One day, while talking to a friend, he finds out that Black families are being terrorized and his dad and the man in the store have been overheard talking about attacking a Black preacher's home and setting it on fire. When

LeRoy, a Black boy William is fishing with, identifies a tree as the "hanging tree," William realizes that the stories of Black families being attacked are likely true. Asking his father about it only prompts his father to get angry. But when William is hidden behind a tree near the road up to his house, he sees something that changes his relationship with his father forever.

Genre: Historical Fiction

Wiles, Deborah. *Freedom Summer.* Illustrated by Jerome Lagarrigue. New York: Atheneum Books for Young Readers, 2001.

Wiles tells the story of two friends, one White and one Black, who live in Mississippi during the civil rights years. The boys get excited about the opening of the town pool and plan to go swimming, only to find out that the pool has been destroyed. In order not to open the pool to Black children, the town has filled it with asphalt. The boys end up planning to do many other things together that are now open to John Henry. The author explains that the story is fiction but based on true events.

Genre: Historical Fiction

Woods, Brenda. *The Red Rose Box.* New York: Putnam's, 2002.

I paused to look at the drinking fountain as we made our way to the door. I was thirsty and there were no signs. I pointed to it and asked Aunt Olivia, "That for white or colored?"

"Anyone who's thirsty, white or colored. No Jim Crow here."[37]

Leah's mother and her mother's sister have not been close in some time; Leah's family lives in poor Sulphur, Louisiana, while Aunt Olivia lives with her wealthy husband in Los Angeles. For Leah's tenth birthday, in 1953, Aunt Olivia sends tickets for Leah, her sister Ruth, her mother, and her grandmother to come visit in California. When they do, Leah is able to see a world very much unlike that in which she lives, a world in which Black people can succeed and be treated equally. When tragedy strikes, Leah and Ruth find themselves living with Aunt Olivia indefinitely. As the family also travels to New York, this book provides an interesting contrast between geographic regions in the time immediately before the civil rights era.

Genre: Historical Fiction

Woodson, Jacqueline. *Coming On Home Soon*. Illustrated by E. B. Lewis. New York: Putnam's, 2004.

> There is snow this morning.
> And a small black kitten scratching against our door.
> There is milk this morning, warm from the cow.
> Grandma says, "You know we can't keep it."
> Then pours milk into a saucer and sets it down on the floor.[38]

During World War II, many women took jobs that had once been exclusively done by men. Because of the call of the armed forces, there was a lack of available men to do them. Woodson's story is of an African American mother who hears about these job openings and seizes the opportunity to work on the railroad. In order to be able to go away and work, she has to leave her young daughter, Ada Ruth, in the care of her mother.

The story is a beautiful sharing about the closeness of Ada Ruth and her mother, who love each other "more than rain" and "more than snow." It is about the days Ada Ruth and her grandma spend together, waiting for word from Ada Ruth's mama. This quiet and tender story is set in winter, and if you listen real close, you can hear the snowflakes fall. This story and the illustrations combine to make this a truly beautiful book.

Genre: Historical Fiction
Award: Caldecott Illustrator Honor

MIDDLE GRADES

Carbone, Elisa. *Storm Warriors*. New York: Knopf, 2001.

> Even with all those men, one mule, and one strong, but skinny, twelve-year-old boy pulling on the drag ropes, it still felt like we were trying to lug an entire steamer through a sea of molasses. By the time we rejoined the rest of the crew, sweat ran down my back and arms. My heart was pounding hard, too. Soon the rescue would begin.[39]

More than anything, Nathan wants to be a surfman at the Pea Island Life-Saving Station, so he studies, practices, and helps in daring storm rescues. Carefully researched, this work of historical fiction is

well-established in a factual context: while Nathan and his family are
created characters, many of the other characters are based on real surfmen. Many of the events are real events, both those set in 1896 and in
the years that precede the novel. After the Civil War, these stations designed to save the lives of sailors in the dangerous Outer Banks of North
Carolina were originally integrated, although Blacks could only serve in
the lower ranks. Over time, the Whites refused to work with the Blacks,
and so Pea Island Life-Saving Station was established as the one all-Black
station, while the other eighteen stations were all White. With the number of young men wanting to be surfmen far exceeding the number of
actual positions, Nathan's dream is only a remote possibility.

The life of Nathan's family before arriving at Pea Island provides a
wealth of historical information. Nathan's grandfather is a freed slave
whose owner was also his father. Near the end of the Civil War, his wife
was sold away by her owner at a neighboring property. He used his early
earnings to place ads in the newspaper trying to find her, as did so many
freed slaves. Years later, he still asks for a dollar from his son each time
they go to town, so that he can continue placing his ads for his long-lost
Dahlia. Nathan's family has moved to the Outer Banks to escape the Ku
Klux Klan after one of their neighbors is found lynched. Because medical care for Blacks is rare in their remote location, Nathan's mother dies
of diphtheria. Clearly, this book deals with difficult issues, but it is a fascinating study not only of racial issues of the time, but also of the generally untold story of these brave surfmen who regularly risked their lives
for others (their motto was "You have to go out, but you don't have to
come back," demonstrating their commitment in the face of danger),
and the aspirations of a young man determined to overcome the odds.

Genre: Historical Fiction

Cooper, Michael L. *The Black Migration: Bound for the Promised Land.*
New York: Lodestar, 1995.

> When the Great Migration began, most African Americans lived in
> fifteen southern states. They were among the poorest and most badly
> treated people in the nation. Black Americans could not vote, run for
> political office or serve on juries. They could be cheated, beaten, or
> even murdered, and the police usually did nothing. For these people,
> the Great Migration was a "second emancipation," an escape from a
> life little better that slavery.[40]

Cooper goes on to say that during this migration, approximately 1 million Black southerners moved to the industrial Northeast and Midwest. Many had been sharecroppers before making their move to the North, where the possibilities for employment had increased with the nation's entrance into World War I. In spite of what seemed like the promise of a better life, African Americans continued to encounter racism and violence that, at times, resulted in race riots where police often did nothing to protect African Americans, and opportunities for education continued to be limited. Cooper tells the story of Paul Robeson, who achieved acclaim as a singer and actor after graduating with a law degree from Columbia University but was unable to practice law because of so few opportunities afforded black lawyers.

Cooper's book is a wonderful resource for young researchers who want to understand the Great Migration, its causes and conditions, its relationship to World War I, and its connections with the Harlem Renaissance.

Genre: Nonfiction/Informational

Fradin, Dennis Brindell, and Judith Bloom Fradin. *Ida B. Wells: Mother of the Civil Rights Movement*. New York: Clarion, 2000.

> She visited places where lynchings had occurred, spoke to the victims' relatives, and corresponded with witnesses. She discovered that black people were routinely lynched for such alleged offenses as horse stealing, barn burning and "talking sassy" to white people. In many cases the lynching victims had been falsely accused but were hunted down because bloodthirsty mobs wanted to kill any black person they could find. Law officers often refused to protect the victims and sometimes participated in the murders. At times, newspapers incited the lynchings, and even announced where and when they would occur in order to attract huge crowds. Incredibly, state governors sometimes knew about upcoming lynchings but refused to stop them. The worst part, Wells realized, was that lynching victims were deprived of the "right to a speedy and public trail," guaranteed to all Americans by the Bill of Rights.[41]

Born in the last years of slavery, Ida B. Wells grew up to become a schoolteacher, journalist, owner and editor of a newspaper, wife, mother of six children, and an activist. She worked with Frederick Douglass, Susan B. Anthony, and Harriet Tubman for the causes of racial equality and women's rights. But one of the things she committed herself to with a passion that often endangered her own life was confronting the horrors of lynching. The practice of lynching became prominent in the late 1800s and the early 1900s and was used to punish African Americans accused of even minor crimes. Used as a tool of intimidation, lynching was also commonly used to frighten would-be voters.

Wells wrote extensively about the lynchings of the time, and she would not let people ignore these horrible acts that were taking place, most often without any legal consequences to the people who were involved. By the time she died in 1931, the era of rampant lynchings had ended, although legalized racial segregation would continue for decades.

Genre: Biography

Freedman, Russell. *The Voice That Challenged a Nation: Marian Anderson and the Struggle for Equal Rights*. New York: Clarion, 2004.

> Soon after the war started, the DAR announced a series of concerts to raise funds for war relief. As a gesture of compromise and goodwill, the Daughters invited Marian Anderson to give the opening concert, a benefit for the United China Relief Fund. She accepted on condition that the audience be completely unsegregated, and after some hesitation the DAR agreed. For the first time in its history, the organization permitted a concert to be held in Constitution Hall with no segregation of any kind in the seating arrangements.[42]

Freedman's biography of Marian Anderson is comprehensive. In the progression of books that can be used to look at the same subject at different reading levels, author styles, and relationship of pictures to text, Freedman's book could be used with Ryan's book, *When Marian Sang*. For young researchers, Freedman's book gives significant facts in great detail.

Genre: Biography
Award: Orbis Pictus Honor Book

Hesse, Karen. *Witness*. New York: Scholastic, 2001.

> I woke up Saturday night
> because the light coming through
> my bedroom window changed.

on the hill across the valley
i saw
a flame
rising.
but it was
no wild fire. It
was a
cross,
burning.[43]

Hesse uses narrative verse to tell the story of the impact of the Ku Klux Klan in Vermont in the early 1920s. Like *Lizzie Bright and the Buckminster Boy*, this is the story of a northern state afflicted by the same discrimination and violence that we often associate with the South during the Jim Crow years. Seeming innocuous and even patriotic at first, the Ku Klux Klan eventually demonstrates their real agenda of terrorizing African Americans and Jews and anyone who is an ally to these groups. The eleven characters whose voices are heard in Hesse's work are fictionalized, but the Ku Klux Klan being active in Vermont in that time period is factual. For twelve-year-old Leonora Sutter, an African American child, and six-year-old Esther Hirsh, a Jew, it is a time of loss of innocence as the world around them takes on a harsh reality.

Genre: Historical Fiction/Narrative Poetry

Moses, Shelia P. *The Legend of Buddy Bush*. New York: Simon and Schuster, 2004.

Pattie Mae's Uncle Buddy arrives back home to Rehobeth Road in Rich Square, North Carolina, in the early 1940s, after living in Harlem. Having been raised by Pattie Mae's grandparents, he migrated north when he was sixteen years old. When he returns to his former hometown, he is returned to the Jim Crow South where a Black man can be accused of a crime by a White person and find his life in danger. Buddy Bush is accused by a White woman of making a pass at her, and Pattie Mae, who was with her uncle when he was accused, sees how quickly his freedom is taken away. When the Klan takes him from his jail cell intending to murder him, he escapes and is found by friends who have come south to help him.

Moses has taken a true event, fictionalized it, and told it through the voice of young Pattie Mae. Born and raised in the same town as the story takes place, Moses has woven her story together with the stories her grandmother told about the legend of Buddy Bush and with her own family's many stories of that period.

Genre: Historical Fiction

Awards: Coretta Scott King Author Honor; National Book Award Nominee

Schmidt, Gary D. *Lizzie Bright and the Buckminster Boy*. New York: Yearling, 2004.

> So he wept. With his hand still on the whale and the whale's eye on him, he wept. He wept for old Mrs. Hurd, and he wept for Mrs. Cobb, and he wept for his father, and he wept for Lizzie Bright. In the open sea, with the land blue in his eyes and the sea green in his hand, he wept.[44]

Schmidt has written a story about an actual island in Maine and the events that happened there in the early 1900s. The friendship that develops between Turner Buckminster, a White newcomer to the town, and Lizzie Bright, an African American girl who lives with her grandfather on Malaga Island, brings a connection between the island and the mainland town of Phippsburg, Maine. The story introduces the reader to well-developed characters that play out one of the most devastating historical events that happened between Whites and Blacks in this rural northern state: Black residents on the island are displaced by White townspeople who wish to make their area a tourist destination. Turner and Lizzie's lives are changed by their friendship, and they change the lives of those around them.

For many northerners, there is a sense that prejudice and discrimination against African Americans is a southern phenomenon, but the racism at the heart of the Jim Crow era existed to some degree throughout the United States. This story, as sad as it is, is a story of the strength of friendship and the hope of children seeing another way, a way of looking beyond race.

Genre: Historical Fiction

Award: Newbery Honor

Sharp, Anne Wallace. *A Dream Deferred: The Jim Crow Era*. Farmington Hills, MI: Lucent, 2005.

> Underlying the Jim Crow system was racism, or the belief that whites are superior in all ways to other races. Throughout the United

States, but particularly in the South, this idea was ingrained in the hearts and minds of whites. As a consequence, for nearly one hundred years after the end of the Civil War, African Americans were unable to participate fully in the American Dream. As late as the early 1940's, thanks to the effects of the Jim Crow system, 90 percent of all African American families lived in poverty, and fewer than 5 percent of black Southerners could vote.[45]

Sharp's well-researched accounts of the Jim Crow era are difficult to read because of their subject matter, but they also make for a book that is difficult to put down. Our history during these years is tragic for the many citizens who were marginalized in almost every facet of American life. Detailed accounts of conditions, events, and individual accomplishments, along with specific historical markers such as the Depression, the Harlem Renaissance, the establishment of the NAACP, and the two world wars, make this a very comprehensive resource for students studying this period of American history.

Genre: Nonfiction/Informational

Taylor, Mildred D. *The Friendship.* Illustrated by Max Ginsburg. New York: Puffin, 1987.

> Stacy nodded. "Yes, sir, that's a fact, but that's the way white folks do. Papa say white folks set an awful store 'bout names and such. He say they get awful riled 'bout them names too. Say they can do some terrible things when they get riled. Say anybody call a white man straight out by his name just lookin' for trouble.[46]

This story has Cassie, Christopher-John, Stacey, and Little Man help out an elderly neighbor they call Aunt Callie Jackson, who asks the children to go to Wallace's Store for medicine. In spite of their parents warning them that the store is not a good place for them to be, they go there to help the older woman out. At the store they run into Mr. Tom Bee, who in his later years has taken to fishing most days. The owner's sons give Tom a hard time when he refers to their father by his first name.

This would seem like the makings of a pretty uneventful story, but it is not. This is the South in the Jim Crow years. The children and Tom Bee leave the store and later have a conversation about the owner's sons' anger at the old man calling their father by his first name. It turns out that John Wallace, the store owner, had told Tom that he could call him by his first name years ago when, as boys, Tom saved John's life. But peer pressure and the enforced segregation and the rules of the Jim Crow years ended up having their way.

This book is little more than fifty pages, but readers will remember it for a long, long time. Because of its length, it makes an excellent read-aloud for middle school classes—but when I read it aloud, I cried so hard at the end, I could hardly talk. There is enormous power in this short story, which once again illustrates Taylor's incredible writing skills.

Genre: Historical Fiction

Award: Coretta Scott King Author Award

Taylor, Mildred D. *Roll of Thunder, Hear My Cry.* New York: Puffin, 1976.

> Papa tilted my chin and gazed softly down at me. "All I can say, Cassie girl—is that it shouldn't be." Then glancing back toward the forest, he took my hand and led me to the house.[47]

Powerful and honest, this story of the Logan family takes place in the South during the Jim Crow years. The brutality and violence of the time is set against a family of enormous love, courage, and wisdom. The characters of Cassie, who tells the story, Stacy, Christopher-John, and Little Man, as well as their parents, will be revisited in other stories by Taylor of the Logan family. These characters are extremely real, and the events of their lives make this one of the richest historical fiction stories for this era.

Taylor writes in her author's note that her father was a storyteller who could paint pictures vividly with characters and dialogue, telling stories with grace and beauty, and I am touched and grateful that she has chosen to share them with her readers.

Genre: Historical Fiction

Award: Newbery Medal Winner

Taylor, Mildred D. *The Well: David's Story.* New York: Puffin, 1995.

> Hammer stepped back and only now unclenched his fists; his face was showing no remorse at what he'd done. If he was scared, he wasn't showing that either. But I was sure enough scared, and I was ready to get out of there. I stared down at Charlie. "What we gonna do, Hammer? What we gonna do?"
>
> Hammer stared down at Charlie too and shrugged, "'Spect there's nothin' we can do now, is there?"

I just looked at him and wondered how long it would be before we both got hung. After all, young as we were, we knew enough to know that black boys of any age didn't go around hitting white boys of any age. Black boy hit white boy, black man hit a white man, he could get hung in a flick of a horse's tail, and that's just the way things were. I ain't hardly lying when I say this David Logan was mighty scared.[48]

Taylor makes the day-to-day events of life in the Jim Crow South come alive in the story of a family who must endure the humiliation and dangers that can be present in even the most benign events. In this book, a Black family has a well that continues to have fresh water while the wells in the surrounding farms have gone dry. Graciously, they share the water with their neighbors, even neighbors who are not respectful or nice to them. After several negative encounters that eight-year-old David Logan and his thirteen-year-old brother, Hammer, have with Charlie Simms, the fourteen-year-old son of one of the meanest men in the neighborhood, Charlie strikes David. Hammer angrily beats up Charlie, and although the Logan boys did not start the fight, Charlie convinces his father and the sheriff that David and Hammer attacked him. The sheriff, pressured by the elder Simms, forces David and Hammer's mother to whip them as punishment. In the end, the Simms children shame their family with a senseless act that harms the whole community, and they never bother the Logan family again.

Like *The Friendship*, this story is short and very powerful. Taylor's use of conversation provides readers with well-developed characters in settings that are authentic and reliably accurate for the period in which they take place.

Genre: Historical Fiction
Award: Jane Addams Older Children's Book Award

Tillage, Leon Walter. *Leon's Story*. Illustrated by Susan L. Roth. New York: Farrar, Straus and Giroux, 1997.

In telling his story, Leon Tillage is continuing his peaceful protesting by helping to educate people. We all need to know and to remember the history over and over again. We all need to help the changes to continue.[49]

This is a true story of Leon Tillage, who was born in 1936, the second oldest of nine children. He tells of growing up in the South in the

Jim Crow years in a sharecropper family. His story is riveting in its simplicity and intensity. The story of his father's death as a result of being deliberately run over by some teenage White boys who had been drinking reveals just how dehumanizing and tragic racism can be. The half-hearted apology of the father of one of the boys and the refusal of the teenager to apologize himself constitute a scene you will not soon forget.

Without any investigation by the town sheriff, this tragedy was never followed up on, nor was there any legal consequence. Through this and other shared experiences, Leon tells the story of a period in our history when a race of people were too often treated with a brutal disregard. In Leon's case, he lived his life without bitterness, and he was eventually honored by the school where he worked as a custodian for almost thirty years.

Genre: Nonfiction/Informational/Biography

CONCLUSION

The Civil War brought an end to slavery but not to injustice. After a brief period of Reconstruction, which resulted in a lost opportunity to create lasting change, the Jim Crow years brought with them laws to segregate and oppress African Americans, particularly in the South. These were years of turbulence and of terror, with lynchings, riots, and everyday indignities that continued for over seventy years. Against this devastating reality, African Americans worked against mighty odds to create brilliant art, literature, music, and dance; they fought valiantly in two world wars and became outstanding athletes in America's "favorite pastime," even without the benefits that were showered on the major league baseball teams. Chapter 9 looks at some of those achievements and the people who worked to create them during the Jim Crow years.

NOTES

1. Foner, *Reconstruction*, 604.
2. Sharp, *A Dream Deferred*, 18.
3. Sharp, *A Dream Deferred*, 9.
4. Sharp, *A Dream Deferred*, 18.

5. Myers, *Now Is Your Time*, 197.
6. Sharp, *A Dream Deferred*, 12.
7. Aliki, *A Weed Is a Flower*.
8. Barasch, *Knockin' on Wood*.
9. Chocolate, *The Piano Man*.
10. Coleman, *White Socks*.
11. Greenfield, *Mary McLeod Bethune*, 24.
12. Harrington, *Going North*.
13. Holiday, *God Bless the Child*.
14. Johnson, *I Dream of Trains*.
15. Krull, *Wilma Unlimited*.
16. McKissack, *Flossie and the Fox*.
17. Miller, *Richard Wright*.
18. Nobisso, *John Blair*.
19. Tobias, *Marian Anderson*.
20. Adair, *George Washington Carver*, 52.
21. Curtis, *Bud, Not Buddy*, 23.
22. English, *Francie*, 174.
23. Grimes, *Talkin' about Bessie*.
24. Hathaway, *Missy Violet and Me*, 4.
25. Johnson, *Onward*, 20.
26. Lasky, *Vision of Beauty*.
27. Lawrence, *Great Migration*.
28. Lester, *The Blues Singers*, introduction.
29. McKissack and McKissack, *Mary McLeod Bethune*, 25.
30. Meltzer, *Mary McLeod Bethune*, 35.
31. Miller, *Joe Louis*.
32. Miller, *Night Golf*.
33. Myers, *Now Is Your Time*, 196–97.
34. Pinkney, *Back Home*.
35. Ryan, *When Marian Sang*.
36. Vander Zee, *Mississippi Morning*.
37. Woods, *Red Rose Box*, 26.
38. Woodson, *Coming On Home Soon*.
39. Carbone, *Storm Warriors*, 6.
40. Cooper, *The Black Migration*, 3.
41. Fradin and Fradin, *Ida B. Wells*, x.
42. Freedman, *Voice That Challenged a Nation*, 74.
43. Hesse, *Witness*, 54.
44. Schmidt, *Lizzie Bright*, 216.
45. Sharp, *A Dream Deferred*, 9.

46. Taylor, *The Friendship*, 37.
47. Taylor, *Roll of Thunder*, 275.
48. Taylor, *The Well*, 30–31.
49. Tillage, *Leon's Story*, 106–7.

BIBLIOGRAPHY OF BOOKS FOR CHILDREN

Adair, Gene. *George Washington Carver: Botanist*. New York: Chelsea House, 1989.

Aliki. *A Weed Is a Flower: The Life of George Washington Carver*. New York: Prentice Hall, 1965.

Barasch, Lynne. *Knockin' on Wood: Starring Peg Leg Bates*. New York: Lee and Low, 2004.

Carbone, Elisa. *Storm Warriors*. New York: Knopf, 2001.

Chocolate, Debbi. *The Piano Man*. Illustrated by Eric Velasquez. New York: Walker, 1998.

Coleman, Evelyn. *White Socks Only*. Illustrated by Tyrone Geter. Morton Grove, IL: Whitman, 1996.

Cooper, Michael L. *The Black Migration: Bound for the Promised Land*. New York: Lodestar, 1995.

Curtis, Christopher Paul. *Bud, Not Buddy*. New York: Delacorte, 1999.

English, Karen. *Francie*. New York: Farrar, Straus and Giroux, 1999.

Fradin, Dennis Brindell, and Judith Bloom Fradin. *Ida B. Wells: Mother of the Civil Rights Movement*. New York: Clarion, 2000.

Freedman, Russell. *The Voice That Challenged a Nation: Marian Anderson and the Struggle for Equal Rights*. New York: Clarion, 2004.

Greenfield, Eloise. *Mary McLeod Bethune*. Illustrated by Jerry Pinkney. New York: HarperCollins, 1977.

Grimes, Nikki. *Talkin' about Bessie: The Story of Aviator Elizabeth Coleman*. Illustrated by E. B. Lewis. New York: Scholastic, 2002.

Harrington, Janice N. *Going North*. Illustrated by Jerome Lagarrigue. New York: Farrar, Straus and Giroux, 2004.

Hathaway, Barbara. *Missy Violet and Me*. Boston: Houghton Mifflin, 2004.

Hesse, Karen. *Witness*. New York: Scholastic, 2001.

Holiday, Billie, and Arthur Herzog Jr. *God Bless the Child*. Illustrated by Jerry Pinkney. New York: HarperCollins, Amistad, 2003.

Johnson, Angela. *I Dream of Trains*. Illustrated by Loren Long. New York: Simon and Schuster, 2003.

Johnson, Dolores. *Onward: A Photobiography of African-American Polar Explorer Matthew Henson*. Washington, DC: National Geographic, 2006.

Krull, Kathleen. *Wilma Unlimited: How Wilma Rudolph Became the World's Fastest Woman*. Illustrated by David Diaz. San Diego: Harcourt, Voyager, 1996.

Lasky, Kathryn. *Vision of Beauty: The Story of Sarah Breedlove Walker*. Illustrated by Nneka Bennett. Cambridge, MA: Candlewick, 2000.

Lawrence, Jacob. *The Great Migration: An American Story*. New York: Harper-Collins, 1993.

Lester, Julius. *The Blues Singers: Ten Who Rocked the World*. Illustrated by Lisa Cohen. New York: Hyperion Books for Children, Jump at the Sun, 2001.

McKissack, Patricia. *Flossie and the Fox*. Illustrated by Rachel Isadora. New York: Scholastic, 1986.

McKissack, Patricia C., and Fredrick L. McKissack. *Mary McLeod Bethune: A Great Teacher*, rev. ed. Berkeley, NJ: Enslow, 2001.

Meltzer, Milton. *Mary McLeod Bethune: Voice of Black Hope*. Illustrated by Stephen Marchesi. New York: Puffin, 1987.

Miller, William. *Joe Louis, My Champion*. Illustrated by Rodney S. Pate. New York: Lee and Low, 2004.

———. *Night Golf*. Illustrated by Cedric Lucas. New York: Lee and Low, 1999.

———. *Richard Wright and the Library Card*. New York: Lee and Low, 1997.

Mitchell, Margaree King. *Uncle Jed's Barbershop*. Illustrated by James E. Ransome. New York: Scholastic, 1993.

Moses, Shelia P. *The Legend of Buddy Bush*. New York: Simon and Schuster, 2004.

Myers, Walter Dean. *Now Is Your Time: The African-American Struggle for Freedom*. New York: HarperCollins, 1991.

Nobisso, Josephine. *John Blair and the Great Hinkley Fire*. Illustrated by Ted Rose. Boston: Houghton Mifflin, 2000.

Pinkney, Gloria Jean. *Back Home*. Illustrated by Jerry Pinkney. New York: Dial Books for Young Readers, 1992.

Ryan, Pam Muñoz. *When Marian Sang*. Illustrated by Brian Selznick. New York: Scholastic, 2002.

Schmidt, Gary D. *Lizzie Bright and the Buckminister Boy*. New York: Yearling, 2004.

Sharp, Anne Wallace. *A Dream Deferred: The Jim Crow Era*. Farmington Hills, MI: Lucent, 2005.

Taylor, Mildred D. *The Friendship*. Illustrated by Max Ginsburg. New York: Puffin, 1987.

———. *Roll of Thunder, Hear My Cry*. New York: Puffin, 1976.

———. *The Well: David's Story*. New York: Puffin, 1995.

Tillage, Leon Walter. *Leon's Story*. Illustrated by Susan L. Roth. New York: Farrar, Straus and Giroux, 1997.

Tobias, Tobi. *Marian Anderson*. Illustrated by Symeon Shimin. New York: Crowell, 1972.

Vander Zee, Ruth. *Mississippi Morning*. Illustrated by Floyd Cooper. Grand Rapids, MI: Eerdmans Books for Young Readers, 2004.

Wiles, Deborah. *Freedom Summer*. Illustrated by Jerome Lagarrigue. New York: Atheneum Books for Young Readers, 2001.
Woods, Brenda. *The Red Rose Box*. New York: Putnam's, 2002.
Woodson, Jacqueline. *Coming On Home Soon*. Illustrated by E. B. Lewis. New York: Putnam's, 2004.

BIBLIOGRAPHY OF REFERENCE WORKS

Foner, Eric. *Reconstruction: America's Unfinished Revolution, 1863–1877*. New York: Harper and Row, 1988.

· 9 ·

Gaining Community, Gaining Voice: The Harlem Renaissance, the Negro Baseball League, and War

Before the Harlem Renaissance began, there were African Americans who distinguished themselves in intellectual and creative fields. After it ended, many more continued to do so. But the sense among African Americans that they had the power to affect their own lives and that their culture should be celebrated was new to the people whose history in the United States had begun with slavery; and it was not to be repeated with a similar outpouring of creative self-assertion until nearly a half century later, after the success of the Civil Rights Movement of the 1960's.[1]

Throughout our country's history, Black men and women in America reached the highest levels of accomplishment. In spite of the great forces that fought against their success, African Americans became great orators, lawyers, artists, writers, scientists, teachers, musicians, athletes, inventors, and much, much more.

THE HARLEM RENAISSANCE

At no other time in our country's history had Blacks experienced the opportunity for accomplishment that they found during the period known as the Harlem Renaissance. Created in part by the migration of Blacks from the South during the war years, the Harlem neighborhood of New York City became a thriving creative community with members who shaped the futures of their chosen fields. Their influence continues to be felt today.

It is generally believed that the Harlem Renaissance began at the end of World War I, around 1919, and ended with the onset of the Great Depression in the early 1930s. Clearly, its impact was profound. Its influence spread across the nation, with literary and artististic pursuits in every major city, whether it was in poetry circles or small theater productions or students interested in painting. As historian John Hope Franklin observed about this phenomenally productive period: "The African-American participant in the Harlem Renaissance inherited a legacy of expression from an earlier generation and, in using that legacy, transformed it into a powerful, relevant statement that would greatly influence succeeding generations."[2]

The books in this section are about or by the artists, authors, dancers, and musicians of the Harlem Renaissance.

EARLY ELEMENTARY

Cooper, Floyd. *Coming Home: From the Life of Langston Hughes*. New York: Philomel, 1994.

> For him, home was a blues song sung in the pale evening night on a Kansas City street corner. Home was the theater where his ma performed, the library where he sat quiet, reading the books he loved. Home was the church, alive with music, where everybody was "brother" and "sister."[3]

Cooper, usually the illustrator, is the storyteller, too, in this story about Langston Hughes. Cooper focuses on Hughes's search for a family as he continues to wish he could live with his father, who has moved to Mexico, and his mother, an aspiring actress. Hughes does a lot of dreaming while he lives with his grandmother, who shares many stories of his ancestors but is poor and elderly and has little else to share. Eventually, living with his Auntie and Uncle Reed, he is amply provided for. As he grows as an author, Hughes begins to realize that he has become part of a much larger family: the Black community.

Genre: Biography

Dillon, Leo, and Diane Dillon. *Rap a Tap Tap: Here's Bojangles—Think of That!* New York: Scholastic, 2002.

There was a man who danced in the street.
Rap a tap tap—think of that![4]

Bojangles has really become a wonderful Harlem story; he is not
only famous for his dancing but is also known for his generosity to his
friends and neighbors. The Dillons have captured the rhythm of Bojangles's dance in this lyrical book that depicts the life of Bill Robinson, who
took the name Bojangles and gained fame as a dancer in the 1930s. The
Dillons' stylized paintings capture not only Bojangles but a variety of
scenes in the community as well. This nicely illustrated picture book is
great for early readers as it repeats a catchy phrase throughout the book.
  Genre: Biography
  Award: Coretta Scott King Illustrator Honor

Duggleby, John. *Story Painter: The Life of Jacob Lawrence*. San Francisco:
Chronicle, 1998.

In 1910, nine out of ten African-Americans lived in the southern
United States, where they had been slaves before the Civil War. But
over the next twenty years, after slavery ended, they fled by the millions to cities in the North. Some left because they had heard that
there were better jobs in the North. Others wanted to escape the
beatings, even killings, that blacks still suffered at the hands of some
white southerners. They felt that in the North their families could
live in safety and comfort.[5]

The story of a person is the story of a time, and this biography provides the reader with an extraordinary window into the early and mid-
1900s through the life of Jacob Lawrence. He was born in 1917, the oldest in a family that became fatherless by the time he was seven. This hard
beginning was made even more difficult as his mother, in search of work,
had to leave the children behind in Philadelphia when she moved to
New York. Being separated from one another and moving from home
to home finally ended when his mother was able to send for the children, and they were reunited in Harlem. The influence of Harlem on
Lawrence was enormous. It provided him with an environment that was
electric with art, music, and literature. It also introduced him to people
who could recognize and support his talents.
  Duggleby takes the reader through the years that followed
Lawrence's move to Harlem and shares the difficulties and obstacles as

well as the remarkable successes that Lawrence encountered along the way. Duggleby points out something that is interesting to note and important for students to understand: that as Lawrence became famous, he was troubled because it appeared at times that his fame was that of a Black artist, not simply an artist. As we read and discuss Black history, this is an important issue to recognize. We must clearly articulate that the greatness of the many people who are mentioned in this history should be thought of in the broadest sense possible.

Genre: Biography

Dunbar, Paul Laurence. *Jump Back, Honey*. Illustrated by Ashley Bryan, Carol Byard, Jan Spivey Gilchrist, Brian Pinkney, and Faith Ringgold. New York: Hyperion Books for Children, 1999.

> So birds of peace and hope and love
> Come fluttering earthward from above,
> To settle on life's window-sills,
> And ease our load of earthly ills:
> But we, in traffic's rush and din
> Too deep engaged to let them in,
> With deadened heart and sense plod on,
> Nor know our loss till they are gone.[6]

The illustrators who created this text brought together a selection of Dunbar's poetry that works well for young readers. As with Langston Hughes's work, many schoolchildren have become familiar with Dunbar's poetry. It also represents Dunbar's versatility writing in both Standard English and in dialect. A poet born just after the Civil War to parents who were former slaves, Dunbar could not afford to go to college, and he worked at menial jobs to help support his mother. Eventually, his poetry brought him national attention, and he became a highly regarded poet of the Harlem Renaissance. Dunbar's use of Black dialect led to some criticism, even from his own mother, but its use creates a lyrical pattern that makes his poetry sing.

Genre: Biography/Poetry

Greenberg, Jan. *Romare Bearden: Collage of Memories*. New York: Abrams, 2003.

> When we look at his paintings, we feel we could be right there with him running through a cotton field in North Carolina or sitting on

the front stoop of a tenement in Harlem. His art celebrates the struggles and triumphs of African American life in the twentieth century. Step inside Bearden's world, where jazz, rhythm, and blues meet a kaleidoscope of shimmering, shimmying colors.[7]

The illustrations that accompany this biography of Bearden are his collages, so the reader can immediately see the relationship between what Greenberg has written and Bearden's artwork. Studying this artist, who really exemplified the collective creativity of the individuals who made up the Harlem Renaissance, is a window that provides a deeper look into what that community of artists brought to the world. In a note at the end of the book, Greenberg shares where she collected information for this book. One source was firsthand accounts that provide not only reliability but also a sense of intimacy with this remarkable artist and his work.

Genre: Nonfiction/Informational

Medina, Tony. *Love to Langston.* Illustrated by R. Gregory Christie. New York: Lee and Low, 2002.

> Harlem is the capital of my world
> black and beautiful and bruised
> like me
> Harlem has soul—it's where black people
> care about black people and everybody's child belongs to the community.[8]

Medina uses the genre of poetry to share the events and themes of Langston Hughes's life. Each poem is accompanied by an illustration that is vibrant and relates well with the text. Each poem is unique in its depiction of everything from Hughes's relationship with his grandmother and his father to his love of Harlem, jazz, and poetry.

I believe it will be interesting for children to see how different genres handle similar material. This relationship can easily be explored using the various biographies of Langston Hughes included in this chapter and this collection of themed poetry. Medina concludes the book with notes on each of the poems that elaborate on that part of Langston's life.

Genre: Biography/Poetry

Michelson, Richard. *Happy Feet: The Savoy Ballroom Lindy Hoppers and Me.* Illustrated by E. B. Lewis. Orlando, FL: Harcourt, Gulliver, 2005.

"When folks are swinging," Whitey sings, "ain't nobody better than nobody! Salt and pepper—equals! Cats and chicks—equals! Everybody just coming to dance."[9]

The fictional narrator of this story is born on the same night as the opening of the Savoy Ballroom in 1926. The Savoy was one of the first integrated ballrooms, as well as one of Harlem's most famous dance clubs. This fun and rhythmic text, with its lively illustrations, describes the opening night of the Savoy and provides a memorable father-and-son trip to the club, incorporating several real figures of the time. Brief biographies of these individuals are provided with the author's notes.

Genre: Historical Fiction

Miller, William. *Zora Hurston and the Chinaberry Tree*. Illustrated by Cornelius Van Wright and Ying-Hwa Hu. New York: Lee and Low, 1994.

> From the tree, she could see as far
> as the lake, as far as the horizon.
> Zora dreamed of fishing in the lake,
> catching bream and catfish in the moonlight.
> Zora dreamed of seeing the cities beyond
> the horizon, of living there one day.[10]

In Miller's story, told in a narrative poetic form, the reader meets Zora Neale Hurston as a child growing up in Eatonville, Florida. Hurston longs to see beyond the horizon, listens obediently to her father, and listens with her heart to her mother when she tells her that the world is hers. When her mother dies, Hurston holds fast to the promise she made to her mother to hold on to who she is. Zora Neale Hurston became a well-known author of the Harlem Renaissance, and from her later biographical and autobiographical work, it appears that she never lost sight of her self-confidence.

Genre: Biography

Monceaux, Morgan. *Jazz, My Music, My People*. New York: Knopf, 1994.

> The musicians in this book are the great rule-breakers of our time. Like all musicians, they listened to the music around them and learned to play what they heard. And then they created new sounds—a distinct American and an African-American music that had never been heard before.[11]

This is a great resource for brief biographies of men and women who played an important part in the creation of the phenomenon that we call jazz. Between Harlem and New Orleans, the music world thrived, with an important common thread being the influence they had on one another. Monceaux describes jazz as an oral tradition, like storytelling, in which one person passes a message on to another. As the message is passed, the personal experiences of the listener gets folded into what is being shared.

Genre: Nonfiction/Informational/Biography

Orgill, Roxane. *If I Only Had a Horn: Young Louis Armstrong*. Illustrated by Leonard Jenkins. Boston: Houghton Mifflin, 2002.

> Louis opened the cupboard. Bare. He lifted the rug where his mother
> hid spare coins. Nothing.
>   "Come on," he said to his little sister, Mama Lucy. "We're going
> to Uncle Ike's."[12]

Orgill tells the story of Armstrong's early life in this picture book for young readers. His early years were very difficult. Born in New Orleans, Armstrong lived in poverty but was also surrounded by the wealth of rich jazz on the streets of the city. His troubles seemed to get much worse when he was arrested and sent to the Colored Waifs' Home for Boys, but while he was there, he learned to play the cornet. His talent soon was evident, and this part of his life story ends with his playing his way to a new cornet with "pass the hat" donations during a street performance.

Although Louis Armstrong was born and grew up in New Orleans, he made his way to Chicago and eventually New York. He found a home in Harlem and is identified with the great musical talent that blossomed there in the Harlem Renaissance.

Genre: Biography

Perdomo, Willie. *Visiting Langston*. Illustrated by Bryan Collier. New York: Henry Holt, 2002.

> Ask me where I'm from
> I'll say Harlem world
> Ask me who I am
> I'll say I'm a Harlem girl[13]

Perdomo tells the story of a young girl who is an aspiring poet. On the day described in this story, she and her father are planning to visit Langston Hughes. Written in verse, the pages tell, in very few words, about where she is with her writing and what Hughes means to her. The illustrations work beautifully with the text and really make the images in the text come alive. Although this is a fictional story, Perdomo grew up in Harlem and shares in his author's notes that Hughes had a reputation for being generous with his time.

Genre: Historical Fiction

Award: Coretta Scott King Illustrator Honor

Pinkney, Andrea Davis. *Duke Ellington: The Piano Prince and His Orchestra*. Illustrated by Brian Pinkney. New York: Hyperion Books for Children, 1998.

> In 1927, Duke Ellington and His Orchestra began a highly successful engagement at Harlem's renowned Cotton Club, a run that lasted five years. By the early 1930's Duke began to produce complex, original arrangements that resembled the music of classical orchestras, yet were still popular among all kinds of music lovers.[14]

This is the story of the brilliant musician Edward Kennedy Ellington as he moved from the "umpy-dump" sounds of a beginner to the accomplished performance of "The Duke" and his orchestra at Carnegie Hall. During his career, Ellington honored his African American heritage with a special musical suite called *Black, Brown, and Beige* that was a pride-filled celebration of Black people. Andrea Pinkney's lyrical language and Brian Pinkney's illustrations capture the movement of the musical theme and work together to make this a real tribute to Duke Ellington.

Genre: Biography

Awards: Coretta Scott King Illustrator Honor; Caldecott Honor

Pinkney, Andrea Davis. *Ella Fitzgerald: The Tale of a Vocal Virtuosa*. Illustrated by Brian Pinkney. New York: Hyperion Books for Children, 2002.

> Ella had her heart set on pretty-steppin' her way to fame—and she didn't need a dance school to do it. She taught *herself* to tap-dance.
>> Determination was her teacher.
>> The sidewalk was her stage.
>> Imagination was her spotlight.[15]

Pinkney tells the story of Ella Fitzgerald playfully, through the voice of Scat Cat Monroe, a fictional cat. The story takes us from Fitzgerald's very early days in Yonkers through her extraordinary career as the jazz singer who created scat. Brian Pinkney's scratchboard illustrations are full of movement and magic. Our little friend Scat Cat Monroe appears in them as the cat that was there "from the get-go."

Fitzgerald's story is part of the story of the Harlem Renaissance, a story that is an important piece of Black history. Hers and the other stories shared in this chapter tell of the outstanding achievements of talented Americans even during the difficult Jim Crow years.

Genre: Historical Fiction/Biography/Fantasy

Raschka, Chris. *Charlie Parker Played Be Bop.* New York: Scholastic, 1992.

This book's title is also in the book as a page of text, and since there are so few words in the whole book, it serves well as a quote. The title is probably enough to give you an idea of where Raschka takes the reader. In fun, rhythmic verse, he *talks* jazz as he describes Charlie Parker and his music. If this does not sound possible, you will surely want to read the book.

Parker is generally regarded as one of the best saxophonists who ever lived. As one of the musicians who began to gain fame at the end of the Harlem Renaissance, he is convincing evidence that, although the Harlem Renaissance was generally regarded as over by the 1940s, jazz is not over, and that artists, including Dizzy Gillespie, Miles Davis, Thelonious Monk, and others, continue the tradition of creative and extraordinary sound.

Genre: Biography/Poetry

Schroeder, Alan. *Satchmo's Blues.* Illustrated by Floyd Cooper. New York: Doubleday Books for Young Readers, 1996.

> "What do you want?" the owner asked. "I'm closing."
> "I want that horn in the window," Louis said.
> The man grunted. "That horn is five dollars, sonny."
> "That horn is mine!" Louis said proudly.[16]

Louis Armstrong became an internationally known musician, but he started out in this world with almost nothing, including food in the cupboard, except the music that surrounded him as he grew up in New

Orleans. Once he made his purchase and learned to play the trumpet, he left New Orleans for Chicago. Eventually he moved to the clubs in Harlem. Armstrong's success continued after the Harlem Renaissance, and he moved from clubs to the film industry, where he appeared in a number of musicals. Considered the "Trumpet King of Swing," Satchmo continued to play until the day he died at the age of sixty-nine.

Genre: Biography

Shange, Ntozake. *Ellington Was Not a Street*. Illustrated by Kadir Nelson. New York: Simon and Schuster Books for Young Readers, 1983.

This book is the poem "Mood Indigo" by Ntozake Shange. It is the reminiscence of a time when Shange was a child and saw some of the great men of her time as visitors in her home. She is the child looking up at, listening to, and being cared for by the adults who surrounded her. The illustrations are a beautiful complement to this personal poem of a time when Ellington Street was a neighborhood, a community. This book offers the reader the opportunity to share Shange's childhood memory of a time when, in spite of Jim Crow and segregation and oppression, a generation found each other and shared their many diverse talents. The book concludes with a brief portrait of the many different people who are introduced through the poem.

Genre: Biography/Memoir

Award: Coretta Scott King Illustrator Award

Taylor, Debbie A. *Sweet Music in Harlem*. Illustrated by Frank Morrison. New York: Lee and Low, 2004.

> C. J. smiled at the old poster on the wall. A young Uncle Click with a snappy black beret blew a gleaming trumpet. C. J. looked at that poster every morning and dreamed of standing onstage, blowing his own sweet music for a roomful of admiring folks.
>
> During the four years he had lived with Uncle Click, C. J. had learned to hold his clarinet just right, to practice every day, and to keep a penny in his shoe for good luck.[17]

What a neat book! In the author's note, Taylor explains that she got the idea for this book from a T-shirt of her husband's that had on it a print of the famous 1958 Art Kane photograph "A Day in Harlem." The story behind the photo is that Kane, newly hired by *Esquire*, was to take a photo to introduce a jazz article. He asked every New York jazz musician he knew of to attend the 10 a.m. photo shoot, not knowing if any would actually show up. Kane's published photo shows fifty-seven jazz musicians and a variety of other people, including a curbful of young boys.

In this book, Uncle Click has misplaced his black hat, and C. J. retraces his steps to find it. As Mr. Garlic of Garlic's Barbershop, Mattie Dee of the Eat and Run Diner, and Miss Canary Alma of the Midnight Melody Club offer up items Uncle Click has forgotten in their establishments (but not the black hat!), they each decide to join in on the photograph, and by the time the photographer arrives, a happy crowd has formed.

Genre: Historical Fiction

LATER ELEMENTARY

Dunham, Montrew. *Langston Hughes: Young Black Poet.* Illustrated by Robert Doremus. New York: Aladdin Paperbacks, 1995.

One of the first exchanges Hughes had when he tried to find a place to live so he could attend Columbia University was with a clerk who wanted to deny him a room when she realized he was African American. Politely, Hughes informed her that he had reserved a room and made payment by mail. Although he was then given a room, disillusioned, he didn't stay long at the university and instead found jobs that would support him as he wrote. This biography, from a series, is a good read for upper elementary students. There are several biographies of Hughes mentioned in this chapter, and the range of reading levels provides an opportunity for differentiated instruction, with students of different reading levels able to contribute to research and conversations about this important person who has contributed to Black history in many, many ways.

Genre: Biography

Goyenar, Alan, ed. *Stompin' at the Savoy: The Story of Norma Miller.* Cambridge, MA: Candlewick, 2006.

Before I went to Europe, I hadn't been interested in the news, but once I was there, I was exposed. Hitler had been just a name until I started hearing about what was happening, that people were being arrested and that anti-Semitism and racism had run amok. We were told we couldn't go to Berlin. Our manager and chaperon, Tim Gale, was Jewish, and we were black. That was the first time we heard about the rumblings of the war to come.[18]

Goyenar worked with Miller to write this book. As he interviewed her, she reminisced about her life, from her childhood with a single mom whose West Indian husband had died of pneumonia after being commandeered to work in a shipyard, through the hard work, disappointments, and triumphs in her career as a renowned dancer. Throughout the editing of this book, Goyenar tried to recapture the essence of the story and reflect the person he had grown to know and admire as he recorded it. We are fortunate that he recognized the powerful story behind this remarkable woman and was inspired to pursue it. Although this is primarily the story of one person—the extraordinarily talented dancer who gained fame during the Harlem Renaissance—it also weaves in other stories of the time, both here in America and in Europe, that give us a larger picture of America's history.

Genre: Biography

Haskins, James. *The Harlem Renaissance*. Brookfield, CT: Millbrook, 1996.

> The real reason why the Harlem Renaissance ended was that the United States was a segregated society and the majority white population never accepted blacks as equals. Those few blacks who managed to gain a white audience ran the risk of having to cater to the paternalistic and condescending attitudes of that audience. When the economy was chugging along nicely, when there was a boosterism of things American by a country flush from victory in war, there could be some liberalization of racial attitudes. But there was no fundamental change in the comparative positions of the two races.[19]

This is another authoritative nonfiction book by the very prolific author James Haskins. Here, he gives the young researcher an easily accessible history of the Harlem Renaissance that is presented in chapters that cover the history and the different aspects of the Renaissance, including chapters entitled "Music, Dance, and Musical Theater," "Poetry and Fiction," and "Painters and Sculptors." The numerous biographical sketches of the many people who made this time and place so notable and the descriptions of the overall events that mark this historical period are comprehensive. For students who are not familiar with the Harlem Renaissance, this book provides a clear window into a fast-paced exciting time that has remained remarkable for the wonderful blossoming of the great works that it produced.

Genre: Nonfiction/Informational

Haskins, James, with Eleanora Tate, Clinton Cox, and Brenda Wilkinson. *Black Stars of the Harlem Renaissance: African Americans Who Lived Their Dreams*. Hoboken, NJ: Wiley, 2002.

> Between about 1916 and about 1940, the area of Manhattan named Harlem by the first Dutch settlers became synonymous with black culture. Up until the turn of the twentieth century, it had been a place of farms, country estates, and areas of recreation for wealthy whites from the more settled areas downtown.[20]

This book is organized to provide biographical sketches of individuals who were part of the Harlem Renaissance. Each profile is easily accessed and can be used by students who are looking at the many different individuals who presented many different talents during this time. *The Harlem Renaissance* by Haskins (above) is a more comprehensive and in-depth view. Both books are helpful, as they allow for the different intentions of the students' research or for differentiated instructional opportunities.

Genre: Nonfiction/Informational

Hughes, Langston. *Black Misery*. Illustrated by Arouni. New York: Oxford University Press, 1969.

> Misery is when you first realize
> So many things bad
> Have black in them,
> Like black cats, black arts, blackball.[21]

This collection of poetry was published after Hughes's death on May 22, 1967. Jesse Jackson wrote the introduction to this book, in which he speaks of his experiences that relate to Hughes's images in these poems. The afterword by Robert O'Meally explains the history of the collection.

The book includes illustrations of a boy lamenting the many ways his life is miserable. The poems are short and are the captions for

Arouni's illustrations. Some might make you smile, but Hughes's humor is layered with a profound sadness that he knew from his own experience. This book of Hughes's poems could be used with the biographies of Hughes mentioned in this section.

Genre: Poetry

Hughes, Langston. *The Dream Keeper and Other Poems*. Illustrated by Brian Pinkney. New York: Knopf, 1994.

From "African Dance":

> The low beating of the tom-toms,
> The slow beating of the tom-toms,
> Low . . . slow
> Slow . . . low—
> Stirs your blood.[22]

Originally published in the early thirties, the poems of Langston Hughes continue to speak to contemporary readers in their eloquence of style and content. Of all the many outstanding authors of the Harlem Renaissance, Hughes has maintained a devoted readership of readers from the very young to the very old.

Genre: Poetry

Jones, Veda Boyd. *Jazz Age Poet: A Story about Langston Hughes*. Illustrated by Barbara Kiwak. Minneapolis, MN: Millbrook, 2006.

> At the white school, Langston sat at the end of the last row, even though the other students were seated in alphabetic order. His teacher didn't want him in the school, and she made hateful comments about his color. She stirred up the students with her remarks, such as warning them not to eat black licorice or they'd turn black like Langston. Some of them chased him home through alleys. He dodged the stones and tin cans they threw at him.[23]

After Hughes's mother had fought to get him enrolled in the White school that was closer to their home, she ended up taking him out of school and taking him to live with his grandmother. Through the stories of his grandmother, he learned about his ancestors and their accomplishments. Although he was lonely with her as his only companion, he came away with a sense of self-confidence, and he successfully confronted the Jim Crow behaviors of his teacher when he was a seventh grader. There were many more opportunities to encounter prejudice, but Hughes prevailed to become one of America's most famous poets. This well-written biography is a good read for later elementary students.

Genre: Biography

Myers, Walter Dean. *Here in Harlem: Poems in Many Voices.* New York: Holiday House, 2004.

> And if you give to Harlem, it always finds a way to give back. When I hear music coming from the apartment windows or from the doors of a storefront church, I know that's Harlem giving me a gift. And it's music that's more than just head music. It's music my soul re-members from way past what my brain knows about.[24]

This is a tender and powerful tribute to the community of Harlem that Myers remembers from his youth. These imaginary words are spoken by the people who live in Myers's memory, and they create neighbors, friends, and relatives for the reader. The many voices that Myers has created speak the language of Harlem: a mail carrier, a sax player, a blues singer, and an undertaker are some of the people you will meet in the poems. Myers took his inspiration for this work from Edgar Lee Masters's *Spoon River Anthology.* As one studies Harlem and its famous artists, writers, and musicians, it is also interesting to look at the great diversity of ordinary people who lived there, during the Harlem Renaissance and at other times.

Genre: Poetry

Porter, A. P. *Jump at de Sun: The Story of Zora Neale Hurston.* Minneapolis, MN: Carolrhoda, 1992.

> On January 7, 1891, Zora Neale Hurston was born into a nation where African Americans were feared and hated. Between Hurston's birth and her tenth birthday, white people in the United States publicly murdered—lynched—1,116 African Americans. . . . Black people were killed for all sorts of reasons, from being successful in business to talking back to a white person.[25]

Porter's biography of Hurston is intense as he tells the story of this complex woman who went from her childhood in rural Florida to become the first African American woman to graduate from Barnard College, then on to Harlem to become one of the most famous women authors of the Harlem Renaissance. Porter provides a comprehensive picture of Hurston as he shares her temper and her talent, her loves and her conflicts, the heights of her success and the lows of her despair. One thing is certain: Hurston lived in troubled times but rose above the obstacles to live her life on her own terms.

Genre: Biography

Walker, Alice. *Langston Hughes: American Poet.* Illustrated by Catherine Deeter. New York: HarperCollins, 2002.

> He always wrote truthfully about black people. He showed that they were beautiful, and sometimes ugly, like most people. He showed that they were sometimes happy and sometimes sad—and that they could laugh even when they were feeling blue. He always thought this ability made them special.[26]

Walker shares the life of Langston Hughes with an honesty that is characteristic of her work in general. The depiction of his relationship with his parents is very well written, and the reader gets a real sense of his father who, unhappy with the way Black people were treated in the United States, went to live in Mexico. This book includes the earthquake that rocked their hotel when the Hughes family reunited in Mexico, which resulted in Hughes's mother packing up and going to Kansas. Later, Hughes's dad tried to get the family back to Mexico, but his mother was not interested in spite of the fact that she needed to work hard at low-status jobs to make a living. Hughes's father was disparaging of African Americans, which was off-putting to his son.

This book is written by the Pulitzer Prize–winning author Alice Walker, and she is writing about someone she met and holds in very high regard. She portrays Hughes in ways that might help give those of us who love his work a greater understanding of his early life.

Genre: Biography

MIDDLE GRADES

Meltzer, Milton. *Langston Hughes.* Illustrated by Stephen Alcorn. Brookfield, CT: Millbrook, 1997.

The critics had hailed him as a poet "who played authentic blues with consummate skill." They used such words as "powerful," "sensitive," "warm," and "lyrical" to describe his poems.[27]

Meltzer's biography of Hughes is rich in detail. Any student in middle school or beyond will find this book a complete history of this fascinating and incredibly talented man. So much of Hughes's life seems bittersweet. After a very humble beginning and working incredibly hard at many jobs, Hughes gained fame as a writer, but a sense of sadness seemed to linger.

Meltzer and Hughes worked together on *The Pictorial History of the Negro in America* (see chapter 1), and through their work on that project, Meltzer, one of the most prolific and effective biographers for children's literature, would have grown to know Hughes, not only as a subject, but also as a friend.

Genre: Biography

Sharp, Anne Wallace. *A Dream Deferred: The Jim Crow Era*. Farmington Hills, MI: Lucent Books, 2005.

> Eventually, the Harlem Renaissance ended as the Great Depression of the 1930's resulted in the flood of wealthy visitors to Harlem being reduced to a trickle and then drying up altogether. Despite the end of this cultural explosion, African Americans had found hope in the works of the movement's artists. This hope would translate into a new appreciation for the potential their own race held and a determination to fight for change throughout America in the decades ahead.[28]

Sharp's book is included here as well as in chapter 8 because, although it is comprehensive of the Jim Crow years, it includes a section on the Harlem Renaissance and its relationship to the larger context of the events in the nation during that time.

THE NEGRO BASEBALL LEAGUES

Although there is no general agreement as to when and where baseball originated, one thing is certain: "from the start, organized baseball tried to limit or exclude African-American participation."[29] Without the resources of the major league White baseball teams, Black athletes formed their own teams that made up what became known as the Negro Baseball Leagues. The leagues included some of the most accomplished players to ever play the game of baseball. But after Jackie Robinson broke the color barrier of the White major leagues in the late 1940s, the Negro Baseball Leagues eventually faded away: "Black baseball had survived the lack of money, the death of Rube Foster, a very rich and well-armed Caribbean dictator, two World Wars, a gasoline crunch, player wars, and racism. But it couldn't survive the major league raids that followed Robinson's success. White teams stripped the black teams of their best players and didn't pay the NAL and NNL owners a dime."[30]

The White leagues had always had more resources and were able to sustain themselves and contract with top players, and the integration of the leagues brought opportunity for Black players to share those resources. The inclusion of all athletes since that time has allowed players to have their athletic talents spotlighted fairly, but the importance of the Negro Baseball Leagues should be remembered, and an important piece of baseball history is falling into place with the inclusion of Black players in the celebrated Baseball Hall of Fame in Cooperstown, New York.

The books in this section highlight some of the players in the Negro Baseball Leagues as well as describe the leagues themselves. The accomplishments of these teams speak to the athletic talent and professional resilience of the players during the Jim Crow years.

EARLY ELEMENTARY

Cline-Ransome, Lesa. *Satchel Paige.* Illustrated by James E. Ransome. New York: Simon and Schuster Books for Young Readers, 2000.

> Got so Satch began to think of his pitches as his children. The "hesitation" was his magic slow ball. The "trouble ball" caused all sorts of havoc. And then there was the "bee ball" which, according to Satch, would "always be where I want it to be."[31]

Satchel Paige's sense of humor and his showmanship and extraordinary talent as a pitcher are highlighted in this picture book of his life. Even from a very young age, Paige showed remarkable talent as a pitcher. With practice and hard work, he developed this talent to become an incredible pitcher, but he was not allowed to play in the major leagues because of the color of his skin. As a player in the Negro Baseball Leagues, he became famous and finally was admitted into the major leagues in 1948, when he was forty-two years old. The major leagues had remained segregated during most of his years of playing in his prime. He only remained with the Cleveland Indians for two years, as he found the rules of the league too restrictive and unnecessary.

One of the stories in the book is about Paige's personal competition with Josh Gibson, another player in the Negro Leagues (see Johnson, *Just Like Josh Gibson*, below). Gibson, one of the best batters, and Paige, one of the best pitchers, played against each other in the 1942 Negro World Series, and Paige playfully struck out his former teammate.

Genre: Biography

Curtis, Gavin. *The Bat Boy and His Violin.* Illustrated by E. B. Lewis. New York: Simon and Schuster Books for Young Readers, 1998.

This story takes place toward the final years of the Negro Baseball Leagues, when Jackie Robinson has integrated the major leagues and the coach of the fictional Negro League team the Dukes is having a terrible season. He blames the team's poor performance in part on having lost many of the best players to the integrated major league teams. The coach's young son, who works as a bat boy for the team, plays the violin. During one game, he begins playing and each team member seems to play exceptionally well. After that, his father encourages him to play during their time at bat. Things go well until an important game, when the violin playing just doesn't seem as effective. Worried that his father will reject his violin playing, he is happy when his father assures him that he has really grown to like his music.

Genre: Historical Fiction
Award: Coretta Scott King Illustrator Honor

Driscoll, Laura. *Negro League: All-Black Baseball.* Illustrated by Tracy Mitchell. New York: Penguin Putnam Books for Young Readers, 2002.

When a black team got to a town, they looked for a black hotel. If there wasn't one, they camped out next to the baseball field. Or they slept on the team bus. Sometimes they weren't allowed to use public bathrooms. Sometimes they weren't even allowed to use the locker rooms at a stadium! It wasn't fair. But the players kept going because they loved baseball.[32]

Writing about a young girl's trip to the Baseball Hall of Fame in Cooperstown, New York, the author describes the creation of the Negro Baseball Leagues and the conditions under which they played. This book also contains brief biographies of most of the famous players of the leagues and the creation of their own World Series. Driscoll writes about the specific teams that were developed and ends with Jackie Robinson joining the major leagues and the eventual end of the Negro Leagues themselves.

Genre: Nonfiction/Informational

Golenbock, Peter. *Teammates*. Illustrated by Paul Bacon. San Diego, CA: Harcourt Brace Jovanovich, 1990.

> Life was very different for the players in the Major Leagues. They were the leagues for white players. Compared to the Negro league players, white players were very well paid. They stayed in good hotels and ate in fine restaurants. Their pictures were put on baseball cards and the best players became famous all over the world.[33]

This is a story about Jackie Robinson, who was hired away from the Negro Baseball Leagues and became a player for the Brooklyn Dodgers. The choice of hiring Robinson was very deliberate. Branch Rickey, the general manager for the Dodgers, thought that Robinson would not only be a great player for the team but would also be able to withstand the enormous hate and prejudice that was likely to face the first Black player in the previously all-White league.

The prediction of outrage and abuse was accurate, and Robinson withstood the many indignities, including having some of his teammates call for his dismissal and being refused lodging in hotels that his teammates stayed in when on the road. In one very difficult game, while fans were hurling jeers and insults at Robinson, a teammate who had grown up in the South but had also grown to admire Robinson expressed support for his teammate in front of a startled crowd.

Genre: Biography

Johnson, Angela. *Just like Josh Gibson*. Illustrated by Beth Peck. New York: Simon and Schuster Books for Young Readers, 2004.

Grandmama says her papa showed up
on that same day,
the day she was born,
with a Louisville slugger and a smile.
He said his new baby would make baseballs fly,
just like Josh Gibson.[34]

A young girl shares the story her grandmother has told her about when she was a girl and wanted to play baseball like Josh Gibson, one of the stars of the Pittsburgh Crawfords baseball team. Her father had practiced playing baseball with her from when she was very young, and although she lived in a time when girls did not usually play baseball with the boys, she was ready to stand in for her cousin, Danny, when he was injured and could not play in an important game. Having practiced with her father and also having played with the boys and watched them play, she stepped up to the plate, dressed in a pretty pink dress, and hit the ball for a win. Her grandmother shares that she had enjoyed the cheers from the crowd.

At the end of the book, Johnson notes the highlights of Josh Gibson's career. Greatly admired by his teammates, Gibson was considered one of the best players in the Negro Leagues. Unfortunately, he died at age thirty-five, just three months before the major leagues began to be integrated when Jackie Robinson signed with the Brooklyn Dodgers.

Genre: Historical Fiction

LATER ELEMENTARY

McKissack, Patricia C., and Fredrick L. McKissack. *Black Diamond: The Story of the Negro Baseball Leagues*. New York: Scholastic, 1994.

Jackie Robinson was a superhero, but he was a human being, too. The constant badgering and insults had taken their toll on his spirit. He'd given it his best, but it didn't seem to be enough. One day it seemed as though he might give up. A Dodger teammate, Pee Wee Reese, who was also a southerner, saw Robinson about to crack under the stress. He walked over to him and put his arm around his shoulder and talked to him calmly. A hush fell over the crowd.[35]

Once again, the McKissacks have teamed up and provided an extraordinarily detailed description of a time in African American history. This time, their work is an account of the formation and performance of the Negro Baseball Leagues. Baseball became popular after the Civil War when soldiers, both Black and White, who had enjoyed playing baseball as an entertaining distraction during the war, returned home and began to establish teams. African Americans who were interested in playing found that the field was closed to them. The National Association of Base Ball Players voted to exclude African American players. As a result, even though some Black players had managed to play on integrated minor league teams and even fewer on the major league teams, by the early 1900s, they were excluded from playing in the all-White major leagues. The Supreme Court decision of *Plessy v. Ferguson*, which upheld segregation, made pursuing this forced exclusion in court a lost cause.

Black teams formed, and these teams were sometimes invited to play against minor league teams, but it was not until 1920 that the Negro National League (NNL) was formed. In 1937 another league, the Negro American League (NAL), was formed. The McKissacks detail the accomplishments of the outstanding players who played during these years, but sadly, even the great players would never reach the acclaim they deserved, because they were not allowed to compete with the other world-class players. Finally, in 1945, Jackie Robinson was signed to play with the Brooklyn Dodgers, and the color line was crossed. With incredible courage and personal conviction, along with amazing skill at the game, Robinson withstood the vicious torments that accompanied his initial appearances. Finally, with Pee Wee Reese's gesture on the field one day, Jackie had the support of his team. He continued to play and became the first Black player inducted into the Baseball Hall of Fame. Eventually the Negro Baseball Leagues disbanded.

Genre: Nonfiction/Informational
Award: Coretta Scott King Author Honor

WORLD WAR I, WORLD WAR II, AND BEYOND

The service of African American soldiers in World War I and World War II has to give all citizens of this nation pause, for here were men and women who had been discriminated against all of their lives, were discriminated against in the armed forces, then returned from their service as veterans and continued to be discriminated against in the country they had risked their lives to defend.

> All of us should reflect on the role African Americans have played in compelling this country to live up to its professed ideals. By insisting on fighting in the War of Independence when they clearly were not wanted, blacks reminded the founding fathers that the American Revolution should bring a better life to all Americans. Black warriors in the Civil War pursued the same course, as did the black men and women who served during World Wars I and II.[36]

Other chapters describe books about the participation and valor of black soldiers in the Revolutionary War and the Civil War, and this chapter includes books about World War I, World War II, and Vietnam, but there is little available to students about the role of Blacks in other wars and conflicts this nation has fought. However, good sources can be found that one might use to inform oneself and one's students about heroism of African Americans in wars up to the present.

The following two sections provide books that can be used to study the participation of African Americans in the two world wars, and a final section includes one book about the war in Vietnam. In both World War I and World War II, Black soldiers experienced racial discrimination in segregated armed services. Eventually the military integrated, however. By the Korean War, Black soldiers had gained "widespread respect," and the Vietnam War "finally put all questions of their courage to rest."[37] The valor of African American soldiers was finally being recognized.

WORLD WAR I

Historian John Hope Franklin provides the context for African Americans' involvement in World War I:

> Woodrow Wilson in 1913 became the first Southern Democrat in the White House since the Civil War. Half of his Cabinet appointees were Southerners. His first Congress was flooded with anti-Negro bills, more than ever before introduced at a single session, and Wilson himself issued orders segregating most Negro federal employees in Washington. In 1915, the year that Booker T. Washington died, there were sixty-nine lynchings. In 1917 the United States entered World War I under the slogan "Make the World Safe for Democracy."[38]

When the all-Black 369th Infantry held their battle position, fighting from trenches for 191 days, they earned the name the "Hell Fighters" from their German opponents. When the 371st Infantry Regiment, fighting alongside the 157th French Division, captured an important position that had been held by the Germans for almost a year, they received accolades for their incredible bravery. During that battle they lost almost half of their men. However, at training camps in the South, the canteens were only available for White soldiers, and it was not unusual for Black trainees to be beaten and discriminated against.

When the draft went into effect, the number of Black soldiers in the army jumped from 2,000 to 200,000. While the Black population equaled 10 percent of the population, they numbered 13 percent of the inductees. Unfortunately, not many books cover the events of World War I from a Black history perspective, but the two included here are exceptional.

LATER ELEMENTARY

Haskins, James, and Kathleen Benson. *Out of the Darkness: The Story of Blacks Moving North, 1890–1940.* New York: Benchmark, 2000.

> Nineteen Fifteen was a watershed year for Black migration. Floods and boll weevil infestations of the cotton crops produced hard times in the South, causing some blacks to leave the land for the cities. But the major spur to migration was World War I. Although the United States stayed out of the war for three years, the nation became a major supplier of war material to its allies in Europe—primarily England and France. The booming industries of the North were starved for labor. And just when those industries could have absorbed as many foreign immigrant workers as came, that supply was choked off.[39]

This is another volume written by historians James Haskins and Kathleen Benson, who have provided young researchers with some of the most reliable nonfiction texts that are written about American history and include African Americans. This one highlights the events that led to the great Black migration from the southern states to the North. Although life was far from perfect for African Americans who moved north, and certainly there were issues of segregation and discrimination, the move was an opportunity to escape an even more hostile setting where Black men especially were being killed for exercising their rights of citizenship or of voting, or for something as simple as addressing a White person in a socially unacceptable way. As usual, Haskins and Benson's work provides a good resource for students who might be interested in the relationship between the Harlem Renaissance and World War I.

Genre: Nonfiction/Informational

Myers, Walter Dean, and Bill Miles. *The Harlem Hellfighters: When Pride Met Courage*. New York: HarperCollins, 2006.

> The Great War soon became the bloodiest conflict known to human experience. No amount of bravery could overcome the technology of the machine gun or the newly developed artillery that sent shells traveling from miles behind the front line into the enemy ranks. The use of modern technology was not consistent at the beginning of the war. While it's hard to imagine in this modern age, the onset of the war actually saw soldiers on horseback, their sabers drawn, charging into ranks of armored vehicles and rapid-firing light weapons.[40]

Myers and Miles provide an interesting and comprehensive book about African American participation in World War I. After a brief history of engagements in earlier wars, they provide a good amount of detail for young researchers about what was in its time considered "the war to end all wars." Individual heroes are recognized as well as the battles waged by the all-Black regiments.

This book also discusses the tension between Black soldiers and White soldiers who were in training together, and between Black soldiers and the townspeople in the areas around the training camps. Sometimes these tensions escalated into race riots. The book concludes with the disappointment felt by returning Black veterans who found themselves discriminated against in spite of the fact that they had risked their lives for their country.

Genre: Nonfiction/Informational

WORLD WAR II

Segregation in the armed forces continued during World War II, and Black men and women again fought for a country where, in many diners across the nation, they could not buy a cup of coffee. Still, they had made some advances since World War I. As John Hope Franklin points out: "The opportunities that African Americans had to serve in the navy were in distinct contrast to those they had had in World War I. Thousands of blacks were trained to perform numerous technical tasks and were given ratings accordingly."[41] The books described in this section provide a glimpse into the lives of African Americans who were in the armed forces during World War II.

EARLY ELEMENTARY

Say, Allen. *The Bicycle Man*. New York: Houghton Mifflin, 1982.

> Two strangers were leaning over the fence and watching us. They were American soldiers. One of them was a white man with bright hair like fire, and the other man had a face as black as the earth. They wore dark uniforms with neck ties, soft caps on their heads, and red stripes on their sleeves. They had no guns.[42]

This story appears to take place at an elementary school on an island in the south of Japan in the spring of the year after World War II when the American forces occupied Japan. The children are having Sportsday, when all the children celebrate sportsmanship by playing games together outside on the playground. The principal makes a speech, prizes are awarded, and parents join the children for lunch. That is the setting when the two American soldiers appear on the scene. The African American soldier borrows a bicycle from the principal of the school and demonstrates many tricks that are enjoyed by all. In the end, the principal awards him the largest prize of all. This is a story from Say's memory of when he was a small child, and it is accompanied by his own illustrations that show some of the traditional customs of Japan.

Genre: Historical Fiction

MIDDLE GRADES

Clinton, Catherine. *The Black Soldier: 1492 to the Present*. Boston: Houghton Mifflin, 2000.

> When the Japanese bombed Pearl Harbor on Sunday, December 7, 1941, Dorie Miller, a black mess cook aboard the U.S.S. Arizona, rushed on deck and saw his captain wounded on the bridge. At great

personal risk, Miller carried his commander to safety. Next he grabbed a machine gun and shot down at least two and perhaps as many as four Japanese planes. After great pressure from black leaders and civil rights groups, this fearless sailor, the son of Texan share-croppers, won the Navy Cross for his brave actions. Miller was never promoted from the ranks of mess duty, despite his proven talents.[43]

Clinton's book is included here although it covers the range of conflicts from precolonial times to the present. Clinton points out that necessity accelerated the roles that Black men and women would play during war. Interestingly enough, the U.S. Marines was the first branch of the armed forces to fully integrate African Americans into their units. Of the 1 million Black men and women who served in World War II, Clinton indicates, three out of four served overseas.

This is an interesting book, and one of the few that includes the service of African Americans in the wars after World War II.

Genre: Nonfiction/Informational

McKissack, Patricia C., and Fredrick L. McKissack. *Red-Tail Angels: The Story of the Tuskegee Airmen of World War II*. New York: Walker, 1995.

The story of the Tuskegee Airmen sheds light on the role of African-Americans in the military, an aspect of American history that has been forgotten or marginalized in many textbooks. Today, it is un-thinkable that until the end of World War II, African-Americans were not allowed to serve in the United Sates Air Force. But in fact they were not.[44]

The McKissacks, well known for their research, have written a comprehensive book chronicling the African Americans who were among the groundbreaking pilots who were trained and served during World War II. Their courage and ability continued the momentum to-ward desegregation of the military. This is an important story and ex-tremely well represented by the McKissacks.

Genre: Nonfiction/Informational

VIETNAM

This section includes the one children's book in print that specifically fo-cuses on the role of African Americans in military actions more recent than World War II. It serves as a follow-up to the books about World Wars I and II even though it is not set during the Jim Crow years. The book is most appropriate for the middle grades.

Canwell, Diane, and Jon Sutherland. *African Americans in the Vietnam War.* Milwaukee, WI: World Almanac Library, 2005.

> The Vietnam War may have been the first major combat deployment of desegregated U.S. troops, but it didn't always feel desegregated to the soldiers fighting the war, nor to the U.S. citizens observing it. In the early years of the war, the statistics show that African Americans especially were being singled out for combat assignments and that more officers were white than black and received less risky assignments.[45]

The U.S. forces in the Vietnam War were integrated by design, but in reality, the segregation and discrimination that existed in our culture continued to create tensions, and Black soldiers often had to fight two battles: one was the enemy they faced in battle, and the other was the attitudes of their comrades that had been impacted by years and years of discrimination. This book includes a comprehensive look from periods when African Americans fought in earlier wars to their involvement in the Vietnam War. It points out that, as time went by, the statistics for Black soldiers in frontline combat became more proportionate to their numbers in the general population.

Throughout this book, it is clear that the relationships between soldiers broke down stereotypes as they shared experiences and found themselves depending on each other in the many dangers of the war. But it is also true that as the war was raging, so were the battles of the civil rights movement. For Black veterans of the Vietnam War, their struggles for equality and justice continued to be a battle they would have to win.

CONCLUSION

Throughout the time of the Harlem Renaissance, the Negro Baseball Leagues, and the major wars of the twentieth century, African Americans fought against discrimination. Richard Wormser describes the struggle in *The Rise and Fall of Jim Crow.*

After seventy long years, the battle waged by African-American against Jim Crow has been won. In the battle, tens of thousands of African-Americans lost their lives simply because they were black. Hundreds of thousands were condemned to chain gangs and convict lease prisons because they were black. Millions lost opportunities to get an education and make a decent living simply because they were black. But despite the systematic attempts of white America to deny blacks their fundamental rights as citizens and human beings, enough African-Americans said "no." Their refusal to accept oppression led to their victory over segregation and disfranchisement.[46]

As we leave the Jim Crow years and look ahead to the civil rights movement, it is important to note the contributions and contributors that led to the movement. Certainly all of the years of courage and resilience, of being part of every fiber of this country's history, started to come together. Soldiers had repeatedly become winners on the battlefield only to come home to humiliating defeat in the land they fought to protect. Creative genius had come forward to give gifts to a society that took those gifts without so much as a "thank you." Millions of slaves had lived and died for the prosperity of the nation. Yes, it was time. Chapter 10 looks at books that depict Martin Luther King Jr., Rosa Parks, and the civil rights movement.

NOTES

1. Haskins, *Harlem Renaissance*, 14.
2. Franklin, *Mirror to America*, 377.
3. Cooper, *Coming Home*.
4. Dillon and Dillon, *Rap a Tap Tap*.
5. Duggleby, *Story Painter*.
6. Dunbar, *Jump Back, Honey*.
7. Greenberg, *Romare Bearden*, 7.
8. Medina, *Love to Langston*.
9. Michelson, *Across the Alley*.
10. Miller, *Zora Hurston*.
11. Monceaux, *Jazz, My Music, My People*, 6.
12. Orgill, *If I Only Had a Horn*.
13. Perdomo, *Visiting Langston*.

14. Pinkney, *Duke Ellington.*
15. Pinkney, *Ella Fitzgerald.*
16. Schroeder, *Satchmo's Blues.*
17. Taylor, *Sweet Music in Harlem.*
18. Goyenar, *Stompin' at the Savoy*, 33.
19. Haskins, *Harlem Renaissance*, 173.
20. Haskins et al., *Black Stars*, 1.
21. Hughes, *Black Misery.*
22. Hughes, *Dream Keeper*, 72.
23. Jones, *Jazz Age Poet*, 10.
24. Myers, *Here in Harlem*, 1.
25. Porter, *Jump at de Sun*, 9.
26. Walker, *Langston Hughes.*
27. Meltzer, *Langston Hughes*, 118.
28. Sharp, *A Dream Deferred*, 3.
29. McKissack and McKissack, *Black Diamond*, 8.
30. McKissack and McKissack, *Black Diamond.*
31. Cline-Ransome, *Satchel Paige.*
32. Driscoll, *Negro League*, 11.
33. Golenbock, *Teammates.*
34. Johnson, *Just like Josh Gibson.*
35. McKissack and McKissack, *Black Diamond*, 140–41.
36. Hughes and Meltzer, *Pictorial History*, 262.
37. Edgerton, *Hidden Heroism*, 230.
38. Franklin, *Mirror to America*, 417.
39. Haskins and Benson, *Out of the Darkness*, 143.
40. Myers and Miles, *Harlem Hellfighters*, 16.
41. Franklin, *From Slavery to Freedom*, 486.
42. Say, *The Bicycle Man.*
43. Clinton, *The Black Soldier*, 60.
44. McKissack and McKissack, *Red-Tail Angels*, 3.
45. Canwell and Sutherland, *African Americans in the Vietnam War*, 17.
46. Wormser, *Rise and Fall*, 130.

BIBLIOGRAPHY OF BOOKS FOR CHILDREN

Canwell, Diane, and Jon Sutherland. *African Americans in the Vietnam War.* Milwaukee, WI: World Almanac Library, 2005.
Cline-Ransome, Lesa. *Satchel Paige.* Illustrated by James E. Ransome. New York: Simon and Schuster Books for Young Readers, 2000.

Clinton, Catherine. *The Black Soldier: 1492 to the Present*. Boston: Houghton Mifflin, 2000.

Cooper, Floyd. *Coming Home: From the Life of Langston Hughes*. New York: Philomel, 1994.

Curtis, Gavin. *The Bat Boy and His Violin*. Illustrated by E. B. Lewis. New York: Simon and Schuster Books for Young Readers, 1998.

Dillon, Leo, and Diane Dillon. *Rap a Tap Tap: Here's Bojangles—Think of That!* New York: Scholastic, 2002.

Driscoll, Laura. *Negro League: All-Black Baseball*. Illustrated by Tracy Mitchell. New York: Penguin Putnam Books for Young Readers, 2002.

Duggleby, John. *Story Painter: The Life of Jacob Lawrence*. San Francisco: Chronicle, 1998.

Dunbar, Paul Laurence. *Jump Back, Honey*. Illustrated by Ashley Bryan, Carol Byard, Jan Spivey Gilchrist, Brian Pinkney, and Faith Ringgold. New York: Hyperion Books for Children, 1999.

Dunham, Montrew. *Langston Hughes: Young Black Poet*. Illustrated by Robert Doremus. New York: Aladdin Paperbacks, 1995.

Golenbock, Peter. *Teammates*. Illustrated by Paul Bacon. San Diego, CA: Harcourt Brace Jovanovich, 1990.

Goyenar, Alan, ed. *Stompin' at the Savoy: The Story of Norma Miller*. Cambridge, MA: Candlewick, 2006.

Greenberg, Jan. *Romare Bearden: Collage of Memories*. New York: Abrams, 2003.

Haskins, James. *The Harlem Renaissance*. Brookfield, CT: Millbrook, 1996.

Haskins, James, and Kathleen Benson. *Out of the Darkness: The Story of Blacks Moving North, 1890–1940*. New York: Benchmark, 2000.

Haskins, James, with Eleanora Tate, Clinton Cox, and Brenda Wilkinson. *Black Stars of the Harlem Renaissance: African Americans Who Lived Their Dreams*. Hoboken, NJ: Wiley, 2002.

Hughes, Langston. *Black Misery*. Illustrated by Arouni. New York: Oxford University Press, 1969.

———. *The Dream Keeper and Other Poems*. Illustrated by Brian Pinkney. New York: Knopf, 1994.

Johnson, Angela. *Just like Josh Gibson*. Illustrated by Beth Peck. New York: Simon and Schuster Books for Young Readers, 2004.

Jones, Veda Boyd. *Jazz Age Poet: A Story about Langston Hughes*. Illustrated by Barbara Kiwak. Minneapolis, MN: Millbrook, 2006.

McKissack, Patricia C., and Fredrick L. McKissack. *Black Diamond: The Story of the Negro Baseball Leagues*. New York: Scholastic, 1994.

———. *Red-Tail Angels: The Story of the Tuskegee Airmen of World War II*. New York: Walker, 1995.

Medina, Tony. *Love to Langston*. Illustrated by R. Gregory Christie. New York: Lee and Low, 2002.

Meltzer, Milton. *Langston Hughes*. Illustrated by Stephen Alcorn. Brookfield, CT: Millbrook, 1997.

Michelson, Richard. *Happy Feet: The Savoy Ballroom Lindy Hoppers and Me*. Illustrated by E. B. Lewis. Orlando, FL: Harcourt, Gulliver, 2005.

Miller, William. *Zora Hurston and the Chinaberry Tree*. Illustrated by Cornelius Van Wright and Ying-Hwa Hu. New York: Lee and Low, 1994.

Monceaux, Morgan. *Jazz, My Music, My People*. New York: Knopf, 1994.

Myers, Walter Dean. *Here in Harlem: Poems in Many Voices*. New York: Holiday House, 2004.

Myers, Walter Dean, and Bill Miles. *The Harlem Hellfighters: When Pride Met Courage*. New York: HarperCollins, 2006.

Orgill, Roxane. *If I Only Had a Horn: Young Louis Armstrong*. Illustrated by Leonard Jenkins. Boston: Houghton Mifflin, 2002.

Perdomo, Willie. *Visiting Langston*. Illustrated by Bryan Collier. New York: Henry Holt, 2002.

Pinkney, Andrea Davis. *Duke Ellington: The Piano Prince and His Orchestra*. Illustrated by Brian Pinkney. New York: Hyperion Books for Children, 1998.

———. *Ella Fitzgerald: The Tale of a Vocal Virtuosa*. Illustrated by Brian Pinkney. New York: Hyperion Books for Children, 2002.

Porter, A. P. *Jump at de Sun: The Story of Zora Neale Hurston*. Minneapolis, MN: Carolrhoda, 1992.

Raschka, Chris. *Charlie Parker Played Be Bop*. New York: Scholastic, 1992.

Say, Allen. *The Bicycle Man*. New York: Houghton Mifflin, 1982.

Schroeder, Alan. *Satchmo's Blues*. Illustrated by Floyd Cooper. New York: Doubleday Books for Young Readers, 1996.

Shange, Ntozake. *Ellington Was Not a Street*. Illustrated by Kadir Nelson. New York: Simon and Schuster Books for Young Readers, 1983.

Sharp, Anne Wallace. *A Dream Deferred: The Jim Crow Era*. Farmington Hills, MI: Lucent Books, 2005.

Taylor, Debbie A. *Sweet Music in Harlem*. Illustrated by Frank Morrison. New York: Lee and Low, 2004.

Walker, Alice. *Langston Hughes: American Poet*. Illustrated by Catherine Deeter. New York: HarperCollins, 2002.

BIBLIOGRAPHY OF REFERENCE WORKS

Edgerton, Robert B. *Hidden Heroism: Black Soldiers in America's Wars*. Cambridge, MA: Westview, 2002.

Franklin, John Hope *From Slavery to Freedom: A History of African Americans*. New York: Knopf, 2000.

————. *Mirror to America: The Autobiography of John Hope Franklin*. New York: Farrar, Straus and Giroux, 2005.

Hughes, Langston, and Milton Meltzer. *A Pictorial History of the Negro in America*, new rev. ed. New York: Crown, 1963.

Wormser, Richard. *The Rise and Fall of Jim Crow: The African-American Struggle Against Discrimination, 1865–1954*. New York: Franklin Watts, 1999.

Martin Luther King Jr., Rosa Parks, and the Struggle for Civil Rights

Let freedom ring. And when this happens, and when we allow freedom to ring—when we let it ring from every village and every ham-
let, from every state and every city, we will be able to speed up that
day when all of God's children—black men and white men, Jews and
Gentiles, Protestants and Catholics—will be able to join hands and
sing in the words of the old Negro spiritual: "Free at last! Free at last!
Thank God Almighty, we are free at last!"[1]

$\mathcal{A}$s the Jim Crow years continued, different world and national events
increasingly challenged the status quo. After World War II, African
Americans returned to most of the same restrictions based on race that
had existed before the war. Now, veterans who had risked their lives
fighting valiantly for the freedoms that this nation espouses came home
to the Jim Crow laws still being rigidly enforced. Frequently, stories of
tension and violence are told, of how veterans in the late 1940s would
challenge the laws and suffer the overwhelming hatred and fear that was
building as the reality of change became more and more likely.

Many historians cite 1954 as the beginning of the civil rights movement. Although for years African Americans had been challenging racist
laws and traditions, these challenges had been individual acts of resistance
or acts of small groups, as in the early slave revolts, but in 1954, the injustice that people saw in the arrest of Rosa Parks came to represent the
injustices that millions felt and would no longer tolerate. For refusing the
demand of a bus driver to relinquish her seat for a White man, Parks was
arrested, and her act led to a bus boycott in Montgomery, Alabama, that
forced the integration of the buses and led to what we know as the civil
rights movement.

After Park's arrest, Martin Luther King Jr., then a young Baptist minister, quickly spearheaded a response that spoke to the nation and formed a first step in what became a march to freedom. Many people joined this march; some became famous for their contributions and some did not. Many people who survived the time between 1954 and 1971 have noted those years as markers for the movement and continue to share the stories of sit-down demonstrations, marches, and protests against laws and restrictions that had enforced a second-class citizenship that would no longer be tolerated. Because of this availability of personal stories, this is likely to be one of the better-known periods of Black history for today's children.

King studied the life of Mohandas Gandhi and his nonviolent response to the colonization of the British in India that ultimately prevailed with the independence of India from the British in 1947. Gandhi had employed ideas of civil disobedience and had become a respected political and spiritual leader. Here in the United States, King's leadership through the turbulent times of the civil rights movement provided the strength of faith and conviction that captured the conscience of the nation. With his eloquent "I Have a Dream" speech, proclaimed on the steps of the Lincoln Memorial during the March on Washington in 1963, Martin Luther King Jr. carved a place in our history that over the years has been acknowledged with a national celebration of his birthday.

EARLY ELEMENTARY

Coles, Robert. *The Story of Ruby Bridges*. Illustrated by George Ford. New York: Scholastic, 1995.

> On Ruby's first day, a large crowd of angry white people gathered outside the Frintz Elementary School. The people carried signs that said they didn't want black children in a white school. People called Ruby names; some wanted to hurt her. The city and state police did not help Ruby.
>
> The President of the United States ordered federal marshals to walk with Ruby into the school building. The marshals carried guns.[2]

This picture book tells the story of Ruby Bridges, a six-year-old child who is selected to begin the process of integration in a White elementary school in 1960. When parents refused to send their children to the school because a Black child was attending, she worked alone with her teacher, Mrs. Henry, learning her school subjects in the cavernous space of an empty classroom.

This remarkable little girl never lost her courage, and in one of the incidents in the book, Ruby pauses in the crowd of demonstrators to pray for the enraged adults who for weeks and months have been demonstrating outside the school, where they jeer at her with terrible racist shouts and banners. When asked why she had stopped in such a dangerous place, she said that she prayed each morning for them but had forgotten that morning until she was close to the school.

In the afterword to his book, Cole shares that, as the school year progressed, several White students started coming to school. After the demonstrators' initial heated and furious response to integration, they begin to give up in their efforts to scare Ruby and defeat the efforts to integrate the schools.

Farris, Christine King. *My Brother Martin: A Sister Remembers Growing Up with the Rev. Dr. Martin Luther King Jr.* Illustrated by Chris Soentpiet. New York: Simon and Schuster Books for Young Readers, 2003.

Told as the memories of a sister and nicely illustrated, this story of King's life has the feel of a family album. The first picture shows baby Martin in a crib while his sister, their parents, grandparents, and Aunt Ida, their grandmother's sister, all look adoringly at the new baby. Farris goes on to tell the many aspects of their home, the story of this loving extended family, and their experiences dealing with the prejudice and segregation of the times. Their mother and their father, a prominent minister in Atlanta, talk to the children as they become increasingly aware of the discrimination around them, and young Martin decides that someday he will "turn the world upside down." Farris includes King's civil rights work and concludes, as the country has, that he made a profound impact working toward his goal.

Genre: Memoir

Giovanni, Nikki. *Rosa*. Illustrated by Bryan Collier. New York: Henry Holt, 2005.

Mrs. Parks was having a good day. Mother was getting over that touch of flu and was up this morning for breakfast at the table. Her husband, Raymond Parks, one of the best barbers in the country, had been asked to take on extra work at the air force base. And the first day of December was always special because you could just feel Christmas in the air.[3]

The day started just like any other, and in fact, things were going very well on a day that will be marked in history. Giovanni's story follows Rosa Parks to work and shows how the day continues to have an easy pace. But as Parks sits in the bus on her way home, she makes a choice that will change the country: she chooses not to get up when the bus driver orders her to give up her seat to a White man. Collier's illustrations are congruent with Giovanni's powerful depiction of the events that surround this key scene from the beginning of the civil rights movement. Both the text and the illustrations provide the reader with an exciting, beautiful, and accurate depiction of this part of Rosa Park's life.

Genre: Biography

Award: Coretta Scott King Illustrator Award

Littlesugar, Amy. *Freedom School, Yes!* Illustrated by Floyd Cooper. New York: Philomel, 2001.

> Brave? Jolie wasn't sure, but she knew, standing there under the stars—Benjamin Banneker's stars—that when it came to school and learning, she was never going to let bein' scared get in her way again.[4]

The author has created this story, set in a fictitious town in the South named Chicken Creek, from the stories shared by three of the more than six hundred volunteers who went into the state of Mississippi to teach African American children and adults who were not receiving a strong education. Most volunteers stayed with families, and Annie is with Jolie and her mother when, on the first night she is there, a brick is thrown through the window with a note attached, telling Annie to leave town. When she and community members continue with plans to start a school, the church is burned to the ground. Persistent, the teacher and students meet outside until a new church is built. Jolie learns about many courageous African Americans in history, and she discovers strength in their stories when she finds herself worried about Annie and the new church building.

Genre: Historical Fiction

Lucas, Eileen. *Cracking the Wall: The Struggles of the Little Rock Nine.* Illustrated by Mark Anthony. Minneapolis, MN: Carolrhoda Books, 1997.

> As Elizabeth walked toward them, someone squirted ink on her dress. A woman screamed in her face. Elizabeth tried to ignore the angry voices. She tried not to show how frightened she was.[5]

In Little Rock, Arkansas, in 1957, nine Black high school students were chosen to attend Central High School, a school of two thousand White students, in an attempt to integrate the school. The Governor of Arkansas, Orval Faubus, spoke angrily about the move to include Black students at the school. He refused to support the students by providing physical protection, and he blocked their entering the school. Finally, President Eisenhower ordered federal troops to the area to protect the students and escort them into the school and through their day.

This period of the civil rights movement was violent, and when the troops left the school, the nine African American students encountered abuse. The following year, Governor Faubus closed the school completely rather than comply with the federal mandate to integrate. Eventually, though, all public schools in the United States were integrated, and the Little Rock Nine, good and dedicated students at the time this story takes place, were seen as heroes.

This book is an easy read but very intense in its content, in the same way as Robert Coles's *The Story of Ruby Bridges.* I was particularly pleased that the author gave a brief profile of each student, which identified the group as nine individuals.

Genre: Nonfiction/Informational

Morrison, Toni. *Remember: The Journey to School Integration.* Boston: Houghton Mifflin, 2004.

> They are trying to scare me. I guess they don't have any children of their own. But didn't grownups used to be little kids who knew how it felt to be scared?[6]

Morrison's book is a sensitive look at the process of school integration through pictures and text with a personal voice. As Ruby Bridges is pictured walking down the school steps surrounded by U.S. marshals, she asks the reader if adults weren't once children, too. For Ruby, it is unimaginable that adults would scare a child with angry shouts and mean looks if they either had children or remembered being a child. It is hoped that all readers would share her thought.

The pictures and text in this book are powerful, presenting the moments of connectedness as children find one another in friendship set against the violence and hatred of the crowd, and the terror children and adults felt as they put themselves on the front line for freedom and justice for all Americans. Honest and powerful, this is an important book to include in any study of school integration.

Genre: Nonfiction/Informational

Myers, Walter Dean. *"I've Seen the Promised Land":The Life of Dr. Martin Luther King, Jr.* Illustrated by Leonard Jenkins. New York: HarperCollins, Amistad, 2004.

> Local police arrested Dr. King just to harass him, and a firebomb was thrown onto the porch of his house.[7]

Myers and Jenkins have paired up to provide a well-illustrated, well-written description of a civil rights leader. With a brief paragraph about his early years, this book essentially begins when King is chosen to lead the Montgomery bus boycott. The challenges he faced as he preached nonviolence, his numerous campaigns for equality, his trip to India to study Gandhi's work, and his unfortunate murder are all discussed completely, but with a sensitivity toward the young reader. This work pairs nicely with Myers and Jenkins's *Malcolm X: A Fire Burning Brightly*.

Genre: Biography

Myers, Walter Dean. *Malcolm X: A Fire Burning Brightly*. Illustrated by Leonard Jenkins. New York: HarperCollins, Amistad, 2000.

> Some said that the police were recording everything Malcolm said. Malcolm knew it was true, but he hadn't come this far to turn back or soften his message about winning freedom, justice, and equality for blacks in America.[8]

Myers has woven together Malcolm X's words and his own understanding of Malcolm X's life and works. Illustrations complement the text well. This book does not shy away from the "dangerous" ideas espoused by Malcolm X, or the situations in his life, but it does make them understandable for young readers. Everything is covered here: from the formative experiences of Malcolm's childhood through his troubles with the law as a young man, his relationship with the Nation of Islam, his trip to Mecca and the very significant changes it effected in his thoughts on race, to his untimely death. In the end, Myers provides a chronology of Malcolm's life, accompanied by quotes from Malcolm. Overall, this is an excellent introduction to Malcolm X for young readers.

Genre: Biography

Parks, Rosa, with James Haskins. *I Am Rosa Parks.* Illustrated by Wil Clay. New York: Dial Books for Young Readers, 1997.

> One day I was riding on a bus. I was sitting in one of the seats in the back section for black people. The bus started to get crowded. The front seats filled up with white people. One white man was standing up. The bus driver looked back at us black people sitting down. The driver said, "Let me have those seats."[9]

This is the story of Rosa Parks in her own words. This book is deliberately written for very young readers and could be readable for first and second graders. It tells about her arrest after she refused to give up her seat on the bus when the driver ordered that she get up. It also includes a brief sketch from her childhood and reminiscences from the civil rights demonstrations that changed the rules about segregated bus service. Published before her death, the book ends with her telling the reader what she is doing in her elder years.

Genre: Biography

Rappaport, Doreen. *Martin's Big Words: The Life of Dr. Martin Luther King, Jr.* Illustrated by Bryan Collier. New York: Hyperion Books for Children, 2001.

> Everywhere in Martin's hometown
> He saw the signs, WHITES ONLY.
> His mother said these signs were
> in all Southern cities and towns
> in the United States.
> Every time Martin read the words,
> he felt bad,
> until he remembered what his mother told him:
> "You are as good as anyone."[10]

Brilliantly illustrated by Bryan Collier, this book combines biographical sketches with King's powerful words. Rappaport has taken a very complex man living in a very turbulent time and made both the man and the time approachable for young children. It is clear in this book that there is strength in people marching together for a cause, in having a movement grounded in peace, and in not being intimidated by violence. It is hard to say much after the eloquence of King, but Rappaport's stories from his life and the illustrations that accompany them are combined with excerpts from King himself, extending his message to even the very young.

Genre: Nonfiction/Information/Biography

Awards: Caldecott Honor; Coretta Scott King Illustrator Honor; Jane Addams Children's Picture Book Award

Ringgold, Faith. *My Dream of Martin Luther King*. New York: Crown, 1995.

> In my dreams, Martin appeared first as a child in a place so huge that it encompassed the whole world and all its people. There were children and old folks, men and women of all colors, races and religions. They carried bags containing their prejudice, hate, ignorance, violence, and fear, which they intended to trade for hope, freedom, peace, awareness, and love.[11]

This story is told as a dream remembered by a young girl who falls asleep as she is listening to Martin Luther King Jr. speak on television. There is a powerful image of a crowd of people moving forward, climbing steps together, singing, "We Shall Overcome." In the dream, King as a child of six discovers that he is no longer welcome to play with a neighbor child who is White. The dream then turns to the heart of some of the protests that landed him in jail, then to events that were part of his adult life and many of the things that marked his incredible career as a civil rights leader. Ringgold's paintings are striking, with bold representations of each scene.

Genre: Historical Fantasy

Ringgold, Faith. *Dinner at Aunt Connie's House*. New York: Hyperion Paperbacks for Children, 1993.

> "I will be the first to speak, I am Rosa Parks. I was born in 1913 in Alabama. I am called the mother of the civil rights movement. In 1955, I was arrested for refusing to sit in the back of the bus.

That incident started the Montgomery bus boycott and inspired Martin Luther King Jr. to devote his life to the civil rights movement."

"But how can you speak? Paintings don't talk like people," Lonnie said.

"Your aunt Connie created us to tell you the history of our struggle. Would you like to hear more?"

We nodded, and the next painting spoke.[12]

When Melody and her family went to visit her Aunt Connie and Uncle Bates in Sag Harbor, she met their adopted son, Lonnie. Together, as their families relaxed on the beach, the children played in the house and encountered some magical paintings that Aunt Connie had painted. Each of the twelve paintings was of an important woman in Black history and each person represented in the painting speaks to the children about their contribution to the struggle for freedom and civil rights. The characters span the time from slavery to the civil rights years. The biographical notes are brief but could introduce children to people they might want to know more about. Ringgold's art illustrates the book, which was inspired by her 1986 work *The Dinner Quilt*, displayed in major museums throughout the country.

Genre: Historical Fantasy

Shore, Diane Z., and Jessica Alexander. *This Is the Dream*. Illustrated by James E. Ransome. New York: HarperCollins, 2006.

These are the diners who sit and who wait at the "WHITES ONLY" counter, ignoring the hate.[13]

The book is told in rhyming verse, and the illustrations are collages of pictures and cut paper along with powerful paintings by James E. Ransome. The story contrasts the situation before the civil rights movement with how things were changed by the movement. Later in the book, there is a scene of a family eating comfortably at a restaurant that is not segregated. As the experiences of schoolchildren, riders on buses, and thirsty people at water fountains are contrasted, the book identifies the marchers and the leaders who made the changes happen with their powerful voices and demands for fair and equal treatment.

Written for younger readers, this book brings the reader to a real understanding of the world before and after the civil rights movement and the work of specific individuals like Thurgood Marshall and Martin

Luther King Jr. in the context of their fellow civil rights workers, both famous and nameless.

Genre: Picture Book

Weatherford, Carole Boston. *Freedom on the Menu: The Greensboro Sit-Ins.* Illustrated by Jerome Lagarrigue. New York: Dial Books for Young Readers, 2004.

> An old white lady came up to the boys. "I'm so proud of you," she said clear as a bell so everyone could hear. "I wish someone had done this sooner."[14]

Connie always enjoyed having time with her mom when they went shopping downtown in Greensboro, North Carolina. When they wanted to get something to eat, though, they could not eat at the lunch counter because it was segregated and African Americans were refused service. But these were changing times and students from the nearby college, North Carolina Agriculture and Technical College, challenged the ban and sat at the counter. Protests and arrests of the many students who joined in from other campuses followed until, months later, diners of all colors were welcome at the lunch counter. Connie learns that challenging segregation is important, even if her sister, an A student who joins the demonstrators, has to go to jail.

Genre: Historical Fiction

LATER ELEMENTARY

Curtis, Christopher Paul. *The Watsons Go to Birmingham—1963.* New York: Delacorte, 1995.

> Momma was the only one who wasn't born in Flint so the cold was coldest to her. All you could see were her eyes too, and they were shooting bad looks at Dad. She always blamed him for bringing her all the way from Alabama to Michigan, a state she called a giant icebox. Dad was bundled up on the other side of Joey, trying to look at anything but Momma. Next to Dad, sitting with a little space between them, was my older brother, Byron.[15]

In this story about the Watsons, a family living in Flint, Michigan, Curtis uses his incredible blend of humor and seriousness to capture the many things that happen within the family. The story is told by Kenny, the ten-year-old son, whose relationship with his older brother Byron is often difficult. In fact, Byron's general behavior has become a concern to his parents, and the family finally has had enough. Plans are made to take Byron to Birmingham, Alabama, to live with his grandmother, who the parents hope will straighten him out. And that is when violence strikes: the bombing of the church in Birmingham in 1963. The story concludes with the individual family members working out their feelings about the events they have just lived through.

This was Curtis's first book, and it was recognized as a Newbery Honor book. It is a very strong read-aloud and can be an excellent independent read for students in the fourth grade and up.

Genre: Historical Fiction

Awards: Coretta Scott King Author Honor; Newbery Honor

Haskins, James. *Delivering Justice: W. W. Law and the Fight for Civil Rights.* Illustrated by Benny Andrews. Cambridge, MA: Candlewick, 2005.

> People, both Black and White, saw Westley as Savannah's hero. He had kept the protest disciplined and peaceful, even in the face of violence. Modestly, he would say, "I was just doing what every black American should be doing."[16]

Throughout telling the story of W. W. Law's efforts to change the discriminatory laws that enforced segregation, Haskins defines much of the language related to the struggle. Chapters are very short and describe different aspects of segregation. Law's life story provides a portrait of the activities of the NAACP's organization for nonviolent protest as well as the cultural pressure to silence leaders. Law could not get a teaching job because of his membership in the NAACP, and although he was reinstated later, he was fired from his job as postal carrier because of his success in organizing protests.

This book contributes wonderful stories of the civil rights era that young children can discuss, and it gives students an opportunity to learn about this important part of American history and another American hero.

Genre: Biography

Award: Jane Addams Children's Book Award

Haskins, James, and Kathleen Benson. *John Lewis in the Lead: A Story of the Civil Rights Movement*. Illustrated by Benny Andrews. New York: Lee and Low, 2006.

> When Dr. King said segregation was wrong, John felt as though Dr. King were speaking directly to him, telling him it was time to get in the way. It was time to turn things upside down in order to set them right side up.[17]

Turn things upside down and set them right side up is what John Lewis has done. This book follows, with nicely illustrated details, Lewis's transitions from a young boy in Alabama through his very active participation in the civil rights movement to his 1986 election and later reelection to the House of Representatives as a representative from Georgia.

This book gives a real, still-active-today face to the civil rights movement. We see John Lewis as a teenager, hearing about the Montgomery bus boycott and being denied a library card. We see his personal successes, such as graduating from seminary and university and getting married and having a child, but we also see the entire civil rights movement through his actions. We watch him participating in the Freedom Rides, being elected chair of the Student Nonviolent Coordinating Committee, speaking at the March on Washington, coordinating voter registration drives, leading the first Selma-to-Montgomery march on Bloody Sunday and the protected, and very well attended Selma-to-Montgomery march two weeks later. We see the violence he endures in the process, and we see his commitment to what he knows to be right. Then we watch him become elected to the city council of Atlanta and later moving into the national political arena as a congressman.

Haskins and Benson provide a clear context for Lewis's life and work. We see the strong influence of Martin Luther King Jr. and how King brought others into the fight for civil rights. We see what is happening in local and national government as Lewis experiences the events of his life.

If one has grown fond of James Haskins's work through these chapters, one might note that this book was published after his death in 2005 and is dedicated to him by his wife and frequent co-author, Kathleen Benson.

Genre: Biography

Nelson, Vaunda Micheaux. *Beyond Mayfield*. New York: Putnam's, 1999.

> Luke stabbed the ground with a stick. "What exactly was Sam doing that made them so mad?"

"Papa says he was helping colored people sign up to vote," Billie said. Alice frowned. "Don't they already vote?"

"The law says they can," Fitch said, "but Daddy says white people down South make them scared to try because something might happen to them."

Mo looked at the ground. "Like with Sam."

"It ain't right," Alice said. She yanked some grass from the ground and threw it.[18]

In this book, a sequel to *Mayfield Crossing*, the work of the Freedom Riders is presented from the viewpoint of children. Sam, who has always been known by his nickname, "Lucky," has just returned to his Pennsylvania town from the navy and asks to be called Sam. He is clearly changed by his experiences in the navy and is soon on his way to join the Freedom Riders. When tragedy strikes, his family and the friends of his little sibling must consider some harsh truths. Busing is also an element of this story, as the Black children find themselves discriminated against in a formerly all-White school.

Genre: Historical Fiction

Robinet, Harriette Gillem. *Walking to the Bus-Rider Blues*. New York: Atheneum, 2000.

It is 1956, and twelve-year-old Alfa lives in poverty in Montgomery, Alabama, with his nearly ninety-year-old great-grandmother, Big Mama, and his sister, Zinnia. Paying the rent each month is a struggle, even though Alfa does his best by working at the local grocery store, stocking groceries. When Alfa and Zinnia are accused of theft, and the rent money starts disappearing, the two children set out to solve the mysteries of the missing money while also dealing with family concerns and the racial issues of Montgomery in the time of the bus boycott.

Genre: Historical Fiction

Award: Jane Addams Children's Book Honor

MIDDLE GRADES

Adoff, Arnold. *Malcolm X*. Illustrated by John Wilson. New York: Crowell, 1970.

Malcom read most about the life of the black man in Africa and Africa. He read that black people had great societies in Africa long before America was discovered. He learned about the kingdoms of Benin, Ghana, and Ethiopia, which began more than five hundred years before the birth of Jesus.[19]

Just before Malcolm Little was born, his home was attacked by the Ku Klux Klan. His father was away at a meeting, and his mother huddled in fear with her three children. Every window in their home was broken. After Malcolm was born, the family moved from Nebraska to Michigan, where Reverend Little continued to challenge the inequities that Blacks were living with and demanded fair treatment. Angry Whites attacked again, and the Littles' house was burned to the ground as fire fighters and police looked on. The family moved again. Reverend Little died in a questionable accident, and Malcolm soon lost his mother as well when she was institutionalized in the state hospital.

Placed in foster care, Malcolm soon was in trouble and sent to a detention center. At school, though, Malcolm was bright and did well. But he realized that in spite of his ability, although his teachers liked him, they did not respect him. When he shared his ambition of becoming a lawyer, he was discouraged from pursuing this career choice.

When Malcolm got into legal trouble as an adult, he was sent to prison. This time he devoured books, reading for many hours a day. He read the work of Black scholars he had never before heard of. He converted to the Muslim religion and became a prominent member of the Nation of Islam. He was angry, and with his brilliance, he spoke for many angry people. After he made two trips to Africa, his religious beliefs changed, and though he remained a Muslim, he left the Nation of Islam. Soon after that decision, he was gunned down and killed. His writings continue to be read and remain important today.

Genre: Biography

Bausum, Ann. *Freedom Riders: John Lewis and Jim Zwerg on the Front Lines of the Civil Rights Movement.* Washington, DC: National Geographic, 2006.

The Freedom Rides changed how people traveled. They revolutionized the civil rights movement by attracting young people and non-Southerners to the cause. They tested and strengthened future leaders of the struggle, both during the rides and with the jail times that followed. They even added a new phrase to the movement—Freedom Rider—a tag often given to people who put their lives on the line for the cause.[20]

Bausum's book tells of the stunningly violent reaction of southerners to the fight for desegregation of public transportation. In spite of the Supreme Court's 1946 decision against segregation on public transportation, it would take the deliberate and committed work of the Freedom Riders to finally see changes in a system that had existed for decades. Bausum reminds readers that Sojourner Truth and Frederick Douglass both challenged the indignities of being physically assaulted for simply sitting where people of color were not allowed to sit in spite of paying the same fares as White people.

Students will read about the movement and about two men who withstood mob attacks and almost fatal experiences while continuing to pressure politicians to protect the rights of all citizens. As news of the shocking attacks on the nonviolent Freedom Riders were broadcast nationwide, with filming often taken at great risk to the cameramen, more and more support came from citizens all over the country. The determination of the Freedom Riders also made it increasingly clear that the movement for civil rights would continue. Two years after the Freedom Rides, the 1963 March on Washington took the movement giant steps forward.

Genre: Nonfiction/Informational

Bridges, Ruby. *Through My Eyes*. New York: Scholastic, 1999.

> When I was six years old, the civil rights movement came knocking at the door. It was 1960, and history pushed and swept me up in a whirlwind. At the time, I knew little about the racial fears and hatred in Louisiana, where I was growing up. Young children never know about racism at the start. It's we adults who teach it.[21]

Thank you, Ruby Bridges, for sharing your remembrances from those days in your childhood when you were a first grader at William Frantz Public School in New Orleans in 1960! In a personal, day-to-day style, Bridges takes the reader into her life as a child who, unaware of the huge implications of her simply going to school, found herself the only Black child in a hostile, all-White school during court-ordered integration. Even though she is an adult looking back into her childhood, she has captured a good deal of the innocence of a child generally accepting things as they were—this despite the angry crowds of adults who demonstrated outside of the school, hurling insults and threats.

Bridges shares some interesting facts, including a visit by John Steinbeck, who had read about the situation surrounding this little girl going to school. She tells of how he had to leave his truck in a distant parking lot, take a cab, and walk the last several blocks to the school. She also describes a letter from Eleanor Roosevelt that her mother read over and over. Sadly, too, there are the other facts she shares: the family could no longer shop at a local store, her father lost his job, and her parents experienced an enormous fear for the family's safety as violent behavior raged in the city toward anyone who supported integration. But Ruby found some measure of safety with her teacher, Mrs. Henry.

Genre: Autobiography
Award: Jane Addams Older Children's Book Award

Crowe, Chris. *Getting Away with Murder: The True Story of the Emmett Till Case.* New York: Dial Books for Young Readers, 2003.

> It wasn't until I was writing a book about the life and works of New-bery-winner author Mildred D. Taylor that I first encountered Emmett. In one of her essays, Taylor made a reference to a fourteen-year-old African American boy who had been murdered in her home state of Mississippi in 1955. I followed up on the reference to Emmett just to make sure it wasn't something I should include in my book about Taylor.[22]

This is an important story about one of the most hideous crimes committed in America that went unpunished by a court system where racial hatred freed murderers. It is also a story of a brave mother who understood that her grief, shared with others who were horrified by the crime committed against her son, had an importance that transcended a family tragedy and allowed a community of Whites and Blacks to share the horror of Emmett Till's brutal death. Crowe brings the details of this case to the reader and helps the reader understand how this young man's death strengthened the commitment to civil rights and propelled the civil rights movement forward.

Genre: Nonfiction/Informational

Crowe, Chris. *Mississippi Trial, 1955.* New York: Penguin, Speak, 2002.

> "I heard them slap the boy a few more times, heard him cry out. Heard car doors open and close; then they drove away with the lights still off." His face turned sad. "Didn't never see the boy alive again."[23]

Hiram, a White boy, has resented his father ever since his father insisted on uprooting the family from Greenwood, Mississippi, to get away from the racism there, so he is eager to have the opportunity to go back to Greenwood to spend the summer of 1955 with his beloved grandfather. Emmett Till is also visiting relatives in the Delta, and his brutal murder leads Hiram to reconsider what he has been taught by both his father and his grandfather. He comes to new understandings about racism and relationships. The fictional story built around the real event draws the reader close to the fictional characters and into the racial setting for a better understanding of this tragic murder of a young African American.

Genre: Historical Fiction

Freedman, Russell. *Freedom Walkers: The Story of the Montgomery Bus Boycott.* New York: Holiday House, 2006.

> "We must not take this as a victory," King told the crowd, "but merely with dignity. When we go back to the buses, go back with a quiet pride. Don't push your way. Just sit where there is a vacant seat. If someone pushes you, don't push back. We must have the courage to refuse to hit . . . we must continue to resist segregation non-violently."[24]

What a powerful book! Freedman's text covers the time of the Montgomery bus boycott, but it also reaches back as far as the 1940s to contextualize the need for the boycott and ahead into the 1960s to discuss several other events of the civil rights movement, and even further into the future to follow up on those who participated in this critical time in our nation's history. Indeed, more than his coverage of the period, it is his focus on the people that really make this work what it is. With chapters focused on Jo Ann Robinson, Claudette Colvin, Rosa Parks, Martin Luther King Jr., and other "boycott heroes," Freedman describes well the efforts of those who became famous for their actions, those who are less well known, and those who will never really be known but whose day-to-day participation in the boycott helped bring an end to legal segregation.

In this well-documented book filled with illustrative photos, Freedman is amazingly clear about the setting of the story. African Americans made up the majority of bus riders in Montgomery, paid the same fares as White passengers, but had to enter and exit the bus at the rear. They were relegated to seats at the rear even if the bus was nearly empty. Yet even those seats would have to be given up if there were not enough seats for Whites. This clarity is also applied to the discussion of the bus boycott itself. Young researchers will easily see how the bus boycott developed, what the demands of the boycotters were, how these issues were resolved, and how the numerous participants played a wide variety of roles toward this resolution.

Freedman's book does not end with the end of the boycott, nor does he paint an unrealistic image of the situation afterwards. He describes how violence and discrimination continued, and he brings the reader through other tragedies, battles, and victories: the 1963 church bombing that killed four girls in Birmingham; the 1963 March on Washington; the 1964 murder of three civil rights workers; sit-ins; the 1964 Civil Rights Act and 1965 Voting Rights Act; and the 1968 Black sanitation workers' strike that brought Martin Luther King Jr. to Memphis, where he was killed.

Genre: Nonfiction/Informational

Hansen, Joyce. *Women of Hope: African Americans Who Made a Difference.* New York: Scholastic, 1998.

> Our goal is to honor courageous, creative women of color whose persistence and vision gave society hopefulness and inspiration—an inspiration we still seek today.[25]

From Ida B. Wells-Barnett, who worked during the Jim Crow years challenging the violence against African Americans, to Mae C. Jemison, the first African American astronaut, the women whose stories are included here have found their way through the limitations that society might have held for them to become leaders in education, medicine, science, and literature. Not only are they incredibly accomplished in their professions, but they also represent a strength of character that truly provides inspiration today. These stories are wonderful examples of grace, intelligence, and courage embodied in women of hope.

Genre: Biography

McKissack, Patricia, and Arlene Zarembka. *To Establish Justice: Citizenship and the Constitution.* New York: Knopf, 2004.

> Literacy tests, in theory, sounded reasonable. But the questions used to test literacy were not reasonable. Sometimes citizens had to recite the entire federal and state constitutions from memory. Citizens were asked to answer ridiculous questions, such as "How high is up?" or "How many angels can dance on the head of a pin?" People who had earned college degrees were declared unqualified to vote because they could not pass these kinds of literacy tests. After a while, a majority of blacks gave up and didn't even try to register to vote.[26]

McKissack and Zarembka have written a very comprehensive description of the politics of this nation and the ongoing struggle, from the nation's beginnings, to afford the rights guaranteed in the Constitution to all of America's citizens. Their book is included in the civil rights chapter because, although justice is a continuing theme throughout the chapters, the authors look at how to actually bring about the concept at the heart of the civil rights movement.

Meltzer, Milton. *There Comes a Time: The Struggle for Civil Rights.* New York: Random House, 2001.

> On August 28 more than 250,000 people, black and white, people of all faiths, from all walks of life, and including 150 congressmen, came together before the Lincoln Memorial in Washington. It was the largest demonstration in American history up to that time. And there, to the huge crowd and to the nation via TV, King gave his famous "I Have a Dream" speech. In it came those unforgettable words: "I have a dream that my four little children will one day live in a nation where they will not be judged by the color of their skin but by the content of their character. . . . I have a dream that one day this nation will rise up and live out the true meaning of its creed: We hold these truths to be self-evident, that all men are created equal."[27]

If we don't find African American history in the lessons taught of American history, it is not Milton Meltzer's fault. He has provided well-researched and authoritative volumes that clearly provide Black history to young readers. Many of his books are described throughout this collection, including his work with Langston Hughes, *The Pictorial History of the Negro in America* (see chapter 1), and his excellent biographies, including one on Frederick Douglass that is extraordinary (see chapter 4).

Here again he has provided the reader with background to a historical period that challenged the nation and everything it stood for.

Genre: Nonfiction/Informational

Myers, Walter Dean. *Malcolm X: By Any Means Necessary*. New York: Scholastic, 1993.

> Malcolm, over his lifetime, had taught himself to deal with all kinds of people. He could talk to "street" people and to college graduates. He was discovering, as were those who worked with him, that he had a genius for organizing, and a genius for reaching places in the African-American soul that organizations like the Urban League and the National Association for the Advancement of Colored People were carefully avoiding. While certain black Americans had made some gains in the United States, most young black men were doing very poorly. They were hopeless, or nearly so. Like Malcolm years before, they had "just given up."[28]

Myers tells Malcolm X's story with honesty, intensity, and great care. In a very detailed biography, he takes the reader through the many complex experiences that were part of Malcolm X's life, from the loss of his father and a struggling childhood, to his very early disillusionment with school and the prospects of a Black man in this culture, to his conversion to Islam while in an archaic prison system. He helps the reader understand Malcolm's rise in his leadership role within the Nation of Islam, his journey into his faith, and his eventual violent death.

In his style of leadership and the fundamental beliefs that guided him, Malcolm X is most often compared with Martin Luther King Jr. Myers writes clearly about each man, their differences, and their contributions during the challenging years of the civil rights movement. Readers are left with sadness and a sense of loss for the brilliant, articulate, and passionate man who was killed while confronting injustice in America.

Genre: Biography

Award: Coretta Scott King Honor Book

Nelson, Marilyn. *A Wreath for Emmett Till*. Illustrated by Philippe Lardy. Boston: Houghton Mifflin, 2005.

> *Rosemary for remembrance*, Shakespeare wrote:
> If I could forget, believe me, I would.
> Pierced by the screams of a shortened childhood.[29]

Nelson is a powerful poet. Here she uses what she calls a "heroic crown of sonnets" to honor Emmett Till, and to consider both the context and the repercussions of his murder. The images are complex, as is the beautiful artwork, but both are explained in notes at the end of the book. Thus, the reader gains much from the beauty of the form and the text, and he or she can also turn to the end of the book for greater explanation. Truly a magnificent work.

Genre: Poetry

Award: Coretta Scott King Author Honor

Thomas, Joyce Carol, ed. *Linda Brown, You Are Not Alone: The* Brown v. Board of Education *Decision*. Illustrated by Curtis James. New York: Hyperion Books for Children, 2003.

> As early as 1896, it was legal to separate blacks and whites, as long as facilities such as water fountains, lunch counters, movie theaters, and schools were "equal." This concept is called *segregation*.[30]

Thomas has collected the reflections of prominent children's literature authors and illustrators regarding the unanimous decision of the U.S. Supreme Court in *Brown v. Board of Education*. In that 1954 decision, the Court struck down the concept that schools could be segregated as long as schools for Black students and White students were equal. Authors, both Black and White, who have contributed to this volume present a great variety of responses, which might help students realize that the decision affected Americans in many different ways. Thomas writes that Linda Brown, after winning the right to attend a White school, had to face many difficult situations. White men, women, and children angrily confronted her when she tried to seek an education in her new school.

Genre: Nonfiction/Informational

NOTES

1. King, "I Have a Dream."
2. Coles, *The Story of Ruby Bridges*.
3. Giovanni, *Rosa*.
4. Littlesugar, *Freedom School, Yes!*
5. Lucas, *Cracking the Wall*, 29.

6. Morrison, *Remember*.
7. Myers, *Dr. Martin Luther King, Jr.*
8. Myers, *Fire Burning Brightly*.
9. Parks, *I Am Rosa Parks*, 8–10.
10. Rappaport, *Martin's Big Words*.
11. Ringgold, *My Dream*.
12. Ringgold, *Aunt Connie's House*.
13. Shore and Alexander, *This Is the Dream*.
14. Weatherford, *Freedom on the Menu*.
15. Curtis, *Watsons*, 2.
16. Haskins, *Delivering Justice*.
17. Haskins and Benson, *John Lewis*.
18. Nelson, *Beyond Mayfield*, 97.
19. Adoff, *Malcolm X*, 17.
20. Bausum, *Freedom Riders*, 64.
21. Bridges, *Through My Eyes*, 4.
22. Crowe, *Getting Away with Murder*, 11.
23. Crowe, *Mississippi Trial*, 169.
24. Freedman, *Freedom Walkers*, 86.
25. Hansen, *Women of Hope*, 5 (foreword by Moe Foner).
26. McKissack and Zarembka, *To Establish Justice*, 74.
27. Meltzer, *There Comes a Time*, 128.
28. Myers, *By Any Means Necessary*, 87–88.
29. Nelson, *A Wreath for Emmett Till*.
30. Thomas, *Linda Brown*, ix.

BIBLIOGRAPHY OF BOOKS FOR CHILDREN

Adoff, Arnold. *Malcolm X*. Illustrated by John Wilson. New York: Crowell, 1970.
Bausum, Ann. *Freedom Riders: John Lewis and Jim Zwerg on the Front Lines of the Civil Rights Movement*. Washington, DC: National Geographic, 2006.
Bridges, Ruby. *Through My Eyes*. New York: Scholastic, 1999.
Coles, Robert. *The Story of Ruby Bridges*. Illustrated by George Ford. New York: Scholastic, 1995.
Crowe, Chris. *Getting Away with Murder: The True Story of the Emmett Till Case*. New York: Dial Books for Young Readers, 2003.
Crowe, Chris. *Mississippi Trial, 1955*. New York: Penguin, Speak, 2002.
Curtis, Christopher Paul. *The Watsons Go to Birmingham—1963*. New York: Delacorte, 1995.

Farris, Christine King. *My Brother Martin: A Sister Remembers Growing Up with the Rev. Dr. Martin Luther King Jr.* Illustrated by Chris Soentpiet. New York: Simon and Schuster Books for Young Readers, 2003.

Freedman, Russell. *Freedom Walkers: The Story of the Montgomery Bus Boycott.* New York: Holiday House, 2006.

Giovanni, Nikki. *Rosa.* Illustrated by Bryan Collier. New York: Henry Holt, 2005.

Hansen, Joyce. *Women of Hope: African Americans Who Made a Difference.* New York: Scholastic, 1998.

Haskins, James. *Delivering Justice: W. W. Law and the Fight for Civil Rights.* Illustrated by Benny Andrews. Cambridge, MA: Candlewick, 2005.

Haskins, James, and Kathleen Benson. *John Lewis in the Lead: A Story of the Civil Rights Movement.* Illustrated by Benny Andrews. New York: Lee and Low, 2006.

Littlesugar, Amy. *Freedom School, Yes!* Illustrated by Floyd Cooper. New York: Philomel, 2001.

Lucas, Eileen. *Cracking the Wall: The Struggles of the Little Rock Nine.* Illustrated by Mark Anthony. Minneapolis, MN: Carolrhoda, 1997.

McKissack, Patricia C., and Arlene Zarembka. *To Establish Justice: Citizenship and the Constitution.* New York: Knopf, 2004.

Meltzer, Milton. *There Comes a Time: The Struggle for Civil Rights.* New York: Random House, 2001.

Morrison, Toni. *Remember: The Journey to School Integration.* Boston: Houghton Mifflin, 2004.

Myers, Walter Dean. *"I've Seen the Promised Land": The Life of Dr. Martin Luther King, Jr.* Illustrated by Leonard Jenkins. New York: HarperCollins, Amistad, 2004.

———. *Malcolm X: By Any Means Necessary.* New York: Scholastic, 1993.

———. *Malcolm X: A Fire Burning Brightly.* Illustrated by Leonard Jenkins. New York: HarperCollins, Amistad, 2000.

Nelson, Marilyn. *A Wreath for Emmett Till.* Illustrated by Philippe Lardy. Boston: Houghton Mifflin, 2005.

Nelson, Vaunda Micheaux. *Beyond Mayfield.* New York: Putnam's, 1999.

Parks, Rosa, with James Haskins. *I Am Rosa Parks.* Illustrated by Wil Clay. New York: Dial Books for Young Readers, 1997.

Rappaport, Doreen. *Martin's Big Words: The Life of Dr. Martin Luther King, Jr.* Illustrated by Bryan Collier. New York: Hyperion Books for Children, 2001.

Ringgold, Faith. *Dinner at Aunt Connie's House.* New York: Hyperion Paperbacks for Children, 1993.

———. *My Dream of Martin Luther King.* New York: Crown, 1995.

Robinet, Harriette Gillem. *Walking to the Bus-Rider Blues.* New York: Atheneum, 2000.

Shore, Diane Z., and Jessica Alexander. *This Is the Dream.* Illustrated by James E. Ransome. New York: HarperCollins, 2006.

Thomas, Joyce Carol, ed. *Linda Brown, You Are Not Alone: The* Brown v. Board of
  Education *Decision.* Illustrated by Curtis James. New York: Hyperion Books
  for Children, 2003.
Weatherford, Carole Boston. *Freedom on the Menu: The Greensboro Sit-Ins.* Illustrated by Jerome Lagarrigue. New York: Dial Books for Young Readers,
  2004.

BIBLIOGRAPHY OF REFERENCE WORKS

King, Martin Luther, Jr. "I Have a Dream." August 28, 1963. www.american
  rhetoric.com/speeches/Ihaveadream.htm.

• 11 •

Telling It Like It Is: Stories of Today

These books, set in contemporary times and portraying families and children having recognizable experiences, provided white children a chance to respond aesthetically to characters who were black and provided black children with black protagonists in literature outside of Black History Month studies. The resulting conversations about these types of books (in which the themes were not about race, yet the characters were black) provided a chance for children to realize the similarities of their positive and challenging experiences. Although the children didn't speak directly to racism issues, the books deepened their sense of community and built the trust critical to open conversations about race.[1]

Contemporary children's literature provides a broad picture of our diverse society. The books that Copenhaver-Johnson shared in her classroom, described above, would not have been available in the years before the late 1960s. Now we have such books detailed in Barbara Thrash Murphy's wonderful volume *Black Authors and Illustrators of Books for Children and Young Adults: A Biographical Dictionary*.[2] But, as much as things have changed and we are seeing many different faces in the children's literature of today, we still have a way to go in bringing multicultural literature into our homes and classrooms.

As this book suggests, one way to create this change is with the inclusion of Black history into the previously White-dominated history of America, not as an add-on, but rather as an integral part of the events that have created and sustained this nation. Even in contemporary children's literature, one sees the shadow of the past, and although a contemporary story may not explicitly speak about the past, its influence is

217

present. As conversations emerge around race in multicultural children's literature, it is important to have a basis for understanding the role race has played in our nation's history. Certainly, having studied the people of the past, one might ask, How might history have been different if Frederick Douglass had been elected president after the Civil War? How many more men and women would have been inventors, statesmen, scholars, and heroes if they had not died in bondage at sea or living in slavery? How might our contemporary world be different if the races had been treated equally?

There continues to be a need to look at race and the advantages that come with the "privilege" of being a particular race. Issues that surround race do come up in contemporary stories, and it is important to share them. One way to begin such a dialogue is to put issues out for students to talk about. Many of the books offered in the previous chapters can do that, but the ones offered here might, in some ways, challenge us to look at today and the many things that remain for us to change.

EARLY ELEMENTARY

Ackerman, Karen. *By the Dawn's Early Light*. Illustrated by Catherine Stock. New York: Aladdin, 1994.

In one of the poems in Ackerman's collection, Josh and Rachel are sad to have their mother leave every night, and they hope that she will someday work during the day, like their friends' parents. For now, they must rely on their Nana to care for them overnight while their mother works. The text alternately describes what the children and their Nana are doing at home and what Mom is doing at work. This book tells of a life that is a reality for many children.

Genre: Realistic Contemporary Fiction

Adoff, Arnold. *Black Is Brown Is Tan*. Illustrated by Emily Arnold McCully. New York: HarperCollins, 1973.

This is the way it is with us this is the way we are.[3]

In 1960, Arnold Adoff and Virginia Hamilton married. At that time, an African American woman and a White man marrying was considered illegal in many states with strict segregation laws. This poem celebrates their family and the extended family of tan uncles and golden-haired aunts, brown and white grandmas. It is full of hugs and kisses, laughter and song. Interracial marriage is now legally protected and generally culturally acceptable as well. It is a phenomenon that is growing, and lines of race, religion, and ethnicity are becoming less divisive in young people's choices of life partners.

Genre: Poetry

Angelou, Maya. *Life Doesn't Frighten Me.* Illustrated by Jean-Michel Basquiat. New York: Stewart, Tabori, and Chang, 1993.

> I go boo
> Make them shoo
> I make fun
> Way they run
> I won't cry
> So they fly
> I just smile
> They go wild
> Life doesn't frighten me at all.[4]

Together, Angelou and Basquiat have created a story of bravery set against the realities that many children live with: loud noises, fighting adults, tormentors at school. This would be a great book to begin conversations about fears and some of the strategies children might use to deal with them.

This is definitely an example of a really great poet and a really great artist combining their talents to create an exceptional offering for children.

Genre: Poetry

Barber, Barbara E. *Allie's Basketball Dream.* Illustrated by Darryl Ligasan. New York: Lee and Low, 1996.

> "Well," Buddy snorted, some guys think girls shouldn't be playin' basketball."
> "That's dumb!" Allie bounced her ball. "My cousin Gwen plays on one of the best high school teams in her state. She's won more than ten trophies!"
> Buddy looked surprised.

"Some girls think boys shouldn't be jumping rope," Allie continued. "They think boys are no good at it. That's dumb, too."[5]

Allie remembers well the first time her father took her to a basketball game at Madison Square Garden. She loved every aspect of the sport and knew right away she wanted to be a professional basketball player. Now her father has given her a basketball, and she learns that she must both practice and have faith in her skills if she is to reach her dream.

Genre: Realistic Contemporary Fiction

Burrowes, Adjoa J. *Grandma's Purple Flowers.* New York: Lee and Low, 2000.

> Grandma lets me rake the leaves
> in the backyard garden
> we planted together.
> "Why do leaves have to fall and die?" I ask.
> "Everything has its time," Grandma tells me.[6]

Hyacinth loves walking to her Grandma's house to spend time with her. She does this in every season and shares the events of the seasons with her grandmother, from gathering her grandmother's purple flowers, to raking leaves, to staying inside on a cold winter day. When Grandma dies, Hyacinth cries and cries, missing her terribly throughout the winter. As soon as spring comes, she finds a way to reconnect with her grandmother. The cut-paper collage illustrations nicely match the brief, gentle text.

Genre: Realistic Contemporary Fiction

Clifton, Lucille. *Everett Anderson's Goodbye.* Illustrated by Ann Grifalconi. New York: Henry Holt, 1983.

> "I don't love Baby Evelyn
> and I don't love Mr. Perry, too,
> and I don't love Christmas or
> Santa Claus
> and I don't love candy
> and I don't love you!"[7]

Clifton's book introduces children to the five stages of grief and shares them through Everett's experience when his father dies. Each stage has Everett expressing his own response to the loss while his loving mother allows him the latitude to express himself until he comes to terms with his father's death.

This is a wonderful book for children to understand what adults sometimes do not: the death of someone you love. Everett is Black, but this concept easily crosses racial lines. It also gives both Black children and White children a concept book with the protagonist being a child of color, something that rarely happens.

Genre: Realistic Contemporary Fiction

Collier, Bryan. *Uptown*. New York: Henry Holt, 2000.

> Uptown is jazz. My grandfather says, "Jazz and Harlem are a perfect match—just like chicken and waffles."[8]

In this nicely illustrated (by the author) picture book, a young boy proudly describes his Harlem. He speaks of the train weaving through uptown, weekend shopping, brownstones, a barbershop, local food, historic family photographs, street ball games, and sisters dressed for church. At the end, the orange sunset has arrived, and the boy is off to watch the Harlem Boys' Choir. This book would pair well with Myers's more complex, but similarly themed, *Harlem*.

Genre: Realistic Contemporary Fiction/Narrative Poetry
Award: Coretta Scott King Illustrator Award

Cooper, Melrose. *Gettin' Through Thursday*. Illustrated by Nneka Bennett. New York: Lee and Low, 1998.

> "Mama, there's nothin' to drink in here." That's my older sister Shawna callin' from behind the 'frigerator door.
> "Faucet ain't broken," Mama calls back.[9]

Every week is the same routine for Andre and his family. Finances run thin on Thursdays, but Mama has a solution for every shortage: water to drink, baking soda to replace toothpaste, leftover sunflower seeds to feed the parakeet. Mama has always promised that if one of the children makes the honor roll, they will drop everything and throw a big celebration. When Andre realizes he is about to make the honor roll, he is sad to also note that the report card will be received on a Thursday. Although Mama cannot immediately make real the celebration she has promised, they throw a "dress rehearsal," with imaginary cake, candles, ice cream, and gifts, that turns out to be nearly as special as the real party that follows.

Genre: Realistic Contemporary Fiction

Crews, Donald. *Bigmama's*. New York: HarperCollins, Greenwillow, 1991.

> Everybody sitting around the table that filled the room—Bigmama, Bigpapa, Uncle Slank, our cousins from down the road, and all of us. We talked about what we did last year. We talked about what we were going to do this year. We talked so much we hardly had time to eat.[10]

This is a story of a family's annual trip back to the grandparents' home in the country. Every year the children and their mother (Dad comes later because he has to work) ride the train to Cottondale. Once there, the children reconnect with everything they remember, and nothing has changed. The magic of the timelessness of visiting Bigmama and Bigpapa and the millions of stars that light up the nighttime sky in the country are remembered forever.

This story offers readers the possibility, still, to find these spaces that exist as a step back in time, into a world that appears to never change.

Genre: Realistic Contemporary Fiction

English, Karen. *Hot Day on Abbott Avenue*. Illustrated by Javaka Steptoe. New York: Clarion, 2004.

> Then, from somewhere down the street, a distant chant.
>
> > Miss Mary
> > Mack, Mack, Mack
> > All dressed in
> > Black, black, black
>
> Kishi and Renee listen.[11]

On one of those "too hot" summer-in-the-city days, two friends, Kishi and Renee, have had an "out" and have decided that they will never be friends again. The things they would naturally have done together, like helping their neighbor Miss Johnson with a crossword puzzle, are just not going to happen, never again. But then, in the distance, the girls hear the jump-rope rhyme and both go to where the chant is coming from. Immediately they find themselves holding the rope for Darlene and Aja to jump. When the ice cream truck comes around, all the girls run to buy their blue ice pop, and Kishi shares hers with her friend and puts the friendship back on track.

Genre: Contemporary Realistic Fiction
Award: Jane Addams Children's Book Honor

Grimes, Nikki. *Meet Danitra Brown*. Illustrated by Floyd Cooper. New York: Lothrop, Lee & Shepard, Mulberry, 1994.

From "Summertime Sharing":

Danitra breaks the Popsicle in two and gives me half.
The purple ice trickles down her chin. I start to laugh.
Her teeth flash in one humongous grin,
Telling me she's glad that I'm her friend without even saying a word.[12]

Danitra Brown and her best friend Zuri Jackson live in the city. In this book of poetry, Zuri introduces the reader to Danitra and to the strength of their friendship. The beautiful illustrations in this text truly occupy the whole page and provide a strong background for the description of the two girls being described in the poems.

Genre: Poetry

Grimes, Nikki. *My Man Blue*. Illustrated by Jerome Lagarrigue. New York: Dial Books for Young Readers, 1999.

Mom sees me eyeing Blue and lets me know
He's her old friend. It's safe to say hello.
She says they both grew up here way back when.
I mumble, "Well, it's news to me!" But then
I throw my shoulders back and take my stance.
He seems alright. I might give him a chance.[13]

Grimes uses the genre of poetry to tell this story of a young boy and an old friend of his mother's who befriends him. In this story, Blue, who missed his own son's early years, spends time with Damon, who does not have a father. The relationship becomes one of gentle support and playfulness that gives both Damon and Blue the rewards of genuine friendship between the two generations. (Another good book that includes intergenerational friendship is Polacco's *Mrs. Katz and Tush*, described below.)

In contemporary society, many children are living with one parent. This story is a depiction of how other people in a child's life, in this case a family friend, can play a significant role. Lagarrigue's illustrations are very compatible with the text in portraying this newly formed father-and-son relationship.

Genre: Realistic Contemporary Fiction

Grimes, Nikki. *Something on My Mind*. Illustrated by Tom Feelings. New York: Dial Books for Young Readers, 1978.

> I don't understand
> how "good" English
> and five times two is ten
> can help buy us more food and extra blankets.
> But Mama says it can
> and she never lied to me.[14]

Published in 1978, this book, with its brief, clear poems and simple drawings, remains a classic. The experiences and thoughts in these brief vignettes are of children living in the city, sharing the concerns of all children. One can imagine each poem being just as true today as when it was first written.

Genre: Poetry

Gunning, Monica. *A Shelter in Our Car*. Illustrated by Elaine Pedlar. San Francisco: Children's Book Press, 2004.

> "Do you remember the sun in Jamaica?" Mama asks. "How brightly it shone after a shower of rain?"
> I do remember. Especially on cold, cloudy days like today. Why did Papa have to die? With Mama's now-and-then day jobs and her working so hard going to community college, it's like having dark, wet days all the time.
> "When I get a steady job there'll be sunshine again," Mama says, as if she read my mind.
> I'm silent. I hear that from Mama all the time, but things are so hard now.[15]

Young Zettie has moved from Jamaica to the city, where her mother is trying to get ahead by going to school and working temporary and day-labor jobs. Despite her mother's best efforts, they are currently sleeping in their car and eating and washing up in a local park. Zettie tries to avoid the snickers of the other children at school, and her mother must avoid the police as she tries to find a place where she can park overnight.

The struggles of homeless children, more common than we want to imagine, are very evident in this book. By the end, though, it appears that this young family is going to be okay, not only because the mother has found employment, but also because they recognize that love is such an important part of shelter.

Genre: Realistic Contemporary Fiction

Howard, Elizabeth Fitzgerald. *Aunt Flossie's Hats (and Crab Cakes Later).* Illustrated by James E. Ransome. New York: Clarion, 1991.

> Aunt Flossie thought for a moment.
> Aunt Flossie almost always thinks a minute before she starts a hat story.
> Then she sniffed the wooly hat.
> "Just a little smoky smell now," she said.[16]

On Sunday afternoons, Sarah and Susan go visit their great-great-aunt Flossie. She always offers them cookies and milk, then lets them go through her boxes and boxes of hats. The children always enjoy hearing the significance of each hat, from the one that survived the great fire in Baltimore, to the one especially made for a parade, to the one that flew into the water on a family walk. This is a nice intergenerational text that touches briefly on the great-great-aunt's history.

Genre: Realistic Contemporary Fiction

Johnson, Angela. *Do like Kyla.* Illustrated by James E. Ransome. New York: Orchard, 1990.

> We sit in front of the big mirror in our room, and Kyla braids her hair with quick fingers.
> I try to do like Kyla in front of the mirror.
> Kyla says, "Beautiful!"
> I do like Kyla and say, "Beautiful!"[17]

This picture book for the youngest of readers shows Kyla and her little sister going through their day, with the little sister imitating all that Kyla does. By the end of the day, Kyla even imitates her little sister. The simple text and colorful illustrations make this fun for a read-aloud.

Genre: Realistic Contemporary Fiction

Johnson, Angela. *The Wedding.* Illustrated by David Soman. New York: Orchard, 1999.

> Me thinking about the wedding
> and Sister leaving me
> and us
> and here
> after the wedding.[18]

Planning and attending her big sister's wedding, Daisy has a range of feelings as she observes the celebration unfolding. Keeping up with the preparations is tiring for a child, but the day of the wedding is beautiful, and Daisy is the flower girl. A festive reception brings everyone to the dance floor. After the wedding has passed, the family gathers and reminisces with pictures of the day.

Again, the face of children's literature is changing to keep current with changes in society. In this case, we have a child and family of color, but the guests at the wedding, in the wedding party, and at the reception party cross racial lines and participate in the ceremony, play, and celebrate together.

Genre: Realistic Contemporary Fiction/Narrative Poetry

Katz, Karen. *The Colors of Us*. New York: Henry Holt, 1999.

> My baby-sitter Candy is like a beautiful jewel,
> bronze and amber. She looks like a princess.[19]

When Lena's mother, who is an artist, tells her that she could mix a color that matches her skin color by mixing red, yellow, black, and white, Lena is surprised and says, "But Mom, brown is brown." This prompts her mom to suggest taking a walk and looking at the many beautiful colors, the variations of color that are her friends' and family's skin colors, and Lena gains a new appreciation for the color brown. This is a wonderful celebration of the variety of skin colors of brown.

Genre: Realistic Contemporary Fiction

Medina, Tony. *Deshawn Days*. Illustrated by R. Gregory Christie. New York: Lee and Low, 2003.

From "In My House":

> My grandma my grandma
> she lives in my house
> Praying or cooking

with me under the table
listening to the grown-ups
telling stories and the kitchen
is warm and the windows wet with the smell of cornbread
and baked chicken[20]

In this book, written as a collection of poetry, ten-year-old Deshawn tells the reader about his house, his family, his friends, and his
school. He describes the richness and the concerns of his urban environment with all their complexity: the busy life of his mother, who
works and attends college; his grandmother, who is so important to him;
his teacher, who introduces her students to worlds beyond themselves. In
one particularly nice poem, he writes about thinking that the television
news is boring until his teacher insists that the students watch in order to
know what is going on around them; he soon comes to realize the differences between childhood fights and adult wars. This is an amazing
work.

Genre: Poetry

Michelson, Richard. *Across the Alley*. Illustrated by E. B. Lewis. New
York: Putnam's, 2006.

"Grandpa was a great violinist in the old country," I tell Willie late
that night.
"But there was a war and the Nazis broke all of his fingers and
worked him like a slave. Grandpa says he was lucky to escape with
his life."
Willie's real quiet now and I wonder if I said something wrong.
Maybe he doesn't know about the Nazis.
"My great-granddaddy was a slave, too," Willie finally says.
"I never knew any white folk that were."
Then we're both real quiet until Willie decides that it's time we
went to bed.[21]

When Willie and his neighbor meet at their bedroom windows
that face each other across an alley, they strike up a friendship. The
narrator is a Jewish boy whose grandfather is teaching him to play the
violin. Willie is African American. His father was a starter in the Negro Baseball Leagues, and he has learned from his father how to throw
a slider. Each teaches the other what they are learning, and in the end,
they share their different talents with their families.

Beautifully illustrated, this story is about children and how they are able to transcend stereotyped roles to do what they really want to do, with a little help from a friend.
Genre: Realistic Contemporary Fiction

Nolen, Jerdine. *In My Momma's Kitchen*. Illustrated by Colin Bootman. New York: HarperCollins, 1999.

> In winter when I come home from school, the warm kitchen fogs the windows. I hug Momma from behind, and she says, "Hello, Sweet Potato Pie. How was school today?" then she drops a taste of peach cobbler into my mouth, and peach juice dribbles down my chin.[22]

The special places in the kitchen of this young girl's home come alive with each story. From her sister getting a scholarship to college to her aunts coming over each week to make a big meal together, telling stories all the while, each story draws you in. In one story, great-aunt Caroline comes to celebrate her ninety-fifth birthday, and much to the girl's surprise, they become friends. Intergenerational and just plain human, this is a wonderful book to share.
Genre: Realistic Contemporary Fiction

Polacco, Patricia. *Chicken Sunday*. New York: Putnam and Grosset, 1992.

> Stewart and Winston were my neighbors. They were my brothers by some solemn ceremony we had performed in their backyard one summer. They weren't the same religion as I was. They were Baptists. Their Gramma, Eula Mae Walker, was my gramma now. My babushka had died two summers before.[23]

This is a story about children who want very much to find a way to purchase something for their grandmother, whom they love dearly. They are mistaken for vandals when they happen to be seen just after some other children cause a disturbance at an old man's hat shop. With the help of their grandmother, they are able to make things right with the man and are even able to make the purchase they had so wanted to make.
As with *Mrs. Katz and Tush*, Polacco tells, in *Chicken Sunday*, a story that is multicultural. The people in the story are of different religions, different ages, and different races. Polacco often says that her stories represent the people she grew up with in her neighborhood. In this case, her friends Stewart and Winston are still her friends.
Genre: Realistic Contemporary Fiction

Polacco, Patricia. *Mrs. Katz and Tush*. New York: Bantam Doubleday Dell
Books for Young Readers, 1992.

> Little Tush grew healthy and strong.
> Mrs. Katz cooked for her,
> brushed her, knitted toys for her,
> and even read to her.
> "Such a person," she'd say as she watched Tush play.
> Mrs. Katz was in love.[24]

When Mrs. Katz's husband dies, a young woman and her son, Larnel, who live in her apartment building, comfort her. Larnel has the idea
to bring her a kitten he has found in the basement of their building, and
as you can tell by the quote above, she falls in love with it. But something else happens as Larnel spends more and more time with Mrs. Katz:
they become friends.

This is a contemporary story for many reasons. Its characters are interracial, intergenerational, and of different religions. An experience like
Mrs. Katz and Larnel's would have been nearly impossible in the centuries, or even decades, before contemporary times.

Genre: Realistic Contemporary Fiction
Award: Jane Addams Children's Book Honor

Raschka, Chris. *Yo! Yes?* New York: Orchard, 1993.

This book has two characters and thirty-two words plus a Hmmm?
and a YOW. Yet, with little text and two characters communicating on
the pages, the message is still clear. There are two boys, one White and
one Black. The Black child is ready to be friends and the White one finally realizes that they can, indeed, be friends.

Genre: Realistic Contemporary Fiction
Award: Caldecott Honor

Woodson, Jacqueline. *The Other Side*. Illustrated by E. B. Lewis. New
York: Putnam's, 2001.

> That summer the fence that stretched through our town seemed
> bigger.
> We lived in a yellow house on one side of it.
> White people lived on the other.
> And Mama said, "Don't climb over that fence when you play."
> She said it wasn't safe.[25]

Two little girls, one on the side of the fence where White people live and the other on the side where Black people live, are each told of the dangers of the other side. Woodson invites children into a story that shows children working through the cautions that so often separate people by race. Clover is Black, and she and her friends play near the fence. Annie is White and is pretty sadly alone. As the story unfolds, Clover and her friends befriend Annie and they play together at the fence and wonder if someday there will be no fence. Discussions about race and segregation with even very young children can be very beneficial. Even though the pictures suggest that this story is taking place in the 1950s, the story could as easily be true today.

Genre: Realistic Contemporary Fiction

Woodson, Jacqueline. *Our Gracie Aunt*. Illustrated by Jon J. Muth, New York: Hyperion Books for Children, 2002.

> "You know how you and Johnson argue sometimes? Well, me and your mama did, too," our Gracie aunt said. "We stopped speaking to each other a long time ago. I don't even remember what we were arguing about. Then me and your mama lost touch."[26]

It is not unusual in our contemporary society to find people struggling with addictions to drugs and alcohol. In this story, two young children are taken to their mother's sister's house when a caseworker determines that their mother is not supervising them. After the caseworker removes them from their apartment, the children guard their emotions even when they are with their aunt. Gradually they begin to open up to her and to enjoy her care, even thought at times their tears "wash out their insides." Eventually they visit their mother, who is in treatment, and she lovingly tells them that their aunt will take care of them and that they will be reunited. Woodson provides a gentle telling of a family in crisis and how they deal with it.

Genre: Realistic Contemporary Fiction

Woodson, Jacqueline. *Visiting Day*. Illustrated by James E. Ransome. New York: Scholastic, 2002.

> Only on Visiting Day
> is there chicken frying
> in the kitchen at 6 A. M.

> and Grandma
> humming soft and low,
> smiling her secret
> just–for–Daddy–and–me smile,
> and me lying in bed
> smiling my just–for–Grandma–and–Daddy smile.[27]

Woodson shares with the reader that even though this story is fiction, it is much like her memories of her favorite uncle being in prison and of visiting him with her grandmother. She remembers these visits as times of laughter and talk and of being so happy to be together that she almost forgot where they were. This book is dedicated to the memory of her Uncle Robert and her grandmother.

For many children, having a parent or relative in prison is part of their life and visiting is part of what makes that separation bearable. For African American children, the odds of having someone close to them in prison is greater because of the disproportionate number of Black men and women who find themselves with inferior educational opportunities and abject poverty. Many are also sentenced to jail for infractions that, if they were White, may have resulted in lesser charges and punishments.

Genre: Realistic Contemporary Fiction

Woodson, Jacqueline. *We Had a Picnic This Sunday Past*. Illustrated by Diane Greenseid. New York: Hyperion Books for Children, 1997.

> Grandma wore her
> blue dress
> with all those flowers on it.
> Brought biscuits and chicken
> and me.[28]

This story about a picnic in a park is narrated by Teeka, who has arrived with her grandmother. The occasion is marked by a lot of fun, and Teeka's comments on everything that is happening make for a light-hearted look at cousins, uncles, and friends of the family. From the caution that Cousin Martha will bring that same dry pie, to Cousin Trevor bringing flowers he picked on his way into the park, the reader meets and gets to know everyone. As everyone joins the group, the playfulness continues until finally the table is set and the picnic begins. Greenseid's

illustrations capture the individual personalities in brightly colored paintings. Readers will find that this was one fun day.
Genre: Realistic Contemporary Fiction

LATER ELEMENTARY

Igus, Toyomi. *Going Back Home: An Artist Returns to the South*. Illustrated
by Michele Wood. San Francisco: Children's Book Press, 1996.

> After segregation ended, my grandmother was able to eat in one of
> these restaurants for the first time. It must have taken a great deal of
> courage. I imagine that she looked like this—dignified, with her head
> held high, but clutching her purse close beside her. Even though she
> looked proud and courageous, deep down inside she was a little bit
> scared![29]

In this artistic work, Michele Wood tells the story of her family's
history through paintings. From herself as a child on her aunt's lap hearing the family stories, through pictures of her ancestors doing slave work
and more recent family members living through Jim Crow years and the
migration north, to reconsidering herself today, Wood beautifully illustrates many elements of African American life and history. This work
serves well as one person's interpretation of her own family's history and
as an artistic representation of that history.
Genre: Memoir

Igus, Toyomi. *I See the Rhythm*. Illustrated by Michele Wood. San Francisco: Children's Book Press, 1998.

> There I see the rhythm of soul,
> in familiar voices that now sing a new message:
> Say it loud—
> I'm black
> and I'm proud.[30]

Although I have placed this in the contemporary chapter, it is really
a retrospective. This artistic history of African American music begins
with the earliest drum rhythms of the 1500s and moves through slave
songs, the blues, ragtime, jazz, swing, bebop, gospel, soul, rock 'n' roll,
funk, and hip hop. The illustrations and artistically placed text truly carry

out the music they describe. In the side margin of each topic, there is also a chronology of that genre of music. This would definitely make for a fun read-aloud for younger children if one only read a portion at a time, but for older children, it will be both an enjoyable read and an informational text. A fun book!

Genre: Realistic Contemporary Fiction

Johnson, Angela. *Toning the Sweep*. New York: Scholastic, 1993.

> "I never said good-bye to my father, Emmie. This new place happened too fast. Ola thought she was saving me from ugliness. Death really. She did her best, and I guess I've never forgiven her for it."[31]

Emmie and her mother are driving out west to pack up Emmie's grandmother, Ola, who has cancer, and bring her back to Cleveland. The experience allows the three generations to consider their individual and shared histories, which include the lynching of Ola's husband in 1964 Alabama, which drove Ola to move away immediately to the desert with her daughter. The memories they share of one another, and the memories Emmie is able to capture from those Ola will be leaving, bring the reader closer to these characters.

Genre: Realistic Contemporary Fiction
Award: Coretta Scott King Author Award

McGrath, Barbara Barbieri. *The Storm: Students of Biloxi, Mississippi, Remember Hurricane Katrina*. Watertown, MA: Charlesbridge, 2006.

This compilation of children's work, a nonfiction/informational book about Hurricane Katrina, is written through many different lenses. McGrath has collected the writing and drawings of children who lived through the storm and the extraordinary devastation that followed. Children tell stories of busily preparing for the storm and quickly finding themselves and their families threatened with homelessness and even possible death. Sadness at the loss of normalcy and hope that things will get better are illustrated with pictures that truly capture the chaos and damage, making this an important contribution to understanding this difficult event and its aftermath.

Genre: Nonfiction/Informational

Smith, Hope Anita. *The Way a Door Closes*. Illustrated by Shane W. Evans. New York: Henry Holt, 2003.

> "Grandmomma,
> Daddy's not coming back, is he?"
> She stops her song but keeps on
> Rocking.
> I'm afraid of her answer, so
> I keep talking.
> "We're supposed to be a family.
> He should've stayed."[32]

This series of poems narrates C.J.'s experiences with his father, from looking at his father in the mirror to get a glimpse of what he will look like as he gets older, to going on a "boys only" outing with his father and brother, to his father's announcement that he has lost his job, to hearing the door close behind his father in a way that tells him his father will not be returning, to the various stages of his grieving process. The poems that depict the time the father is gone are especially poignant. In the end, it seems that the family will have a happy ending.

Genre: Poetry

Woodson, Jacqueline. *Last Summer with Maizon*. New York: Bantam Doubleday Dell, 1990.

> "Maizon took a test in May. If she passes, she's going to go to this big private school in Connecticut. Every night I pray she doesn't get accepted."[33]

Eleven-year-old Maizon and Margaret are best friends. When Maizon gets a scholarship to a private school, she moves away, despite her nervousness that she might be the only Black girl at her new school. She leaves Margaret grieving not only her best friend, but also her father who has just died. Still, Margaret finds strengths she didn't know she had. In less than three months, though, Maizon is back, having faced unexpected prejudice and resentment.

Genre: Realistic Contemporary Fiction

Woodson, Jacqueline. *Locomotion*. New York: Putnam's, 2003.
"Line Break Poem":

> Ms. Marcus
> says
> line breaks help
> us figure out
> what matters
> to the poet
> *Don't jumble your ideas*
> Ms. Marcus says
> *Every line*
> *should count.*[34]

Woodson always amazes me with how complete a character she creates with so few words, and this is no exception. Lonnie loses both his parents in a fire and is separated from his sister through the foster care system. His teacher encourages him to write, and through the course of sixty poems, he goes through a range of emotions in telling his story. As they read this young boy's experience in the pages of a book, children in the foster care system, and there are many, may find something that helps them deal with their own situation.

Genre: Realistic Contemporary Fiction/Poetry
Award: Coretta Scott King Author Honor

MIDDLE GRADES

Flake, Sharon G. *The Skin I'm In*. New York: Hyperion Paperback for Young Readers, 1998.

> Seems like people been teasing me all my life. If it ain't about my color, it's my clothes. Momma makes them by hand. They look it, too—lopsided pockets, stitching forever unraveling. I never know when a collar's gonna fall off, or a pushpin gonna stick me and make me holler out in class. I stopped worrying about that this year now that Charlese lends me clothes to wear. I stash them in the locker and change into them before first period. I'm like Superman when I get Charlese's clothes on. I got a new attitude, and my teachers sure don't like it none.[35]

Maleeka Madison is twelve years old and struggling with the fact that many things make her vulnerable to teasing. The situation compounds itself, as teasing tends to do, since she feels terrible about herself and that just makes the situation worse. But she begins to find her way away from a destructive friend and closer to someone who has expressed caring and support.

This is a great story for middle school, where many young people feel the vulnerability of some aspect of themselves and are afraid of teasing and bullying. It brings up issues of color within the race and of classism that, if not talked about, can silently torment children.

Genre: Realistic Contemporary Fiction
Award: Coretta Scott King New Talent (Author) Award

Grimes, Nikki. *The Road to Paris*. New York: Putnam's, 2006.

> *Home* was such a funny word. For most kids, home was where your mom and dad lived, where you felt safe, where the bogeyman was merely make-believe. Home was where you knew every square inch of the place by heart, where you could wake up in the middle of the night and know exactly where you were without even opening your eyes. Paris didn't have a place like that. She didn't even have an address she'd lived at long enough to memorize, no single place that felt familiar as all that. Except maybe the city itself.[36]

For Paris, home was more a person, and that person was Malcolm. Neither family nor house can define home for Paris, whose father left the family when she was four. The father of her older brother, Malcolm, didn't even stay that long. Because of issues related to their mother's alcoholism and depression, the siblings end up in foster care. When they run away to their grandmother, she returns them to the system. Although they have come to rely on one another, they are now split up and Paris finds herself living with the Lincoln family. She misses her brother terribly and faces racism as a biracial child in a mostly white neighborhood, but she does come to a new understanding of herself and of family during the time she lives with the Lincolns.

Once again, Grimes has created a very honest, contemporary portrayal of life. She always conveys well the essence of her characters, and here we experience both the fragile and the strong elements of ten-year-old Paris.

Genre: Contemporary Realistic Fiction
Award: Coretta Scott King Award Honor

Johnson, Angela. *The First Part Last*. New York: Simon and Schuster Books for Young Readers, 2003.

> I look at the adoption papers stacked in front of me, then fold them in half before I tear them.
> "No, I don't know anything about raising a kid. I'm sixteen and none of these people on the wall look like the kind of family me and Feather's gonna be. But I'm doing it."[37]

On his sixteenth birthday, Bobby's girlfriend, Nia, tells him that she is pregnant. Together, they consider their options and it seems that they have decided on adoption, although they both clearly have concerns about this option. When eclampsia puts Nia into a persistent vegetative state and their baby girl is born, Bobby makes the tough decision to raise their daughter, Feather. Once again, Johnson succeeds at drawing readers in, compelling them to care deeply about the characters.

Genre: Realistic Contemporary Fiction

Award: Coretta Scott King Author Award

Johnson, Angela. *The Other Side: Shorter Poems*. New York: Orchard, 1998.

> I loved and hated the place.
> Not enough room in the world
> To tell my feelings about Shorter.
> And now they're pullin' it all down.[38]

"Shorter" in the title of this book refers to both the length of the poems and the name of the town that is their focus: Shorter, Alabama. In this book, Johnson uses her poetry to describe her memories of the town where she grew up and her feelings about the town being demolished. Through the brilliant imagery of the poems themselves and Johnson's black-and-white family photographs woven though the book, it is easy to picture oneself growing up alongside her in Shorter.

Genre: Poetry

Award: Coretta Scott King Author Honor

Woodson, Jacqueline. *Miracle's Boys*. New York: Puffin, 2000.

> "I wish the last time had been something else. I wish it had been me sitting on the couch next to her making her laugh. I used to make

her laugh all the time. I wish that was the way she got to remember *me*. Not with no handcuffs on."[39]

In this book, Woodson describes the lives of three boys after their parents have both died. Ty'ree must pass up his admission to MIT to stay and care for young Lafayette and for Charlie, who has recently been released from a juvenile detention center. In their urban struggles against poverty, gangs, and police violence, they must also struggle to find their identities as individuals and as brothers. A tough story, but one that really draws the reader in.

Genre: Realistic Contemporary Fiction

Awards: Coretta Scott King Author Award; National Book Award Nominee

CONCLUSION

The books described in this chapter provide a wide range of experiences that children of today can relate to their own lives. There tend to be fewer of the nonfiction and informational books seen in past chapters, and more realistic fiction and contemporary poetry. As with all exceptional literature, they possess quality in the elements of style, character development, and authenticity of setting and plot. They are stories of life in the city, relationships within families and communities, people of all races living together, and people facing difficult times, but most of all, they are good stories about life.

NOTES

1. Copenhaver-Johnson, "Talking to Children," 20.
2. Murphy, *Black Authors and Illustrators*, see chapter 13.
3. Adoff, *Black Is Brown Is Tan*.
4. Angelou, *Life Doesn't Frighten Me*.
5. Barber, *Allie's Baseball Dream*.
6. Burrowes, *Grandma's Purple Flowers*.
7. Collier, *Uptown*.
8. Clifton, *Everett Anderson's Goodbye*.
9. Cooper, *Gettin' Through Thursday*.

10. Crews, *Bigmama's*.
11. English, *Hot Day*, 15.
12. Grimes, *Meet Danitra Brown*.
13. Grimes, *My Man Blue*.
14. Grimes, *Something on My Mind*.
15. Gunning, *Shelter in Our Car*.
16. Howard, *Aunt Flossie's Hats*.
17. Johnson, *Do like Kyla*.
18. Johnson, *The Wedding*.
19. Katz, *The Colors of Us*.
20. Medina, *Deshawn Days*.
21. Michelson, *Across the Alley*.
22. Nolen, *In My Momma's Kitchen*.
23. Polacco, *Chicken Sunday*.
24. Polacco, *Mrs. Katz and Tush*.
25. Woodson, *The Other Side*.
26. Woodson, *Our Gracie Aunt*.
27. Woodson, *Visiting Day*.
28. Woodson, *We Had a Picnic*.
29. Igus, *Going Back Home*.
30. Igus, *I See the Rhythm*.
31. Johnson, *Toning the Sweep*, 98.
32. Smith, *The Way a Door Closes*.
33. Woodson, *Last Summer with Maizon*, 1.
34. Woodson, *Locomotion*, 4.
35. Flake, *The Skin I'm In*, 4.
36. Grimes, *Road to Paris*, 30.
37. Johnson, *The First Part Last*, 124.
38. Johnson, *The Other Side*, 2.
39. Woodson, *Miracle's Boys*, 126.

BIBLIOGRAPHY OF BOOKS FOR CHILDREN

Ackerman, Karen. *By the Dawn's Early Light*. Illustrated by Catherine Stock. New York: Aladdin, 1994.

Adoff, Arnold. *Black Is Brown Is Tan*. Illustrated by Emily Arnold McCully. New York: HarperCollins, 1973.

Angelou, Maya. *Life Doesn't Frighten Me*. Illustrated by Jean-Michel Basquiat. New York: Stewart, Tabori, and Chang, 1993.

Barber, Barbara E. *Allie's Basketball Dream*. Illustrated by Darryl Ligasan. New York: Lee and Low, 1996.

Burrowes, Adjoa J. *Grandma's Purple Flowers*. New York: Lee and Low, 2000.

Clifton, Lucille. *Everett Anderson's Goodbye*. Illustrated by Ann Grifalconi. New York: Henry Holt, 1983.

Collier, Bryan. *Uptown*. New York: Henry Holt, 2000.

Cooper, Melrose. *Gettin' Through Thursday*. Illustrated by Nneka Bennett. New York: Lee and Low, 1998.

Crews, Donald. *Bigmama's*. New York: HarperCollins, Greenwillow, 1991.

English, Karen. *Hot Day on Abbott Avenue*. Illustrated by Javaka Steptoe. New York: Clarion, 2004.

Flake, Sharon G. *The Skin I'm In*. New York: Hyperion Paperbacks for Young Readers, 1998.

Grimes, Nikki. *Meet Danitra Brown*. Illustrated by Floyd Cooper. New York: Lothrop, Lee & Shepard, Mulberry, 1994.

———. *My Man Blue*. Illustrated by Jerome Lagarrigue. New York: Dial Books for Young Readers, 1999.

———. *The Road to Paris*. New York: Putnam's, 2006.

———. *Something on My Mind*. Illustrated by Tom Feelings. New York: Dial Books for Young Readers, 1978.

Gunning, Monica. *A Shelter in Our Car*. Illustrated by Elaine Pedlar. San Francisco: Children's Book Press, 2004.

Howard, Elizabeth Fitzgerald. *Aunt Flossie's Hats (and Crab Cakes Later)*. Illustrated by James E. Ransome. New York: Clarion, 1991.

Igus, Toyomi. *Going Back Home: An Artist Returns to the South*. Illustrated by Michele Wood. San Francisco: Children's Book Press, 1996.

———. *I See the Rhythm*. Illustrated by Michele Wood. San Francisco: Children's Book Press, 1998.

Johnson, Angela. *Do like Kyla*. Illustrated by James E. Ransome. New York: Orchard, 1990.

———. *The First Part Last*. New York: Simon and Schuster Books for Young Readers, 2003.

———. *The Other Side: Shorter Poems*. New York: Orchard, 1998.

———. *Toning the Sweep*. New York: Scholastic, 1993.

———. *The Wedding*. Illustrated by David Soman. New York: Orchard, 1999.

Katz, Karen. *The Colors of Us*. New York: Henry Holt, 1999.

McGrath, Barbara Barbieri. *The Storm: Students of Biloxi, Mississippi, Remember Hurricane Katrina*. Watertown, MA: Charlesbridge, 2006.

Medina, Tony. *Deshawn Days*. Illustrated by R. Gregory Christie. New York: Lee and Low, 2003.

Michelson, Richard. *Across the Alley*. Illustrated by E. B. Lewis. New York: Putnam's, 2006.

Nolen, Jerdine. *In My Momma's Kitchen.* Illustrated by Colin Bootman. New York: HarperCollins, 1999.

Polacco, Patricia. *Chicken Sunday,* New York: Putnam and Grosset, 1992.

———. *Mrs. Katz and Tush.* New York: Bantam Doubleday Dell Books for Young Readers, 1992.

Raschka, Chris. *Yo! Yes?* New York: Orchard, 1993.

Smith, Hope Anita. *The Way a Door Closes.* Illustrated by Shane W. Evans. New York: Henry Holt, 2003.

Woodson, Jacqueline. *Last Summer with Maizon.* New York: Bantam Doubleday Dell, 1990.

———. *Locomotion.* New York: Putnam's, 2003.

———. *Miracle's Boys.* New York: Puffin, 2000.

———. *The Other Side.* Illustrated by E. B. Lewis. New York: Putnam's, 2001.

———. *Our Gracie Aunt.* Illustrated by Jon J. Muth. New York: Hyperion Books for Children, 2002.

———. *Visiting Day.* Illustrated by James E. Ransome. New York: Scholastic, 2002.

———. *We Had a Picnic This Sunday Past.* Illustrated by Diane Greenseid. New York: Hyperion Books for Children, 1997.

BIBLIOGRAPHY OF REFERENCE WORKS

Copenhaver-Johnson, Jeane. "Talking to Children about Race: The Importance of Inviting Difficult Conversations." *Childhood Education* 83:1 (2006): 12–22.

Murphy, Barbara Thrash. *Black Authors and Illustrators of Books for Children and Young Adults: A Biographical Dictionary,* 3rd ed. New York: Garland, 1999.

· *12* ·

Selection and Inclusion of Children's Literature about American History: A Critique

> Literature can make learning history more meaningful. It also creates a positive reading environment and can be more interesting than textbooks. Unlike textbooks, books on literature are not encyclopedic. Thus, the use of literature in teaching history enables students to learn important facts as well as profound and abstract concepts.[1]

$\mathcal{W}$hen writers set out to write a book about a particular subject in history, they take with them on that journey what they "know" about the subject and what they "feel" about the subject. These two ingredients have a powerful impact on what a writer presents to the reader, and this book is no exception.

I came to address the topic of children's literature and its importance to the study of American history from years of teaching children's literature to preservice and practicing teachers in college courses, professional development workshops, and other presentations on the subject, as well as in the process of writing journal articles and co-authoring a textbook. I also came to see the importance of children's literature in my classrooms when I was a public schoolteacher in Maine, particularly when I was with children who had been in residential facilities because of behavior issues but who would crowd together quietly to hear a good story, and when I was with readers who were reluctant and unmotivated because they did not see themselves in textbooks and had not heard stories read aloud. There is just something about a good story.

As the mother of seven children, all of whom love a good story, I have watched them relish the chance to roam through shelves and shelves of books as soon as they could reach them. Through my various experiences, I came to see how children's literature has the potential to draw children not just to learn to read, but also to find a reason to read: to meet people like themselves in whom they can see themselves, and to meet people living different lives so they can vicariously experience possibilities outside their own world, and then see the thread of humanity that encircles both.

I came to an awareness of the importance of children's literature to the study of Black history as students reflected on the books we shared in my children's literature classes. They were unfamiliar with the roles that African Americans had played in every aspect of American history. Many students, both Black and White, did not know when slavery first began in the colonies; how slavery continually changed over 250 years, as the nation developed with slavery as a major institution in the South (with implications for the entire country); what happened during Reconstruction; and the role African Americans played in World War I and World War II.

I began to ask several questions before I would present a book or issue to the class: What do Juneteenth celebrations commemorate? When was the Harlem Renaissance? How did the Jim Crow era get its name? Who was York? How did the U.S. Constitution address the issue of the slave trade? At one presentation, a single participant raised her hand and said she knew the answer to who York was because she had been in my children's literature class. I was amazed, but more than that I was disappointed. I could understand why many students would not be familiar with York or with where the term Jim Crow originated. But Juneteenth is celebrated in many cities across the country. And one has to imagine that students who have progressed through all of the American history classes that took place in their elementary, middle, and high school experiences would know about how the important and contentious issues surrounding slavery were addressed in the creation of the Constitution. Further, the Harlem Renaissance is a significant component of any study of literature, art, music, or dance. To not know the Harlem Renaissance is to not know any of these fields with breadth or depth.

So, what I "know" comes from a background in literacy and children's literature along with a background in social studies and wide reading in history. What I "feel" has been impacted by the sheer joy that I have experienced with young readers, with great children's literature, and with sadness and frustration about the dearth of knowledge about

African American contributions to this nation that students come away with, even with Black History Month celebrated in most states. This absence of Black history in the study of American history concerns me in several significant ways.

First, if we don't learn of the significant contributions of African Americans to this country's history, how will that incomplete history impact the perception of African Americans and the many struggles that still exist for civil rights? The practice of omission has been pervasive in American history texts and in children's literature. Until Nancy Larrick confronted the absence of African American representation in story, authorship, and illustration in her 1965 article "The All-White World of Children's Books," little was written about, written by, or illustrated by people of color. In that article, first published in the *Saturday Review of Books*, Larrick quotes a district librarian for the Central and East Harlem Area of New York who said that there had been a cultural lobotomy, and that "it is no accident that Negro history and Negro identification have been forgotten. Our society has contrived to make the American Negro a rootless person."[2]

This omission from history texts implies that the contributions of African Americans were not, and are not, significant, and it serves to perpetuate two myths that are destructive to the very fiber of our nation. One is that African Americans accepted, and continue to accept, a subordinated role. The second is that they lacked, and continue to lack, the desire or ability to engage fully in the broad range of events in the history of this nation. If these myths go unchallenged, they create a sense of White supremacy and contribute to an elitist sense of segregation in the minds of all students.

Sharing texts, even those that speak to the injustices of slavery, the disappointments of Reconstruction, the horrendous violence of the Jim Crow years, and the years of struggle for basic civil rights that have been part of our history, gives children and young people an opportunity to talk about race. In many ways, it is because of our history that race is so difficult to talk about, but its importance is critical to the discussion of Black history. In fact, as Jeane Copenhaver-Johnson notes, "the temptation among many well-meaning whites to resist acknowledging the importance or even the presence of race only reinforces blindness to the harmful effects of racism."[3]

Clinical psychologist Beverly Daniel Tatum, the dean at Mount Holyoke College, is the author of *Why Are All the Black Kids Sitting Together in the Cafeteria?* She states,

> I think it's important to acknowledge that race matters, that color-blind is not the goal. That it's not necessarily divisive to acknowledge difference. That the more comfortable the teacher is talking about issues of race and racism, the more comfortable students will be. And that students really need that guidance. When you create opportunities for young people to talk about these issues in a safe space—there's a lot of engagement. Young people are trying to make sense of the world, and they need help. Racism is one of those things that is hard to understand. Whether you teach algebra or auto mechanics, this issue affects young people's lives and they're going to want to talk about it in some meaningful way.[4]

Race, she says, matters to everyone, and "everybody's life is affected by the fact that we live in a society built on systems of privilege and disadvantage." This greatly influences "how we view the world, who we come into contact with, how we think about ourselves and other people."[5]

According to Copenhaver-Johnson, even preschoolers have been observed demonstrating "understandings of the privilege that whiteness carries" and "defining who is and who is not 'other' in their efforts to negotiate their own identities." She observes that White teachers and parents tend to be reluctant to discuss race, while "Black families report long explicit discussions with their children about race, privilege, discrimination, and relationships between members of different ethnic groups." She also points out that "one of the many dire consequences of [White] adult denial is that young children of color tend to bear the burdens of racism without acknowledgement and support from their caregivers."[6] Attributable to fear of saying the wrong thing, or simply not noticing the impact of racism since it is "not on the radar of many white parents and teachers because whiteness is so rarely scrutinized," Copenhaver-Johnson says, the absence of conversation about race creates a "culture of silence."[7]

My second concern is that we will not learn from history, and thus some negative aspects of it could be repeated. Particularly in the case of Black history, restrictive, discriminatory laws that were legislatively imposed and supported by the judiciary had an enormous impact. We continue to live in a nation that is very segregated and where there are many inequities. We are currently engaged in conversations about what it means to have social equity and, where it doesn't exist, how we can provide support for such equity. Dialogue generated by a more complete picture of history will surely inform the larger conversations and perhaps give all constituencies a greater understanding of each other.

Finally, we cannot understand the present, which is on a continuum with the past and is greatly influenced by it, until we broaden our study of American history to include the contributions of everyone.

WHAT TO LOOK FOR IN THE LITERATURE THAT WE USE WITH CHILDREN

Not all books that have African American characters or that highlight a Black person or event in history will necessarily be authentic, relevant, or even accurate. In this chapter, I address several important aspects of looking at books you may want to include in the study of American history and what you may want to look for. In order to better explain what I mean, I provide a look at a variety of books and compare them. First, we will look at books that address the same event in history: the writing of the Constitution of the United States. Second, we will look at books that provide information about an individual named York, who accompanied Lewis and Clark as a member of the well-known expedition that explored the territory west of the Mississippi. We will also look at genre and how multiple genre sources for the same subject can add depth and understanding to the subject being studied. Finally, we will look at visual representations of some of the different times and events that are often studied in American History classes, and we will look for inclusion and the quality of inclusion of African Americans.

A LOOK AT TWO BOOKS ABOUT THE CONSTITUTION

What would you think about a book documenting the writing of the Constitution for young readers that does not mention the very significant struggle between the northern and southern delegates about the issue of slavery?

The first book we will look at focuses on the writing of the Constitution. This book has been reprinted from its original publication in the late 1980s and continues to be available. (You will notice that in this chapter, I may not identify by name a book about which I have concerns—I do not want to unfairly undermine books that might be good in many other ways.) Written primarily for early elementary students, this is a picture book, and its language is appropriate to the students for whom it is intended. But what about the illustrations? In the illustrations of the inner circle of delegates, we would not necessarily expect to see African Americans. However, we can most certainly imagine that there would be Black people in the casual street scenes and in the crowds of enthusiastic citizens assembled in celebration—yet in this book's illustrations, there are none.

Even more difficult to understand is the complete absence of any mention of the issues and conflicts that arose about how to deal with slavery. It is important to note that it was one of the major areas of contention and was resolved by a compromise between the North and the South. The compromise for the North was that each slave would be counted as only three-fifths of a person so that the South would not be overrepresented because of its large slave population. The compromise for the South was that the slave trade would not be eliminated until 1808, which allowed the trade to continue intensely until then to provide slaves for the plantations in the South. Not one word about this is seen in the book. Yet, that knowledge would be valuable when history lessons bring students to the year 1863, almost a hundred years later during the Civil War, when Lincoln signed the Emancipation Proclamation, freeing the slaves in the Confederate South.

In contrast, *Shh! We're Writing the Constitution*, by Jean Fritz and illustrated by Tomie dePaola, provides early elementary students with a greater amount of text. Fritz raises the issues about slavery in the main text, then elaborates on them in notes at the back of the book. The illustrations do not, however, include anyone of color.

I would conclude that the first book has left out such a significant piece of the story of the Constitution that it misrepresents the writing of that document. Even for early elementary students, it is important to know that this is an important document both for its content and for who the "founding fathers" were who wrote it, and they also need to understand that the rights guaranteed in the Constitution did not apply to women,

African Americans, or Native Americans. It is also important that they know that the issues that surrounded slavery were discussed and bitterly argued during that time. This awareness is also important as it impacts later on the Civil War: although slavery did not start the war, the concerns that the North had with slavery did lead to the eventual freeing of slaves.

YORK AND THE LEWIS AND CLARK EXPEDITION

Rhoda Blumberg's award-winning book *York's Adventures with Lewis and Clark: An African-American's Part in the Great Expedition* (discussed in chapter 3) is a great resource for young researchers, and as good research does, it provides us with an expectation of the important details we should find in other sources dealing with the same subject. Although a book that is intended for later elementary and middle school would be expected to have more details and to be more complete than books for younger readers, all should be accurate. The absence of important facts may lead to inaccurate portrayals. In Blumberg's depiction of York, the times, the expedition, and the events afterward, she provides important facts and insights that could also be included in books for early elementary readers.

Blumberg's book is well researched and presents an extraordinary human being who was a major contributor to the success of the Lewis and Clark Expedition. York had been Clark's slave from when they were both barely teenagers, and when Clark was asked by Lewis to accompany him on the expedition to explore the territory west of the Mississippi for President Jefferson, it was expected that Clark would bring his slave and personal servant, York.

York was a large and very able worker, and as the historical documents show, he contributed to the success of the expedition in every way.[8] He was particularly successful in helping the expedition engage with the indigenous people encountered along the way, since many had not seen a Black man before, and his ability to relate to them made him quite popular.

To me it is most profound, though, that when the expedition returned successfully, York remained Clark's slave, even though he allegedly risked his own life to save Clark's life in a flood. As a slave, he was also not given the same rewards that others on the expedition received: "The government rewarded each enlisted man on the list with double pay and 320 acres of land. Lewis and Clark each received double pay and 1600 acres of land. Because York was a slave, York was not eligible for money or land."[9] Although Blumberg admits she would like to have been able to write a happy ending for this biography, she could not, for even though York asked Clark for his freedom, according to Blumberg, it was only after about ten years that he would eventually be freed.

With all of the information in the Blumberg book, I began to look at other volumes on this topic that are frequently included in classroom libraries. One, a picture book from a popular series of history books, is very disappointing. The author barely mentions York and never includes any stories of York's unique relationship with the indigenous people the expedition encountered. With that as an omission, the reader might not come away with the expectation that surely Clark would free him. In fact, there is no mention of York at the conclusion of the story, although the author includes in his notes in the back of the book that York was refused his freedom when he requested it but was eventually freed some years later. The greatest omission comes with the statement that members of the expedition were rewarded with land and money for their courageous and successful expedition without indicating that York, because he was a slave, received nothing. This book dismisses an important member of the expedition whose contributions, from all accurate accounts available, factored heavily in its success. I would not recommend a book with these omissions and weaknesses.

A third book detailing the Lewis and Clark Expedition introduces a few of the original members of the expeditionary corps early in the book with small portraits identifying each person and a brief statement about each. The author even includes Lewis's dog. York is described as Clark's faithful slave, large, powerful, and the only Black member of the corps. He is also described as a childhood playmate of Clark. The book includes brief quotes from letters that were written by Lewis and Clark during the expedition, and the illustrations go nicely with the text. However, the illustration of York where the author is talking about the Indians' fascination with his physical appearance and playfulness I found stereotypical. York is pictured again, twice, but not mentioned again at all, and although the hailstorm is mentioned, there is no mention of York racing to rescue Clark. In this case, it is important to remember that the author has taken the text from letters written by Lewis and Clark, and that although Blumberg found a source that indicated Clark was aware of York's concern for his safety, this author either did not see the same document or chose to ignore it.

In another book that actually focuses specifically on York as part of the expedition, the author assumes the voice of York. This is problematic for me. I have serious concerns about this approach for young readers, since it implies an intimacy with this person, his life, and what he would have been thinking that would be very difficult to have. On one page, York is described as almost forgetting he was Clark's slave. This is a serious flaw in this type of biography, for even though York was an active member of the Corps of Discovery and was even allowed to express his opinion about where to camp for the winter they spent on the West Coast, his forgetting he was Clark's slave, for even one moment, could have easily met serious punishment. Later, the author is clear about the relationship between slave and master when, at the end of the journey, Clark refuses to free York and states that he was never legally freed. The illustrations are not stylized, and the scene with York entertaining the Corps and the Indians receives very different treatment than in the previous book. The illustrations throughout the book are, in fact, beautiful, and they contribute greatly to the text. Nevertheless, that the author claims to get inside York's head seems problematic.

Carol Johmann's *The Lewis and Clark Expedition: Join the Corps of Discovery to Explore Uncharted Territory*, illustrated by Michael Kline, is another book that looks at the expedition as a whole. Obviously a book dealing with the whole cast of characters that took part in the expedition will treat York differently than one that is focused on him as a participant, and that has certainly had an impact on the information that is shared in the books mentioned so far. All of the drawings of the people in this book are in a cartoon style, and although York looks pretty silly holding a rabbit by the ears in his introductory picture, everyone else looks pretty silly, too. This book is a collection of facts, descriptions, and plenty of activities that children can do related to this topic, from making a keelboat out of wood to making moccasins and learning the sign language used by the Shoshone Indian nation so that they could communicate with people outside of their nation.

I must admit that when I first saw the book, I made an assumption that it would not include the information I was now looking for about York, but I was mistaken. I was impressed by the inclusion of what I believe are important facts that someone studying this expedition should know. The author includes the fact that when York asked for his freedom, it angered Clark, and that there was a contradiction in the fact that York was so much an active participant in all aspects of the expedition yet would remain a slave. These are important observations that often do not exist in books about the expedition. However, in her description of what happened to the individual corps members, Johmann describes York as going from being "essentially a free man who shouldered his share of duties and hardships on the journey, back to being a slave."[10] This is a confusion that I see in books about York's "freedom" during the expedition. York was always a slave. To be "essentially a free man" is far, far, far from being free. You are not "essentially free" if you still do not have any rights.

Many sources cite the fact that both York and Sacagawea were able to "vote" on where the party would camp over the winter when they were on the West Coast, and that their voting was an acknowledgement of their equality in the group. As much as I would like to think that was the case, there is more evidence that they were likely included in the decision-making because they were the most knowledgeable. The "rights" that vote represented were exclusive to this decision. In fact, Clark would never have seen York as anything but a slave, nor would Lewis, who, when he heard of York's request for freedom, agreed with Clark that he should not be freed. I am concerned because to even begin to understand the life of a slave, it is important to know that slavery is an institution of dehumanization, and what we look at today with respect to what should happen was extremely different from what existed then. Even though Thomas Jefferson wrote that "All men are created equal," his home, Monticello, was "like all plantation homes—built by slave labor, supported by slaves who raised the rice, indigo, sugar, tobacco, and cotton."[11]

Johmann's book is particularly interesting because, even though it is a project/activity book, the author chooses to include information about York that adds to our understanding of his importance to the expedition and of slavery itself.

Last, but certainly not least, a book worth sharing is Laurence Pringle's biography of York, *American Slave, American Hero: York of the Lewis and Clark Expedition* (discussed in chapter 3). This book is well researched, could be presented in early elementary grades, and also could be used as a good companion book for later elementary students along with Blumberg's biography of York. One of the reasons Pringle decided to write about York was his concern about misinformation or omission of information about this important member of the expedition.

When the Public Broadcasting Service provided a study of York as a segment, the piece brought together historians to detail who York was and the part he played in the expedition. They share that "York is virtually unknown to almost all blacks and whites alike. Yet as the journals of the expedition testify, this first black man to cross the continent north of Mexico played a meaningful role in our young nation's first exploration of the American West."[12] Most of what is discussed in this PBS documentary is consistent with Blumberg's work; however, although the documentary does share that York received adulation from the crowds that welcomed the Corps of Discovery when they returned east, it does not share that he received no remuneration.

REPRESENTATION IN CHILDREN'S PICTURE BOOKS

Picture books make representation very explicit. When you pick up the book, whether you can read the words or not, you are able to understand a great deal about what the author and illustrator are trying to convey. When you couple that with the content that children are likely to take from pictures that are provided to depict historical events, they have even more meaning.

One book that comes to mind is *A Slave Family* by Bobbie Kalman and Amanda Bishop. The illustrations are predominantly photographs taken at Colonial Williamsburg, a reenactment colonial village in Williamsburg, Virginia, that attracts tourists from around the world. The story begins with the voice of a slave girl who is frightened about her move to the plantation master's home to become a servant to the daughter of the plantation owner. Throughout the story, there are descriptions of the life of the slaves on the plantation, and although the written text is accurate about many of the details of a slave's life, the photos give the impression that there was an abundance of free time, that there was a good deal of interaction between slave and owner, and that slaves were provided with nice clothing and clean, well-maintained quarters. After looking at the book and reading even its worst statements about punishments and the absence of a slave's rights, I came away feeling that the book had minimized the tragedy of enslavement.

Other books on colonial America give the impression that African Americans didn't exist in the colonies at all. For instance, *If You Lived in the Time of the American Revolution*, by Kay Moore and illustrated by Daniel O'Leary, does not have a single person of color in any of the scenes, and only on page sixty-five, when Phillis Wheatley is mentioned, is there a picture of an African American.

In Jean Fritz's book *George Washington's Breakfast*, a modern little White boy named George Allen, who was born on the same month and day as George Washington, enjoys finding out things about his namesake. He knows about him being the first president and about the horses he rode, but he wants to know what he ate for breakfast. His grandmother does not know the answer but promises to cook it for him if he can find out. He works with his imagination to create a scene in Washington's kitchen, and the illustrator, Paul Galdone, depicts the scene: two White women, presumably the cooks, are standing and talking about preparing Washington's breakfast. Now, with the slaves that both George and Martha Washington owned, it is very unlikely that he would have hired White cooks to work in his kitchen. With all of the things George Allen knew about George Washington, he did not know that his plantation workers were African American slaves. Of course George Allen is not real, but for the children who read this book, this omission will create a different reality of Washington than would have existed had the slaves been mentioned. This also avoids the contradiction that exists in the study of George Washington as slave owner and freedom fighter.

In reviewing a book on World War I, I searched page after page for representation of African Americans I knew had fought in that war, and I found none. The three soldiers of color I did find turned out to be British West African troops. Again, the omission of a mention either in writing or in pictures leads to a conclusion that African Americans were not there, in spite of an estimated 350,000 Black troops and their strong desire to serve, even in an army characterized by discrimination and segregation. When I see this in books from well-respected publishers, I am reminded of the fact that even well-researched material can be selective and exclusive in its presentation.

LOOKING THROUGH THE LENSES OF DIFFERENT GENRES

Including a variety of works related to the same subject can have benefits for students. Books written at different reading levels can provide opportunities for differentiated instruction, allowing a number of students to work on the same subject but at their own reading level. The caution, of course, is that all of the material needs to be accurate.

Another consideration when selecting books to share on the same subject is to bring together books written in different genres. I will use as an example three books about the murder of Emmett Till, each of which is discussed in chapter 10. All three books are written at a middle school level with consideration of the readability and the concept load, which is great, considering the hideous crime that was committed.

Chris Crowe's *Getting Away with Murder* is a nonfiction/informational book about fourteen-year-old Emmett Till, the murder, and the trial. It provides students with well-researched information about the time, the crime that was committed, and the injustice of the courts. It describes how Till's mother and her decision to have his tortured body viewed by the community enraged and moved people to social civil rights action.

Another book by Chris Crowe, *Mississippi Trial, 1955*, is historical fiction, placing the true events of the murder within a story. Given what he knows about the time and setting of the murder, Crowe is able to create a story that is plausible. It is told from the viewpoint of a White boy who knew Till and who discovers the hatred and violence of the South during the Jim Crow years. Along with a story that he has created, Crowe incorporates parts of the actual events with accuracy.

Marilyn Nelson's *A Wreath for Emmett Till* is a book of poems that relate to the story of Emmett Till in another way. Through the genre of poetry, Nelson writes of the teenager and his mother, the crime, and the injustices that followed. It is a tribute, a wreath, symbolic and passionate. It is the crystallization of language that is poetry, that carries so much meaning in so few words, that is both fragile and strong.

REPRESENTATION IN CHILDREN'S LITERATURE

Looking at *The Journey of the One and Only Declaration of Independence* by Judith St. George, which is illustrated by Will Hillenbrand, I noticed that the artist had very clearly thought about the inclusion of people of color in his illustrations. In every picture where the story portrays the present, he has people of color, but in every picture from the past, all of the people in the illustrations are White, except for one person half-hidden behind a tree. It makes me wonder, since he was so conscientious in his illustrations of the present day, if he was unaware of just how many African Americans would likely have been on the streets, in the crowd of listeners, or busily doing different jobs. Whatever the reason, their absence in the illustrations gives the impression that they were not involved in the times, and worse yet, that they were not relevant to history.

My observations so far have led to several conclusions regarding representation. One is that many books are written about the events in American history without any representation of African Americans. That is no surprise, because in many ways that is what prompted me to create this book. What I now suspect is that many of the authors do not know the history, and when they collect data to support the integrity of their book, they don't think to include African Americans because of their own misinformation, which was formed through the systematic exclusion of African Americans in our history books over time. Thus, many illustrators of today who are aware of the importance of representation feel comfortable including people of color in contemporary illustrations but might not be sure of where to picture people of color in historical texts. But African Americans have been present in our country's entire history, and although they would not authentically be among of the framers of the Constitution, there were likely slaves in the room, and certainly there were Black citizens in the crowds of interested Americans.

This partial inclusion is often present in books about the western expansion. Popular books about this topic often mention the soldiers of the African American Ninth Cavalry, often referred to as "Buffalo Soldiers," but Blacks have no inclusion in the many other facets of that era: no Black pioneers, no Black cowboys, no Black gold miners. In one such book, even though there is an illustration and a one-sentence description of the Ninth Cavalry, the terms "Ninth Cavalry," "African American," and "Buffalo Soldiers" do not appear in the index.

SUGGESTIONS FOR WHAT TO LOOK FOR IN NONFICTION/INFORMATIONAL BOOKS

A good way to determine the criteria for reviewing nonfiction comes from looking at the characteristics shared by the winners and honor books of the Orbis Pictus Award, given each year by the National Council of Teachers of English. The award is specifically given to works of nonfiction, and the criteria for selection were developed in 1989:

- Accuracy—facts current and complete, balance of fact and theory, varying points of view, stereotypes avoided, author's qualifications adequate, appropriate scope, authenticity of detail.
- Organization—logical development, clear sequence, interrelationships indicated, patterns provided (general-to-specific, simple-to-complex, etc.).
- Design—attractive, readable, illustrations complement text, placement of illustrative materials appropriate and complementary, appropriate media, format, type.
- Style—writing is interesting, stimulating, reveals author's enthusiasm for subject, curiosity and wonder encouraged, appropriate terminology, rich language.

Because this is a teacher's organization, the committee also looks at the usefulness of the book to the classroom.[13]

The nonfiction books described in the previous chapters have not all won an award, but they deserve to be included because of their fine examples of the above criteria.

SUGGESTIONS FOR
WHAT TO LOOK FOR IN HISTORICAL FICTION

Many of the books that have been cited in the previous chapters are from the genre of historical fiction. They are not considered nonfiction because part of the book is made up, but there are certainly threads that run between fiction and fact that are significantly important to their selection.

The Scott O'Dell Award is given each year to the best historical fiction children's book, and several of the books that have been identified for classroom inclusion are among the winners. The criteria for evaluating historical fiction are included in *Children's Literature: An Invitation to the World*, a text that I co-authored with Diana Mitchell and Pamela Waterbury. The questions one should ask are:

- Is fact distinguished from fiction?
- From the inside jacket flap, acknowledgments, or authors note, can you get a sense of the research the author did and learn what sources were used?

- Do the action and plot develop out of the time period? If the book could be set in any other time period with the same conflicts present, it is not historical fiction.
- Do the characters jump to life and make the reader feel connected to them? Do they express attitudes and beliefs consistent with the time period?
- Are the historical setting and events woven into the story in seamless ways, or do the characters spout history lessons? Are the themes significant ones?
- Does the writing bring the story to life?
- Is the story authentic in language, details, and of the times?[14]

Historical fiction might take many different forms, from diaries, journals, and letters to first-person narratives, time travel, and more. One of the genres that gets special attention is picture books, where "the illustrator carries much of the burden of telling the story," and where "the drawings must be accurate if the illustrator is to contribute effectively to the story and its authenticity."[15]

AUTHENTICITY AND ITS
RELATIONSHIP TO BLACK HISTORY

As Connie Wilson Anderson explains about reviewing children's books,

> It is important that instructional resources used in classrooms be relevant to African-American children because it affects their academic achievement. Activities and lessons that encourage children to read about history should include resources, fiction and non-fiction, written by African-American authors. How teachers use their knowledge and understanding of African-American heritage can enhance the teaching-learning process and may increase the willingness of students to learn by helping them to identify with their past. Historically relevant content is a meaningful support system recommended as a vehicle to connect teachers with students.[16]

Certainly as we look at books through all of the lenses that we have talked about in terms of quality, we can feel safe that the books possess positive qualities for inclusion in our classrooms or on our bookshelves at home, but one last feature must be taken seriously if we are to create an opportunity for learning: authenticity. As Rudine Sims Bishop states, "One of the most sensitive current issues in the field of literature in general and children's literature as well is the issue of cultural authenticity. . . . Almost always the controversies are about books written by someone from a different cultural background, usually Euro-American."[17] Although this criticism and concern continues to this day, there seems to be a general agreement that if authors and illustrators work to inform themselves, they may be able to write an authentic book outside of their own culture. However, that is not easy, and books that do not meet that standard are often written when "the author was unaware of the nuances of day-to-day living in the culture portrayed in the book, or that the distortions and misrepresentations are reflections of an ethnocentric, biased, or at worst, racist point of view."[18]

For many people, authenticity might be the hardest feature to determine, particularly if we are looking outside our own cultures. How do we know authenticity? How can we avoid stereotypes? And does it matter if the author is a member of the group being written about?

Bishop provides some guidance for the selection of individual books and suggests some questions to ask:

- Look for the point of view the author takes toward his or her subject. Does the author assume a paternalistic attitude?
- Examine relationships between characters from different cultures. Do people of color lead or follow?
- Analyze the way people of color are characterized. Are main characters well-rounded and fully developed?
- Examine the language, both of the narrator or the author, and the fictional characters. Do the writers avoid racially offensive terms (e.g., savage, primitive)?
- Examine the language of the characters. Is the language accurate, and appropriate to the historical period?
- Look carefully at the pictures.
- Look for accuracy.
- Information should be factual and up to date.
- Consider the background of the author.
- Consider the possible effect on a child's self-esteem.[19]

OTHER THINGS TO CONSIDER

In addition to all of the considerations above, I would suggest that you diversify your collection. We usually have to grow our collections a little at a time. Books can be expensive. Every time I teach a course in children's literature, students tell me that instead of their usual requests for holiday and birthday gifts, they simply give lists of children's books to relatives and friends. As you build gradually in the area of books for Black history, you may want to select works discussed in the preceding chapters for a broad range of representation, or focus on one era initially, but within each area, select from different genres that can address your focus of interest. For each book you select, make a deliberate choice based on guidelines such as those outlined above. That will provide for the strongest collection. I often remind students that to have a great conversation about a book, you need to begin with a great book.

NOTES

1. Van Middendorp and Lee, "Literature for Children and Young Adults," 117.
2. Larrick, "All-White World," 67.
3. Copenhaver-Johnson, "Talking to Children about Race," 13.
4. Tatum interview, 42.
5. Tatum interview, 42.
6. Copenhaver-Johnson, "Talking to Children about Race," 14.
7. Copenhaver-Johnson, "Talking to Children about Race," 13.
8. Public Broadcasting Service, "York's Experience," Lewis and Clark companion website to the Ken Burns film. It is interesting that on the PBS website, there is this comment from Clark's journal that seems to contradict everything that has been written about York's extraordinary physical abilities:

> August 25, the captains, together with nine men, including York, hiked nearly 20 miles to examine "Spirit Mound," a place of "little people" feared by superstitious Indians. The outing, made on a hot, muggy day, was commented upon by Clark in an entry that is totally at odds with York's traditional image of having been a giant of superb physique and stamina. Clark wrote, "we returned to the boat at Sunset, my servent nearly exosted with heat thurst and fatigue, he being fat and unaccustomed to walk as fast as I went was the cause." [spelling errors in the original]

9. Blumberg, *York's Adventures,* 76. It is worth noting that the PBS program on York mentioned that York received adulation from the crowds welcoming

the expedition on their return, but they did not mention that he received no remuneration.

10. Johmann, *The Lewis and Clark Expedition*, 102.
11. Meltzer, *Slavery: A World History*, 153.
12. Public Broadcasting Service, "York."
13. National Council of Teachers of English, "Criteria."
14. Mitchell, Waterford, and Casement, *Children's Literature*, 288.
15. Mitchell, Waterford, and Casement, *Children's Literature*, 283.
16. Anderson, "Examining Historical Events," 36.
17. Bishop, "Multicultural Literature," 40–41.
18. Bishop, "Multicultural Literature," 42.
19. Bishop, "Multicultural Literature," 50.

BIBLIOGRAPHY OF BOOKS FOR CHILDREN

Blumberg, Rhoda. *York's Adventures with Lewis and Clark: An African-American's Part in the Great Expedition.* New York: HarperCollins, 2004.

Crowe, Chris. *Getting Away with Murder.* New York: Dial, 2003.

———. *Mississippi Trial, 1955.* New York: Puffin, 2003.

Fritz, Jean. *George Washington's Breakfast.* 1969. Reprint. New York: Putnam's, 1998.

———. *Shh! We're Writing the Constitution.* Illustrated by Tomie dePaola. 1967. Reprint. New York: Putnam's, 1997.

Johmann, Carol. *The Lewis and Clark Expedition: Join the Corps of Discovery to Explore Uncharted Territory.* Illustrated by Michael Kline. Topeka, KS: Sagebrush, 2003.

Kalman, Bobbie, and Amanda Bishop. *A Slave Family.* New York: Crabtree, 2002.

Moore, Kay. *If You Lived in the Time of the American Revolution.* Illustrated by Daniel O'Leary. New York: Scholastic, 1998.

Nelson, Marilyn. *A Wreath for Emmett Till.* Boston: Houghton Mifflin, 2005.

St. George, Judith. *The Journey of the One and Only Declaration of Independence.* Illustrated by Will Hillenbrand. New York: Philomel, 2005.

BIBLIOGRAPHY OF REFERENCE WORKS

Anderson, Connie Wilson. "Examining Historical Events through Children's Literature." Review of *Days of Jubilee: The End of Slavery in the United States; Mississippi Morning; Free at Last! Stories and Songs of Emancipation; Going North; Remember: The Journey to School Integration. Multicultural Education* 14:1 (2006): 36–38.

Bishop, Rudine Sims. "Multicultural Literature for Children: Making Informed Choices." In *Teaching Multicultural Literature in Grades K–8*, ed. Violet J. Harris, 37–53. Norwood, MA: Christopher-Gordon, 1992.

Copenhaver-Johnson, Jeane. "Talking to Children about Race: The Importance of Inviting Difficult Conversations." *Childhood Education* 83:1 (2006): 12–22.

Larrick, Nancy. "The All-White World of Children's Books." *Saturday Review*, September 11, 1965, 63–67.

Meltzer, Milton. *Slavery: A World History*. New York: Da Capo, 1993.

Mitchell, Diana, Pamela Waterford, and Rose Casement. *Children's Literature: An Invitation to the World*. Boston: Allyn and Bacon, 2002.

National Council of Teachers of English. "Criteria." NCTE Orbis Pictus Award for Outstanding Nonfiction for Children. www.ncte.org/elem/awards/orbispictus/106877.htm?source=gs.

Public Broadcasting Service. "York's Experience." Lewis and Clark companion website to the Ken Burns film. www.pbs.org/lewisandclark/inside/york.html.

Tatum, Beverly Daniel. Interview. *Techniques* 74:2 (1999): 42.

Van Middendorp, Judy E., and Sharon Lee. "Literature for Children and Young Adults in a History Classroom." *Social Studies* 85:3 (1994): 117–120.

· 13 ·

Outstanding Authors and
Illustrators of Children's Literature

Books by, about, and for African-Americans have increased in number over the past decade. However, most literature for children continues to exclude the African American culture. It is important to continue to write and illustrate books of quality that express this heritage and have them available not only to Black readers but for the edification of all readers.[1]

$\mathscr{F}$or too many years, African Americans were excluded from the authorship and art of children's literature. In 1987, Barbara Rollock first compiled a dictionary of Black authors and illustrators. In her second edition, published in 1992, she notes that her intention is not to isolate these authors and illustrators, but rather to provide a single volume of reference for those interested in Black authors and illustrators and their contributions to children's literature.[2]

The need to highlight these authors and illustrators in such a work is further illustrated by an experience Andrea Pinkney recounts of attending a presentation by a highly respected children's literature scholar who was speaking about the history of picture books. The audience was made up predominantly of young editorial assistants and junior editors, many of whom would be likely editors and publishers of the future. Pinkney attended with a colleague who was new to the world of children's literature illustration, and they were the only Black attendees in the audience.

The lecture and slide presentation of exemplary books was chronological and as the speaker began to bring in the books of the sixties, seventies, eighties, and nineties, Pinkney waited to hear the names of African American authors and illustrators whom she would have expected to hear mentioned for their outstanding work, work that had won the Caldecott as well as the Coretta Scott King Award. To her astonishment, none of the authors or illustrators of color were mentioned. Not one.[3]

Pinkney describes the experience as isolating and notes that she was saddened for her friend, an aspiring new illustrator, and for the young attendees in the audience, "many of whom were not even aware of what they'd missed."[4] Pinkney's experience is a powerful argument for observing and celebrating the Coretta Scott King Award for children's literature authored or illustrated by a person of color, the list of which appears at the end of this chapter.

I include in this chapter some of the authors and illustrators whose work appears in this book. They are powerful in their creative abilities, in their contributions to children's literature, and in their dedication to sharing a broad range of authentic African American experiences across the last four hundred years. Their contributions have marked a turning point in children's literature and the study of American history.

White people see history differently, partly because they have experienced a different history, but also because they see themselves in history differently: "As more races, religions, and ethnicities have become represented in the literature in our classrooms, we have provided children with stories that open windows into the lives of people different from themselves, windows that open to tolerance, empathy, compassion and celebrations of diversity."[5]

This chapter shares some observations I arrived at while gathering this collection of children's literature for literacy (reading, writing, listening, speaking, visual representation, and visual interpretation) and social studies/American history/Black history. It is clearly a personal response to the work I've included throughout the chapters. I also share some of the resources that readers can use to find biographical details of these authors and illustrators and help our understanding of the lens through which they have written their books or visualized their subjects. Also, students enjoy learning more about their favorite authors and illustrators. The chapter concludes with a list of the Coretta Scott King Award winners and honorees from 1984 to the present (the award actually goes back to 1970, but many of the early winners are, unfortunately, out of print). You will see several authors' and illustrators' names repeated from year to year.

IN MEMORY

Several of the authors who played a very large part in the literature that supports an authentic history of the Black experience are no longer with us. Some are included here in great appreciation of their contributions to this important history.

Tom Feelings (1933–2003)

The work of Tom Feelings spanned decades and often captured, with brutal honesty, the history of slavery. *The Middle Passage* (discussed in chapter 3) is a testament to the tragic journey of captive Africans bound for slavery in the Americas. *Soul Looks Back in Wonder* (see chapter 1), which he edited and illustrated, reflects his intense spiritual connection with the past.

No one website seems to have comprehensive coverage of Feelings, but two sites maintained by the National Conference of Artists of New York provide information about his life and work. The first, http://ncanewyork.com/feelings.htm, provides a profile, while tributes from his friends can be found on http://ncanewyork.com/feelings/tom _feelings_tribute.htm. The publisher Penguin Group also offers a Tom Feelings page on their website, http://us.penguingroup.com.

Virginia Hamilton (1936–2002)

Another extraordinary scholar and author is Virginia Hamilton, who wrote texts rich and deep. Her characters' voices resonate with honesty and soulfulness. Her informational book *Many Thousand Gone: African Americans from Slavery to Freedom* (discussed in chapter 3) profiles many significant early Americans of color as well as lesser-known people of accomplishment. Over the course of her long career, her work was very versatile and includes folklore and fantasy as well as realistic and historical fiction.

Hamilton's official website is very complete on many aspects of her career, and much of it is in her own words: www.virginiahamilton.com/ home.htm.

James Haskins (1941–2005)

James Haskins had an active academic life at the University of Florida for over thirty years. He contributed over one hundred nonfiction/informational books to the study of Black history in children's literature. He was truly extraordinary, and his work will remain a powerful resource for anyone wanting to know more about Black history. I have included many of his books throughout the chapters, and each time I picked one up and read it, I was informed. He did not talk down to his reader but instead wrote of a very complex history with clarity and readable text. He knew the history, and the richness of his work cannot be praised too highly.

For years, I have suggested that teachers read great informational books for young readers if they are interested in a subject. Often, adult books on a historical topic are intensely scholarly and intended for academic study. Haskins's work presents an opportunity to read well-researched books about a number of subjects to get informed. A picture, biographical information, and a list of his published works can be found on his professional page at the University of Florida website: www.english.ufl.edu/faculty/jhaskins/.

AUTHORS

The following authors are significant contributors to the depth and breadth of children's literature.

Christopher Paul Curtis

Curtis stunned the world of children's literature with his first book, *The Watsons Go to Birmingham—1963* (discussed in chapter 10). It won a Newbery Honor and the Coretta Scott King Award, and everyone marveled at how Curtis could write with humor that made your sides hurt as you laughed out loud in a book dealing with one of the saddest tragedies of the civil rights era, the murder of four little girls in a bombed Birmingham church. Curtis's second book, *Bud, Not Buddy* (discussed in chapter 8), earned the Newbery Medal and the Coretta Scott King Award, which was the first time anyone received both awards at the same time.

Christopher Paul Curtis maintains a website within the Random House website: www.randomhouse.com/features/christopherpaulcurtis/. Here one can find a biography and pictures of Curtis, a list of the books he has written, and even his advice for young writers.

Angela Johnson

A very prolific writer, Johnson has won many awards, including a 2003 MacArthur Foundation "Genius Grant," which is given to individuals who show potential in their field. She is a poet and an author of both picture books and chapter books (several are featured in chapter 11).

Because Johnson lives in Ohio, she is featured on a website called Ohioana Authors: www.ohioana-authors.org. This site provides a brief biography, a list of her work and awards, and her connection to Ohio, where she was born and later attended Kent State University. But the neatest thing is the audio clip that you can play from National Public Broadcasting.

Julius Lester

I have included Lester's work in several different chapters. One that makes me cry just to think of it is *Day of Tears* (described in chapter 3). While reading that particular book, I was greatly affected by Lester's giving voice to individuals who lived during the horrible ordeal of the largest slave sale in history. No, I won't ever forget it, and it is a tribute to Lester's work and image craft that it is carved into my mind and heart. Sometimes one just has to realize that there is probably no way to adequately talk about an artist's work, and the only way to engage with it is to become part of it by reading it. A useful website for learning about this author is his page for Houghton Mifflin: www.eduplace.com/kids/hmr/mtai/lester.html. Also see his faculty page for the University of Massachusetts at Amherst, where he is a professor emeritus: www.umass.edu/judaic/faculty/juliuslester.html. One thing you will discover is that Lester is an avid photographer.

Patricia C. McKissack and Fredrick L. McKissack

Two exceptional researchers who have published a great deal of nonfiction/informational work on Black historical concerns are Patricia C. McKissack and Fredrick L. McKissack. A number of their works are discussed in various chapters in this text. They have been working for decades, often together and sometimes individually, and their well-researched books offer a great deal to the integrity of the history they share. Patricia McKissack, formerly a middle school teacher, demonstrates a good sense of language and content load in the stories they have written for young readers. Factual background for both authors can be found at the

Houghton Mifflin page, www.eduplace.com/kids/hmr/mtai/mckissack. html. Patricia C. McKissack's page at the Random House website is also good and is especially detailed: www.randomhouse.com/author/results. pperl?authorid=20049.

Milton Meltzer

Milton Meltzer has written extensively about the African American experience in American history, and he has contributed much excellent, credible research over a long period of time, providing young scholars with accurate information to build understandings. Metzer worked with Langston Hughes on an early nonfiction/informational text for Black history, and he also offers many works where the voices of people, both famous and simple, are recorded. One of the most exquisite books on Frederick Douglass, *Frederick Douglass: In His Own Words*, is edited by Meltzer and illustrated by Stephen Alcorn. Although it is currently out of print, used copies can be found fairly easily, and it is well worth having. It is one of the best books that chronicle Douglass's life and work, and it is beautiful as well, with powerful woodcuts on the subject. Because he is not a person of color, his books have not been eligible for the Coretta Scott King Award; however, he has received numerous awards, including the National Book Award and the Christopher Award.

I have been grateful for Meltzer's work, as it has informed those who would listen of the extraordinary history of African Americans in America's history. The best website for Meltzer is the National Book Foundation's site. Meltzer is a five-time nominee for the National Book Award and his response to the topic "The Book That Changed My Life" is posted on their website: www.nationalbook.org/bookchanged _mmeltzer_nbm.html.

An interesting biography of Meltzer is on the site for the Worcester Polytechnic library, the George C. Gordon Library, where he is cited as a Worcester Area Writer: www.wpi.edu/Academics/Library/ Archives/WAuthors/meltzer/bio.html. This site shares information about Meltzer from his beginnings in 1915, growing up in Worcester, Massachusetts, as the son of immigrant parents, to the present.

Walter Dean Myers

Although Myers is best known as a prolific author of young adult literature, you will find some of his work in several chapters of this book, including *I've Seen the Promised Land: The Life of Dr. Martin Luther King, Jr.*; *Malcolm X: A Fire Burning Brightly*; *Malcolm X: By Any Means Necessary*; and *Now Is Your Time! The African-American Struggle for Freedom*. The last two of these books received the Coretta Scott King Award. Most author websites provide readers with a brief biographical sketch and a listing of the author's work, often including the awards they have won. The best site for reading about Myers was compiled by individuals at Rutgers University: www.scils.rutgers.edu/~kvander/myers.html.

Mildred D. Taylor

Mildred D. Taylor's work is imbedded in my soul. It got there without my ever intending it to have that profound an influence. Her book *The Friendship* (discussed in chapter 8), a mere fifty-three pages long, is a thunderbolt of harsh reality, and as difficult as it is to have as part of me now, I am grateful.

Taylor has received awards for her literary genius, with high praise for her characters and her ability to tell a powerful story. She has also received some criticism about her inclusion of words that are derogatory or mean but that accurately depict the language that would have been used, particularly during slavery and the Jim Crow years. Her response is that, as painful as these words are, they are authentic to the times, and to not use them in her books would paint an inaccurate picture of the terrible times people lived through, that the degradation that is inherent in the language of the times was part of the violence imposed on African Americans in every part of our culture.[6] When I hear discussions about writing outside of one's culture, I think of Mildred Taylor and ask the question: Could a White person have written one of her stories? The answer for me is no.

The best website I found for Taylor has her acceptance speech for the 1997 Alan Award for young adult literature: http://scholar.lib.vt.edu/ejournals/ALAN/spring98/taylor.html. A site offered by a literacy specialist at the University of Indiana School of Education, Mei-Yu Lu, has a listing of many other websites one can use to study Taylor's work: www.indiana.edu/~reading/ieo/bibs/taylor.html.

Jacqueline Woodson

Woodson's work is very much a part of chapter eleven, as she provides picture books and stories of today. Several of her stories have been

Coretta Scott King Award winners, and she has been nominated for the National Book Award and American Library Association Awards as well. In her books, the protagonist is often African American and provides a way for children to see themselves as central to the story. The importance of this is measured by the absence of African Americans as protagonists in contemporary children's literature. The family structure that is present in her stories is usually strong and loving, though it is often interrupted by the death of a parent from natural or accidental causes. In one of her books, *I Hadn't Meant to Tell You This*, the protagonist, Lena, is White, and her confidante is Black. In a later book, *Lena*, a Black family helps and supports Lena and her sister as they try in vain to find protection with their White relatives.[7] One departure from Woodson's contemporary stories is her book *Show Way* (discussed in chapter 5), where she traces her ancestry and considers a distant relative born into slavery.

Woodson maintains her own website at www.jacquelinewoodson. com. Fun to browse, this site has links to her books, frequently asked questions, and places and dates for where she will be presenting. It is very personable and speaks directly to the visitor.

A Family of Authors and Illustrators—The Pinkneys

Here is an amazing family. Jerry Pinkney, the extraordinary watercolorist whose work has won many awards over his career, is the husband of Gloria Pinkney, who is a children's literature author. Together, they are the parents of the award-winning artist in the scratchboard medium, Brian Pinkney, who is the husband of Andrea Pinkney, an author in her own right. Jerry and Gloria's other son, Myles, has also worked in children's literature as a photography illustrator, and his wife, Sandra, is an author.

When Jerry Pinkney talks at book signings or conferences, he has a quiet, down-to-earth style, and I have never come away thinking that he sees himself as a dynastic family patriarch. However, this is a remarkable family with great success in the creation of children's literature, and one cannot help but be enormously impressed. As you review the awards listed at the end of this chapter, you will see the significant contributions that this family of authors and illustrators has made to the world of children's literature.

Jerry Pinkney

Jerry Pinkney has a website provided by Houghton Mifflin: www.edu place.com/kids/hmr/mtai/jpinkney.html. Here, Pinkney talks about his process of creating his watercolors and about how he became an illustrator.

Another site is provided by Penguin Group Publishing: http://us .penguingroup.com/nf/Author/AuthorPage/0,,1000013120,00.html. This site is more comprehensive and includes what Pinkney has illustrated, how he became an illustrator, and his focus on multicultural and African American themes.

Brian Pinkney

Brian Pinkney's medium is almost unique to him in the world of picture book illustration. That medium is scratchboard, a technique of painting over an already painted or white surface and scratching off the applied paint (usually black) to make a drawing. His work is very identifiable because of the dramatic effect offered by this technique. In some of his illustrations, he paints over what is already there from the scratchboard work to highlight different parts of the illustration. Brian Pinkney also has a website provided by Houghton Mifflin: www.eduplace.com/kids/hmr/mtai/bpinkney.html. This site tells of his growing up with an illustrator father and an author mother and how he studied for a career as an illustrator.

ILLUSTRATORS

The following illustrators contribute to the depth and breadth of the visual representations of children's literature. Their work is often the first thing you see when you are looking for that special book, and the artists that are shared here have styles that are easily recognized because of each artist's amazing abilities.

E. B. Lewis

Lewis's medium is watercolor. His paintings seem to capture the soul of the characters in the books he illustrates. The interplay between the story and his illustrations is remarkable. Two works that stand out are *Coming On Home Soon* (discussed in chapter 8) and *The Other Side* (see chapter

11), both written by Jacqueline Woodson. Lewis has an "artistrator" webpage at www.eblewis.com/default2.asp, which includes a biographical sketch, information about the books he has illustrated, and his current activities.

Floyd Cooper

Cooper's medium is oil wash on illustration board. His illustrations often have a dreamlike quality, and as with E. B. Lewis, his artwork takes the reader deeper into the story. Cooper has a website provided by Houghton Mifflin: www.eduplace.com/kids/hmr/mtai/fcooper.html. This site describes how Cooper became a children's literature illustrator. It also has a brief description of how he does the oil wash illustrations.

CONCLUSION

Multicultural children's literature has changed the faces our children see as they explore the texts we consider valuable for reading aloud, for shared reading, and for students to read together or individually. If we continue to include high quality books that offer equal representation without privilege, a new canon in children's literature that is more inclusive of all children within our culture will continue to grow.[8]

One important source for excellent books to share with children is the list of Coretta Scott King Award winners and honorees.[9] The books that have been awarded provide excellent literature for all children of all races. Many have won other prestigious awards, but this award has a special importance because it is awarded solely to authors and illustrators of color. Books are judged on the cultural competency with which they have been written and illustrated and their merits in representing a culture that until the last fifty years was at best underrepresented or at worst maligned. The awards include Author Award, Illustrator Award, New Talent Award (Author), New Talent (Illustrator), Author Honor Awards, and Illustrator Honor Awards.

Listed below are the Coretta Scott King Award winners from 1970 to 2006. Honorees are included from 1978 to 2006. Many of the earlier books are no longer in print.

2007

Author Award—Draper, Sharon. *Copper Sun*. Simon and Schuster, Atheneum.
Illustrator Award—Weatherford, Carole Boston. *Moses: When Harriet Tubman Led Her People to Freedom*. Hyperion, Jump at the Sun.
John Steptoe New Talent Award—Jones, Traci L. *Standing against the Wind*. Farrar, Straus and Giroux.
Author Honor—Grimes, Nikki. *The Road to Paris*. Putnam's.
Illustrator Honor—Myers, Walter Dean. *Jazz*. Illustrated by Christopher Myers. Holiday House.
Illustrator Honor—Roessel, David, and Arnold Rampersad. *Poetry for Young People: Langston Hughes*. Sterling.

2006

Author Award—Lester, Julius. *Day of Tears: A Novel in Dialogue*. Hyperion, Jump at the Sun.
Illustrator Award—Giovanni, Nikki. *Rosa*. Illustrated by Bryan Collier. Henry Holt.
New Talent—Adoff, Jaime. *Jimi and Me*. Hyperion, Jump at the Sun.
Author Honor—Bolden, Tonya. *Maritcha: A Nineteenth-Century American Girl*. Abrams.
Author Honor—Grimes, Nikki. *Dark Sons*. Hyperion, Jump at the Sun.
Author Honor—Nelson, Marilyn. *A Wreath for Emmett Till*. Illustrated by Philippe Lardy. Houghton Mifflin.
Illustrator Honor—Christie, R. Gregory. *Brothers in Hope: The Story of the Lost Boys of Sudan*. Lee and Low.

2005

Author Award—Morrison, Toni. *Remember: The Journey to School Integration*. Houghton Mifflin.
Illustrator Award—Shange, Ntozake. *Ellington Was Not a Street*. Illustrated by Kadir A. Nelson. Simon and Schuster.
New Talent (Author)—Hathaway, Barbara. *Missy Violet and Me*. Houghton Mifflin.
New Talent (Illustrator)—Roberts, Brenda C. *Jazzy Miz Mozetta*. Farrar, Straus and Giroux.
Author Honor—Moses, Shelia P. *The Legend of Buddy Bush*. Simon and Schuster, Margaret K. McElderry Books.
Author Honor—Flake, Sharon G. *Who Am I without Him? Short Stories about Girls and the Boys in Their Lives*. Hyperion, Jump at the Sun.

Author Honor—Nelson, Marilyn. *Fortune's Bones: The Manumission Requiem*. Front Street.
Illustrator Honor—Holiday, Billie, and Arthur Herzog Jr. *God Bless the Child*. Illustrated by Jerry Pinkney. HarperCollins, Amistad.
Illustrator Honor—Hamilton, Virginia. *The People Could Fly: The Picture Book*. Illustrated by Leo and Diane Dillon. Random House, Knopf.

2004

Author Award—Johnson, Angela. *The First Part Last*. Simon and Schuster.
Illustrator Award—Bryan, Ashley. *Beautiful Blackbird*. Atheneum.
New Talent (Author)—Smith, Hope Anita. *The Way a Door Closes*. Henry Holt.
New Talent (Illustrator)—Cox, Judy. *My Family Plays Music*. Illustrated by Elbrite Brown. Holiday House.
Author Honor—McKissack, Patricia C., and Fredrick L. McKissack. *Days of Jubilee: The End of Slavery in the United States*. Scholastic.
Author Honor—Woodson, Jacqueline. *Locomotion*. Grosset and Dunlap.
Author Honor—Draper, Sharon. *The Battle of Jericho*. Atheneum.
Illustrator Honor—Nelson, Vaunda Micheaux. *Almost to Freedom*. Carolrhoda.
Illustrator Honor—Nolen, Jerdine. *Thunder Rose*. Illustrated by Kadir Nelson. Silver Whistle.

2003

Author Award—Grimes, Nikki. *Bronx Masquerade*. Dial.
Illustrator Award—Grimes, Nikki. *Talkin' about Bessie: The Story of Aviator Elizabeth Coleman*. Illustrated by E. B. Lewis. Scholastic, Orchard.
New Talent (Author)—McDonald, Janet. *Chill Wind*. Farrar, Straus and Giroux, Frances Foster Books.
New Talent (Illustrator)—DuBurke, Randy. *The Moon Ring*. Chronicle.
Author Honor—Woods, Brenda. *The Red Rose Box*. Putnam's.
Author Honor—Grimes, Nikki. *Talkin' about Bessie: The Story of Aviator Elizabeth Coleman*. Illustrated by E. B. Lewis. Scholastic, Orchard.
Illustrator Honor—Dillon, Leo, and Diane Dillon. *Rap a Tap Tap: Here's Bojangles—Think of That!* Scholastic, Blue Sky.
Illustrator Honor—Perdomo, Willie. *Visiting Langston*. Illustrated by Bryan Collier. Henry Holt.

2002

Author Award—Taylor, Mildred. *The Land*. Penguin Putnam, Phyllis Fogelman Books.

Illustrator Award—McKissack, Patricia C. *Goin' Someplace Special*. Illustrated by Jerry Pinkney. Atheneum, an Anne Schwartz Book.
New Talent (Illustrator)—Wiles, Deborah. *Freedom Summer*. Illustrated by Jerome Lagarrigue. Atheneum.
Author Honor—Flake, Sharon G. *Money-Hungry*. Hyperion, Jump at the Sun.
Author Honor—Nelson, Marilyn. *Carver: A Life in Poems*. Hyperion: Jump at the Sun.
Illustrator Honor—Rappaport, Doreen. *Martin's Big Words*. Illustrated by Bryan Collier. Hyperion, Jump at the Sun.

2001

Author Award—Woodson, Jacqueline. *Miracle's Boys*. Putnam's.
Illustrator Award—Collier, Bryan. *Uptown*. Henry Holt.
Author Honor—Pinkney, Andrea Davis. *Let It Shine! Stories of Black Women Freedom Fighters*. Illustrated by Stephen Alcorn. Harcourt, Gulliver.
Illustrator Honor—Rappaport, Doreen. *Freedom River*. Illustrated by Bryan Collier. Hyperion, Jump at the Sun.
Illustrator Honor—Rockwell, Anne. *Only Passing Through: The Story of Sojourner Truth*. Illustrated by R. Gregory Christie. Random House.
Illustrator Honor—Howard, Elizabeth Fitzgerald. *Virgie Goes to School with Us Boys*. Simon and Schuster.

2000

Author Award—Curtis, Christopher Paul. *Bud, Not Buddy*. Delacorte.
Illustrator Award—Siegelson, Kim L. *In the Time of the Drums*. Illustrated by Brian Pinkney. Hyperion, Jump at the Sun.
Author Honor—English, Karen. *Francie*. Farrar, Straus and Giroux.
Author Honor—McKissack, Patricia C., and Frederick L. McKissack. *Black Hands, White Sails: The Story of African-American Whalers*. Scholastic.
Author Honor—Myers, Walter Dean. *Monster*. HarperCollins.
Illustrator Honor—Mollel, Tololwa M. *My Rows and Piles of Coins*. Illustrated by E. B. Lewis. Clarion.
Illustrator Honor—Myers, Christopher. *Black Cat*. Scholastic.

1999

Author Award—Johnson, Angela. *Heaven*. Simon and Schuster.
Illustrator Award—Igus, Toyomi. *I See the Rhythm*. Illustrated by Michele Wood. Children's Book Press.
New Talent (Author)—Flake, Sharon. *The Skin I'm In*. Hyperion, Jump at the Sun.

New Talent (Illustrator)—Chocolate, Debbie. *The Piano Man*. Illustrated by Eric Velasquez. Walker.

Author Honor—Grimes, Nikki. *Jazmin's Notebook*. Dial.

Author Honor—Hansen, Joyce, and Gary McGowan. *Breaking Ground, Breaking Silence: The Story of New York's African Burial Ground*. Henry Holt.

Author Honor—Johnson, Angela. *The Other Side: Shorter Poems*. Scholastic, Orchard.

Illustrator Honor—Thomas, Joyce Carol. *I Have Heard of a Land*. Illustrated by Floyd Cooper. HarperCollins, Joanna Cotler Books.

Illustrator Honor—Curtis, Gavin. *The Bat Boy and His Violin*. Illustrated by E. B. Lewis. Simon and Schuster.

Illustrator Honor—Pinkney, Andrea Davis. *Duke Ellington: The Piano Prince and His Orchestra*. Illustrated by Brian Pinkney. Hyperion.

1998

Author Award—Draper, Sharon M. *Forged by Fire*. Atheneum.

Illustrator Award—Schroeder, Alan. *In Daddy's Arms I Am Tall: African Americans Celebrating Fathers*. Illustrated by Javaka Steptoe. Lee and Low.

Author Honor—Haskins, James. *Bayard Rustin: Behind the Scenes of the Civil Rights Movement*. Hyperion.

Author Honor—Hansen, Joyce. *I Thought My Soul Would Rise and Fly: The Diary of Patsy, a Freed Girl*. Scholastic.

Illustrator Honor—Bryan, Ashley. *Ashley Bryan's ABC of African American Poetry*. Atheneum, Jean Karl.

Illustrator Honor—Myers, Walter Dean. *Harlem*. Illustrated by Christopher Myers. Scholastic.

Illustrator Honor—Giakite, Baba Wague. *The Hunterman and the Crocodile*. Scholastic.

1997

Author Award—Myers, Walter Dean. *Slam*. Scholastic.

Illustrator Award—Schroeder, Alan. *Minty: A Story of Young Harriet Tubman*. Illustrated by Jerry Pinkney. Dial.

New Talent (Author)—Southgate, Martha. *Another Way to Dance*. Delacorte.

Author Honor—McKissack, Patricia C., and Fredrick L. McKissack. *Rebels against Slavery: American Slave Revolts*. Scholastic.

Illustrator Honor—Adedjouma, Davida, ed. *The Palm of My Heart: Poetry by African American Children*. Illustrated by R. Gregory Christie. Lee and Low.

Illustrator Honor—Lauture, Denize. *Running the Road to ABC*. Illustrated by Reynold Ruffins. Simon and Schuster.

English, Karen. *Neeny Coming, Neeny Going.* Illustrated by Synthia Saint James. BridgeWater Books.

1996

Author Award—Hamilton, Virginia. *Her Stories.* Scholastic, Blue Sky.
Illustrator Award—Feelings, Tom. *The Middle Passage: White Ships/Black Cargo.* Dial.
Author Honor—Curtis, Christopher Paul. *The Watsons Go to Birmingham—1963.* Delacorte.
Author Honor—Williams-Garcia, Rita. *Like Sisters on the Homefront.* Delacorte.
Author Honor—Woodson, Jacqueline. *From the Notebooks of Melanin Sun.* Scholastic, Blue Sky.
Illustrator Honor—Hamilton, Virginia. *Her Stories.* Illustrated by Leo Dillon and Diane Dillon. Scholastic, Blue Sky.
Illustrator Honor—San Souci, Robert. *The Faithful Friend.* Illustrated by Brian Pinkney. Simon and Schuster.

1995

Author Award—McKissack, Patricia C., and Fredrick L. McKissack. *Christmas in the Big House, Christmas in the Quarters.* Scholastic.
Illustrator Award—Johnson, James Weldon. *The Creation.* Illustrated by James E. Ransome. Holiday House.
New Talent (Author)—Draper, Sharon. *Tears of a Tiger.* Simon and Schuster.
Author Honor—Hansen, Joyce. *The Captive.* Scholastic.
Author Honor—Woodson, Jacqueline. *I Hadn't Meant to Tell You This.* Delacorte.
Author Honor—McKissack, Patricia C., and Fredrick L. McKissack. *Black Diamond: The Story of the Negro Baseball League.* Scholastic.
Illustrator Honor—Shelf, Angela. *The Singing Man.* Illustrated by Terea Shaffer. Holiday House.
Illustrator Honor—Grimes, Nikki. *Meet Danitra Brown.* Illustrated by Floyd Cooper. Lothrop, Lee & Shepard.

1994

Author Award—Johnson, Angela. *Toning the Sweep.* Scholastic, Orchard.
Illustrator Award—Fogelman, Phyllis. *Soul Looks Back in Wonder.* Illustrated by Tom Feelings. Dial.
Author Honor—Thomas, Joyce Carol. *Brown Honey in Broom Wheat Tea.* Illustrated by Floyd Cooper. HarperCollins.

Author Honor—Myers, Walter Dean. *Malcolm X: By Any Means Necessary.* Scholastic.

Illustrator Honor—Thomas, Joyce Carol. *Brown Honey in Broom Wheat Tea.* Illustrated by Floyd Cooper. HarperCollins.

Illustrator Honor—Mitchell, Margaree King. *Uncle Jed's Barbershop.* Illustrated by James E. Ransome. Simon and Schuster.

1993

Author Award—McKissack, Patricia C. *Dark Thirty: Southern Tales of the Supernatural.* Knopf.

Illustrator Award—Anderson, David A. *The Origin of Life on Earth: An African Creation Myth.* Illustrated by Kathleen Atkins Wilson. Sights.

Author Honor—Walter, Mildred Pitts. *Mississippi Challenge.* Knopf.

Author Honor—McKissack, Patricia C., and Fredrick L. McKissack. *Sojourner Truth: Ain't I a Woman?* Scholastic.

Author Honor—Myers, Walter Dean. *Somewhere in the Darkness.* Scholastic.

Illustrator Honor—Wahl, Jan. *Little Eight John.* Illustrated by Wil Clay. Lodestar.

Illustrator Honor—San Souci, Robert. *Sukey and the Mermaid.* Illustrated by Brian Pinkney. Four Winds.

Illustrator Honor—Williams, Sherley Anne. *Working Cotton.* Illustrated by Carole Byard. Harcourt.

1992

Author Award—Myers, Walter Dean. *Now Is Your Time: The African American Struggle for Freedom.* HarperCollins.

Illustrator Award—Ringgold, Faith. *Tar Beach.* Crown.

Author Honor—Greenfield, Eloise. *Night on Neighborhood Street.* Illustrated by Jan Spivey Gilchrist. Dial.

Illustrator Honor—Bryan, Ashley, ed. *All Night, All Day: A Child's First Book of African American Spirituals.* Atheneum.

Illustrator Honor—Greenfield, Eloise. *Night on Neighborhood Street.* Illustrated by Jan Spivey Gilchrist. Dial.

1991

Author Award—Taylor, Mildred. *The Road to Memphis.* Dial.

Illustrator Award—Price, Leontyne. *Aida.* Illustrated by Leo Dillon and Diane Dillon. Harcourt.

Author Honor—Haskins, James. *Black Dance in America.* Crowell.

Author Honor—Johnson, Angela. *When I Am Old with You.* Scholastic, Orchard.

1990

Author Award—McKissack, Patricia C., and Fredrick L. McKissack. *A Long Hard Journey: The Story of the Pullman Porter*. Walker.

Illustrator Award—Greenfield, Eloise. *Nathaniel Talking*. Illustrated by Jan Spivey Gilchrist. Black Butterfly.

Author Honor—Greenfield, Eloise. *Nathaniel Talking*. Illustrated by Jan Spivey Gilchrist. Black Butterfly.

Author Honor—Hamilton, Virginia. *The Bells of Christmas*. Harcourt.

Author Honor—Patterson, Lillie. *Martin Luther King, Jr. and the Freedom Movement*. Facts on File.

Illustrator Honor—San Souci, Robert. *The Talking Eggs*. Illustrated by Jerry Pinkney. Dial.

1989

Author Award—Myers, Walter Dean. *Fallen Angels*. Scholastic.

Illustrator Award—McKissack, Patricia C. *Mirandy and Brother Wind*. Illustrated by Jerry Pinkney. Knopf.

Author Honor—Berry, James. *A Thief in the Village and Other Stories*. Scholastic, Orchard.

Author Honor—Hamilton, Virginia. *Anthony Burns: The Defeat and Triumph of a Fugitive Slave*. Knopf.

Illustrator Honor—Greenfield, Eloise. *Under the Sunday Tree*. Illustrated by Amos Ferguson. Harper.

Illustrator Honor—Stolz, Mary. *Storm in the Night*. Illustrated by Pat Cummings. Harper.

1988

Author Award—Taylor, Mildred D. *The Friendship*. Dial.

Illustrator Award—Steptoe, John. *Mufaro's Beautiful Daughters: An African Tale*. Lothrop.

Author Honor—De Veaux, Alexis. *An Enchanted Hair Tale*. Harper.

Author Honor—Lester, Julius. *The Tales of Uncle Remus: The Adventures of Brer Rabbit*. Dial.

Illustrator Honor—Langstaff, John, ed. *What a Morning! The Christmas Story in Black Spirituals*. Illustrated by Ashley Bryan. Macmillan.

Illustrator Honor—Rohmer, Harriet, et al., eds. *The Invisible Hunters: A Legend from the Miskito Indians of Nicaragua*. Illustrated by Joe Sam. Children's Press.

1987

Author Award—Walter, Mildred Pitts. *Justin and the Best Biscuits in the World.* Lothrop.

Illustrator Award—Dragonwagon, Crescent. *Half a Moon and One Whole Star.* Illustrated by Jerry Pinkney. Macmillan.

Author Honor—Bryan, Ashley. *Lion and the Ostrich Chicks and Other African Folk Tales.* Atheneum.

Author Honor—Hansen, Joyce. *Which Way Freedom.* Walker.

Illustrator Honor—*Lion and the Ostrich Chicks and Other African Folk Tales.* Atheneum.

Illustrator Honor—Cummings, Pat. *C.L.O.U.D.S.* Lothrop.

1986

Author Award—Hamilton, Virginia. *The People Could Fly: American Black Folktales.* Illustrated by Leo Dillon and Diane Dillon. Knopf.

Illustrator Award—Flournoy, Valerie. *The Patchwork Quilt.* Illustrated by Jerry Pinkney. Dial.

Author Honor—Hamilton, Virginia. *Junius over Far.* Harper.

Author Honor—Walter, Mildred Pitts. *Trouble's Child.* Lothrop.

Illustrator Honor—Hamilton, Virginia. *The People Could Fly: American Black Folktales.* Illustrated by Leo Dillon and Diane Dillon. Knopf.

1985

Author Award—Myers, Walter Dean. *Motown and Didi.* Knopf.

Author Honor—Boyd, Candy Dawson. *Circle of Gold.* Scholastic: Apple.

Author Honor—Hamilton, Virginia. *A Little Love.* Philomel.

1984

Author Award—Clifton, Lucille. *Everett Anderson's Good-bye.* Holt.

Special Citation—King, Coretta Scott, ed. *The Words of Martin Luther King, Jr.* Newmarket.

Illustrator Award—Walter, Mildred Pitts. *My Mama Needs Me.* Illustrated by Pat Cummings. Lothrop.

Author Honor—Hamilton, Virginia. *The Magical Adventures of Pretty Pearl.* Harper.

Author Honor—Haskins, James. *Lena Horne.* Coward-McCann.

Author Honor—Thomas, Joyce Carol. *Bright Shadow.* Avon.

Author Honor—Walter, Mildred Pitts. *Because We Are.* Morrow.

1983

Author Award—Hamilton, Virginia. *Sweet Whispers, Brother Rush.* Philomel.
Illustrator Award—Mugabane, Peter. *Black Child.* Knopf.
Author Honor—Lester, Julius. *The Strange New Feeling.* Dial.
Illustrator Honor—Adoff, Arnold. *All the Colors of the Race.* Illustrated by John Steptoe. Lothrop.
Illustrator Honor—Bryan, Ashley. *I'm Going to Sing: Black American Spirituals.* Atheneum.
Illustrator Honor—Caines, Jeanette. *Just Us Women.* Illustrated by Pat Cummings. Harper.

1982

Author Award—Taylor, Mildred. *Let the Circle Be Unbroken.* Dial.
Illustrator Award—Guy, Rosa. *Mother Crocodile: An Uncle Amadou Tale from Senegal.* Illustrated by John Steptoe. Delacorte.
Author Honor—Childress, Alice. *Rainbow Jordan.* Coward-McCann.
Author Honor—Hunter, Kristin. *Lou in the Limelight.* Scribner's.
Author Honor—Mebane, Mary E. *Mary: An Autobiography.* Viking.
Illustrator Honor—Greenfield, Eloise. *Daydreamers.* Illustrated by Tom Feelings. Dial.

1981

Author Award—Poitier, Sidney. *This Life.* Knopf.
Illustrator Award—Bryan, Ashley. *Beat the Story Drum, Pum-Pum.* Atheneum.
Author Honor—De Veaux, Alexis. *Don't Explain: A Song of Billie Holiday.* Harper.
Illustrator Honor—Greenfield, Eloise. *Grandmama's Joy.* Illustrated by Carole Byard. Collins.
Illustrator Honor—Zaslavsky, Claudia. *Count on Your Fingers African Style.* Illustrated by Jerry Pinkney. Crowell.

1980

Author Award—Myers, Walter Dean. *The Young Landlords.* Viking.
Illustrator Award—Yarborough, Camille. *Cornrows.* Illustrated by Carole Byard. Coward-McCann.
Author Honor—Gordy, Berry. *Movin' Up.* Harper.
Author Honor—Greenfield, Eloise, and Lessie Jones Little. *Childtimes: A Three-Generation Memoir.* Harper.

Author Honor—Haskins, James. *Andrew Young: Young Man with a Mission*. Lothrop.
Author Honor—Haskins, James. *James Van Der Zee: The Picture Takin' Man*. Dodd.
Author Honor—Southerland, Ellease. *Let the Lion Eat Straw*. Scribner's.

1979

Author Award—Davis, Ossie. *Escape to Freedom*. Viking.
Illustrator Award—Grimes, Nikki. *Something on My Mind*. Illustrated by Tom Feelings. Dial.
Author Honor—Patterson, Lillie. *Benjamin Banneker*. Abingdon.
Author Honor—Peterson, Jeanne W. *I Have a Sister, My Sister Is Deaf*. Harper.
Author Honor—Hamilton, Virginia. *Justice and Her Brothers*. Greenwillow.
Author Honor—Fenner, Carol. *Skates of Uncle Richard*. Random House.

1978

Author Award—Greenfield, Eloise. *Africa Dream*. Illustrated by Carole Bayard. Crowell.
Illustrator Award—Greenfield, Eloise. *Africa Dream*. Illustrated by Carole Bayard. Crowell.
Author Honor—Faulkner, William J. *The Days When the Animals Talked: Black Folk Tales and How They Came to Be*. Follett.
Author Honor—Glass, Frankcina. *Marvin and Tige*. St. Martin's.
Author Honor—Greenfield, Eloise. *Mary McLeod Bethune*. Crowell.
Author Honor—Haskins, James. *Barbara Jordan*. Dial.
Author Honor—Patterson, Lillie. *Coretta Scott King*. Garrard.
Author Honor—Stewart, Ruth Ann. *Portia: The Life of Portia Washington Pittman, the Daughter of Booker T. Washington*. Doubleday.

1977

Author Award—Haskins, James. *The Story of Stevie Wonder*. Lothrop.

1976

Author Award—Bailey, Pearl. *Duey's Tale*. Harcourt.

1975

Author Award—Robinson, Dorothy. *The Legend of Africana*. Johnson.

1974

Author Award—Mathis, Sharon Bell. *Ray Charles*. Illustrated by George Ford. Crowell.

Illustrator Award—Mathis, Sharon Bell. *Ray Charles*. Illustrated by George Ford. Crowell.

1973

(Note that prior to 1974, awards were given to authors only.)

Robinson, Jackie, with Alfred Duckett. *I Never Had It Made: The Autobiography of Jackie Robinson*. Putnam.

1972

Fax, Elton C. *17 Black Artists*. Dodd.

1971

Rollins, Charlemae. *Black Troubadour: Langston Hughes*. Rand McNally.

1970

Patterson, Lillie. *Martin Luther King, Jr.: Man of Peace*. Garrard.

NOTES

1. Murphy, *Black Authors and Illustrators*, xviii.
2. Rollock, *Black Authors and Illustrators*.
3. Casement, "Changing the Face," 13.
4. Pinkney, "Awards," 536.
5. Casement, "Changing the Face," 13.
6. Davis-Undiano, "Mildred D. Taylor," 12.
7. *I Hadn't Meant to Tell You This* and *Lena* are not discussed further in this book, but they are well worth checking out. Woodson is such a prolific writer, I was not able to include all of her excellent work.
8. Casement, "Democratic Representation," 46.
9. American Library Association, "Coretta Scott King Award."

BIBLIOGRAPHY OF BOOKS FOR CHILDREN

Feelings, Tom. *The Middle Passage.* New York: Dial, 1995.

Feelings, Tom, ed. and illus. *Soul Looks Back in Wonder.* New York: Dial, 1993.

Hamilton, Virginia. *Many Thousand Gone: African Americans from Slavery to Freedom.* Illustrated by Leo Dillon and Diane Dillon. New York: Knopf, 1993.

Lester, Julius. *Day of Tears: A Novel in Dialogue.* New York: Hyperion Books for Children, Jump at the Sun, 2005.

Meltzer, Milton, ed. *Frederick Douglass: In His Own Words.* Illustrated by Stephen Alcorn. San Diego, CA: Harcourt, 1995.

Myers, Walter Dean. *"I've Seen the Promised Land": The Life of Dr. Martin Luther King, Jr.* Illustrated by Leonard Jenkins. New York: HarperCollins, Amistad, 2004.

———. *Malcolm X: By Any Means Necessary.* New York: Scholastic, 1993.

———. *Malcolm X: A Fire Burning Brightly.* Illustrated by Leonard Jenkins. New York: HarperCollins, Amistad, 2000.

———. *Now Is Your Time: The African-American Struggle for Freedom.* New York: HarperTrophy, 1991.

Taylor, Mildred D. *The Friendship.* Illustrated by Max Ginsburg. New York: Puffin, 1987.

BIBLIOGRAPHY OF AUTHOR, ILLUSTRATOR, AND AWARD WEBSITES

American Library Association. "Coretta Scott King Award." www.ala.org/ala/emiert/corettascottkingbookaward/corettascott.htm.

Curtis, Christopher Paul. "Christopher Paul Curtis." Random House. www.randomhouse.com/features/christopherpaulcurtis/.

Fisher, Marilyn, et al. "Learning about Walter Dean Myers." www.scils.rutgers.edu/~kvander/myers.html.

Hamilton, Virginia. www.virginiahamilton.com/home.htm.

Houghton Mifflin. "Meet the Author/Illustrator: Floyd Cooper." www.eduplace.com/kids/hmr/mtai/fcooper.html.

———. "Meet the Author: Julius Lester." www.eduplace.com/kids/hmr/mtai/lester.html.

———. "Meet the Author: Patricia and Fredrick McKissack." www.eduplace.com/kids/hmr/mtai/mckissack.html.

———. "Meet the Illustrator: Brian Pinkney." www.eduplace.com/kids/hmr/mtai/bpinkney.html.

———. "Meet the Illustrator: Jerry Pinkney." www.eduplace.com/kids/hmr/mtai/jpinkney.html.

Lewis, E. B. "e. b. lewis, artistrator." www.eblewis.com/default2.asp.

Lu, Mei-Yu. "Mildred D. Taylor." www.indiana.edu/~reading/ieo/bibs/taylor.html.

Meltzer, Milton. "The Book That Changed My Life." National Book Foundation. www.nationalbook.org/bookchanged_mmeltzer_nbm.html.

National Conference of Artists of New York. "In Tribute to Tom Feelings: May 19, 1933–August 25, 2003." http://ncanewyork.com/feelings/tom_feelings_tribute.htm.

National Conference of Artists of New York. "Profile on Tom Feelings." http://ncanewyork.com/feelings.htm.

Ohioana Authors. "Angela Johnson." www.ohioana-authors.org/johnson/index.php.

Penguin Group (USA). "Tom Feelings." http://us.penguingroup.com/nf/Author/AuthorPage/0,,1000010711,00.html.

———. "Jerry Pinkney." http://us.penguingroup.com/nf/Author/AuthorPage/0,,1000013120,00.html.

Random House. "Patricia McKissack." www.randomhouse.com/author/results.pperl?authorid=20049.

Taylor, Mildred D. "Acceptance Speech for the 1997 Alan Award." *Alan Review* 25:3 (1998). http://scholar.lib.vt.edu/ejournals/ALAN/spring98/taylor.html.

University of Florida. "Professor James Haskins." www.english.ufl.edu/faculty/jhaskins/.

University of Massachusetts, Amherst. "Julius Lester, professor emeritus." www.umass.edu/judaic/faculty/juliuslester.html.

Woodson, Jacqueline. "Jacqueline Woodson: Books for Children and Young Adults." www.jacquelinewoodson.com/.

Worcester Polytechnic Institute. "Worcester Area Writers: Milton Meltzer." www.wpi.edu/Academics/Library/Archives/WAuthors/meltzer/bio.html.

BIBLIOGRAPHY OF REFERENCE WORKS

American Library Association. "Coretta Scott King Award." www.ala.org.

Casement, Rose. "Changing the Face of the Children's Literature Canon." *Michigan Reading Journal* 36:1 (2003): 9–14.

———. "Democratic Representation in Children's Literature." *Democracy and Education* 14:3 (2002): 45–47.

Davis-Undiano, Robert Con. "Mildred D. Taylor and the Art of Making a Difference." *World Literature Today* 72:2 (2004): 11–13.

Murphy, Barbara Thrash. *Black Authors and Illustrators of Books for Children and Young Adults: A Biographical Dictionary*, 3rd ed. New York: Garland, 1999.

Pinkney, Andrea. "Awards That Stand on Solid Ground." *Horn Book Magazine* 77:5 (2001): 535–39.

Rollock, Barbara. *Black Authors and Illustrators of Books for Children and Young Adults: A Biographical Dictionary*, 2nd ed. New York: Garland, 1992.

Glossary

abolitionists—the name given to people who worked to end slavery in the years before emancipation.

Black Codes of the 1860s—state and local laws, established primarily in the South, to restrict the rights of Black citizens.

Black History Month—the period each February dedicated to the study of the contributions and experiences of African Americans. Black History Month was established in 1976 by the Association for the Study of African-American Life and History as an extension of the earlier Negro History Week, originated by Carter Woodson in 1926.

Black Indians—those African Americans who, during or after legalized slavery, settled in Indian settlements, and their descendants.

Brown v. Board of Education—the 1954 Supreme Court decision that, by overturning the decision of *Plessy v. Ferguson*, ended legalized segregation in public schools and had widespread implications for other forms of segregation.

Buffalo Soldiers—the name given to troops of African American soldiers, many of whom were stationed in the western territories in the late 1800s. This term was used from the 1860s until 1951, when the last all-Black regiment was disbanded.

buffoon—someone whose behavior is characterized as foolish.

Cape Bianco—a city on the western coast of Africa that was used in the 1400s as a port in the slave trade.

civil rights movement—the period of social activism in the mid-1900s through which African Americans finally were afforded many of America's legal and social opportunities. The events commonly cited as the beginning and end of this period are the 1954 *Brown v. Board of Education* Supreme Court decision and the Civil Rights Act of 1968, signed into law by President Lyndon Johnson.

consanguinity—a relationship through shared ancestry.

contraband—a dehumanizing term used to describe escaped slaves as stolen property.

Corps of Discovery—the name given by President Thomas Jefferson to the group of individuals who embarked on the Lewis and Clark Expedition.

emancipation—the granting of freedom. In Black history, this term is most commonly used to refer to the 1863 freeing of slaves by the Emancipation Proclamation.

Fifteenth Amendment—the 1870 amendment to the U.S. Constitution that ensured the right to vote to all citizens.

Fisk Free Colored School—the original name of what is now Fisk University, established in 1866 to educate newly freed slaves.

Fourteenth Amendment—the 1868 amendment to the U.S. Constitution that ensured the rights of citizenship to former slaves.

Freedman's Bureau—a government department established by Congress in 1865 to assist former slaves during Reconstruction. Its good work was ended when funds were cut after the election of Rutherford B. Hayes in 1877.

Freedom Riders—participants in nonviolent demonstrations in 1961 in which Black and White citizens, many of whom were college students, rode interstate buses to challenge segregation laws.

Fugitive Slave Act—passed in 1850, this law was intended to bolster an earlier fugitive slave law passed in 1793 by requiring authorities not only to return slaves to their masters but also to arrest anyone accused of being a slave. The far-reaching possibilities of this law bolstered antislavery sentiment in the North.

gag rule—a rule that is intended to stop publication or free speech on a particular issue.

Gao—the name of an ancient and present-day city on the Niger River in Mali, western Africa.

generations—as a measure of time, "generation" refers to the time it takes for humans to grow up and produce their own offspring.

Great Migration—the term given to the movement of African Americans from the southern states to the northern states between the

1910s and the 1950s, as they sought to escape Jim Crow laws and find better jobs.

Gullah baskets—baskets made in a West African traditional style, primarily by African American women in the southeastern United States.

Harlem Hellfighters—members of the 369th Infantry Regiment from New York, the first African American regiment of World War I, who fought valiantly for our country in Europe during this war.

Harlem Renaissance—the cultural movement between 1919 and the mid-1930s in which a community of African American writers, artists, musicians, and dancers in the neighborhood of Harlem in New York City created an incredible legacy of great works.

Horn of Africa—the peninsula that extends out from the eastern coast of Africa; the continent's easternmost point.

indentured servants—in American history, the term is used for people who have entered into a contract to work as a servant for a particular period of time in exchange for passage to the colonies.

indigenous people—people who have lived in an area since the earliest times and predate any other people who are exploring or settling in the area.

intermarried—a term used to describe people married to someone of a different race, ethnicity, or religion.

Jenné—an ancient city on the Niger River in Africa.

Jim Crow—the name given to a White minstrel performer who performed with a black face and acted as a fool. His portrayal was used to characterize African Americans with insulting and dehumanizing stereotypes.

Jim Crow era—the years after Reconstruction when discriminatory laws and acts of violence threatened the freedom of African Americans throughout the United States but especially in the South. The era ended with the gains of the civil rights movement.

Jubilee Singers—a group of singers from Fisk University who gained international prominence during Reconstruction by singing spirituals to raise money for the university.

Ku Klux Klan—a still-active white supremacy group first established in 1866 that is especially well known for their violence and intimidation against African Americans in the years following the Civil War and during the Jim Crow years.

lynching—violence (usually murder by hanging) committed by a group or informal mob as a retribution for a real or perceived crime or for social reasons. In our country, the lynching of Black citizens by White citizens occurred with alarming frequency during the period of legalized slavery and through the mid-1900s. Its purpose was often to establish the superiority of Whites and to intimidate, as in its use to keep slaves from attempting escape and in keeping African Americans from voting.

Malaga Island—an island off the coast of Maine where African Americans settled and established a community for generations until White townspeople violently destroyed their property, forced residents to leave, and placed some children and adults against their will in institutions, causing their premature deaths.

manumission papers—legal documents stating that a person has been freed from slavery.

manumission settlements—(rare) settlements set up by former slave owners for their freed slaves.

maroon settlements—populations of fugitive slaves who settled in areas throughout North, Central, and South America.

Middle Passage—the months-long sea voyage of slave transportation from Africa to the Americas. Many slaves did not survive this harrowing experience.

minstrel show—a genre of entertainment that became popular after the Civil War in which a White performer with his face painted black does comic skits by acting foolish with negative characterizations of Black people.

Montgomery bus boycott—the refusal of Blacks to ride the buses of Montgomery, Alabama, for over a year, despite great hardships. This boycott was a key demonstration in the early civil rights movement. The boycott, planned in advance by E. D. Nixon, spearheaded by Martin Luther King Jr., and begun by Rosa Park's refusal to give up her seat to a White bus passenger on December 1, 1955, led to integration of the buses a little more than a year later.

NAACP—the National Association for the Advancement of Colored People was established in the early 1900s to fight Jim Crow laws and segregation. It grew in prominence during the civil rights movement in the 1960s and 1970s and remains committed to issues of social justice.

National Negro Business League—an organization founded in 1900 by Booker T. Washington to advance the economic success of African Americans in business.

Negro Baseball Leagues—the organizations of all-Black professional baseball teams that played between 1920 and 1948, during which time Black players were effectively banned from playing in the White major leagues. Jackie Robinson joining the Brooklyn Dodgers in 1947 began the integration of professional baseball teams, although a few Black teams continued to play until the 1960s.

Pea Island Life-Saving Station—First built in 1868, from 1878 until it was decommissioned in 1947, this was the only all-Black life-saving station of those established in the Outer Banks to rescue troubled ships. The surfmen here became renowned after their heroic rescue of the crew of the *E. S. Newman* during a terrible storm in 1896.

Plessy v. Ferguson—the 1896 Supreme Court decision that upheld legalized segregation with its "separate but equal" ruling.

Reconstruction—the period immediately following the Civil War (1865–1877) that was intended to address the serious issues that faced the country. The many significant advancements made during that time included the Thirteenth and Fourteenth Amendments. However, some gains were later lost, and Reconstruction came to an end with the election of Rutherford B. Hayes, who removed federal troops from the South, thus taking away protections for the newfound rights of African Americans.

Redcoats—the name given to British soldiers in the colonial period because of their red uniforms.

requiem—a piece of music or a literary work written to commemorate someone who has died; a religious service commemorating the dead.

retainers—a word that was sometimes used to refer to slaves, as was the word "servant." Both of these words implied that the slave was serving willingly, denying the reality that the slave was owned by his or her master.

sharecroppers—individuals who farm another person's land in return for a portion of the crops.

slave revolts—also known as slave rebellions, these were armed uprisings by slaves against the institution of slavery. Perhaps the most well-known slave rebellion in America was that led by Nat Turner in 1831.

Society of Friends—also known as Quakers, this group maintained a strong opposition to slavery, and many of its members were abolitionists active in the Underground Railroad.

sweetgrass—a perennial grass commonly found in the coastal areas of the southern United States and used to make sweet-smelling baskets.

Thirteenth Amendment—the 1865 amendment to the U.S. Constitution that abolished slavery.

Timbuktu—an ancient city on the Niger River in Mali.

Underground Railroad—the many routes, developed at great risk to everyone involved, through a series of safe houses and safe people to assist slaves on their escape to the North and to freedom.

Credits

CHAPTER 1

From: *The Village That Vanished* by Ann Grifalconi, illustrated by Kadir Nelson, copyright © 2002 by Ann Grifalconi, text. Used by permission of Dial Books for Young Readers, A Division of Penguin Young Readers Group, A Member of Penguin Group (USA) Inc., 345 Hudson Street, New York, NY 10014. All rights reserved.

CHAPTER 2

Excerpt from *Molly Bannaky* by Alice McGill. Text copyright © 1999 by Alice McGill. Reprinted by permission of Houghton Mifflin Company. All rights reserved.

Excerpt from *Circle Unbroken* by Margot Theis Raven, pictures by E. B. Lewis. Text copyright © 2004 by Margot Theis Raven. Pictures copyright © 2004 by E. B. Lewis. Reprinted by permission of Farrar, Straus and Giroux, LLC.

CHAPTER 3

What Are You Figuring Now? A Story about Benjamin Banneker, by Jeri Ferris and illustrated by Amy Johnson. Copyright © 1998 by Jeri Ferris. Reprinted with the permission of Carolrhoda Books, a division of Lerner Publishing Group, Inc. All rights reserved. No part of this excerpt may be used or reproduced

From *Days of Tears* by Julius Lester. Copyright © 2005 by Julius Lester. Reprinted by Permission of Hyperion Books for Children.

Excerpted from "Not My Bones" from *Fortune's Bones: The Manumission Requiem* by Marilyn Nelson (Front Street an imprint of Boyds Mill Press, 2003). Reprinted with the permission of Boyds Mill Press, Inc. Text copyright © 2003 by Marilyn Nelson.

From *The Old African* by Julius Lester, illustrated by Jerry Pinkney, copyright © 2005 by Julius Lester, text. Used by permission of Dial Books for Young Readers, A Division of Penguin Young Readers Group, A Member of Penguin Group (USA) Inc., 345 Hudson Street, New York, NY 10014. All rights reserved.

Excerpt from *The Escape of Oney Judge: Martha Washington's Slave Finds Freedom* by Emily Arnold McCully. Text copyright © 2007 by Emily Arnold McCully. Reprinted by permission of Farrar, Straus and Giroux, LLC.

Revolutionary Poet: A Story about Phillis Wheatley by Maryann Weidt and Illustrated by Mary O'Keefe Young. Copyright © 1997 by Maryann Weidt. Reprinted with the permission of Millbrook Press, a division of Lerner Publishing Group, Inc. All rights reserved. No part of this excerpt may be used or reproduced in any manner whatsoever without the prior written permission of Lerner Publishing Group, Inc.

CHAPTER 4

Almost to Freedom by Vaunda Micheaux Nelson and illustrated by Colin Bootman. Copyright © 2003 by Vaunda Micheaux Nelson. Reprinted with the permission of Carolrhoda Books, a division of Lerner Publishing Group, Inc. All rights reserved. No part of this excerpt may be used or reproduced in any manner whatsoever without the prior written approval of Lerner Publishing Group, Inc.

From *Minty: A Story of Young Harriet Tubman* by Alan Schroeder, copyright © 1996 by Alan Schroeder, text. Used by permission of Dial Books for Young Readers, A Division of Penguin Young Readers Group, A Member of Penguin Group (USA) Inc., 345 Hudson Street, New York, NY 10014. All rights reserved.

CHAPTER 5

From *Crossing Bok Chitto: A Choctaw Tale of Friendship and Freedom* by Tim Tingle. Illustrated by Jeanne Rorex Bridges. El Paso, TX: Cinco Puntos, 2006. www.cincopuntos.com.

From *Pink and Say* by Patricia Polacco, copyright © 1994 by Patricia Polacco. Used by permission of Philomel Books, A Division of Penguin Young Readers Group, A Member of Penguin Group (USA) Inc., 345 Hudson Street, New York, NY 10014. All rights reserved.

From *Show Way* by Jacqueline Woodson, illustrated by Hudson Talbott, copyright © 2005 Jacqueline Woodson, text. Used by permission of G. P. Putnam's Sons, A Division of Penguin Young Readers Group, A Member of Penguin Group (USA) Inc., 345 Hudson Street, New York, NY 10014. All rights reserved.

CHAPTER 6

From *More Than Anything Else* by Marie Bradby. Scholastic Inc./Orchard Books. Copyright © 1995 by Marie Bradby. Reprinted by permission.

CHAPTER 7

From *Black Cowboy, Wild Horses: A True Story* by Julius Lester, copyright © 1998 by Julius Lester, text. Used by permission of Dial Books for Young Readers, A Division of Penguin Young Readers Group, A Member of Penguin Group (USA) Inc., 345 Hudson Street, New York, NY 10014. All rights reserved.

Aunt Clara Brown: Official Pioneer by Linda Lowery and illustrated by Janice Lee Porter. Copyright © 1999 by Linda Lowery. Reprinted with the permission of Carolrhoda Books, a division of Lerner Publishing Group, Inc. All rights reserved. No part of this excerpt may be used or reproduced in any manner whatsoever without the prior written approval of Lerner Publishing Group, Inc.

CHAPTER 8

CHAPTER 9

From *Coming Home: From the Life of Langston Hughes* by Floyd Cooper, copyright © 1994 by Floyd Cooper. Used by permission of Philomel Books, A Division of Penguin Young Readers Group, A Member of Penguin Group (USA) Inc., 345 Hudson Street, New York, NY 10014. All rights reserved.

From *Jump Back, Honey* by Paul Laurence Dunbar. Copyright © by Paul Laurence Dunbar. Illustrations © 1999 by Pinkney. Reprinted by Permission of Hyperion Books for Children.

Jump at de Sun: The Story of Zora Neale Hurston by A. P. Porter and foreword by Lucy Ann Hurston. Copyright © 1992 by Carolrhoda Books. Reprinted with the permission of Carolrhoda Books, a division of Lerner Publishing Group, Inc. All rights reserved. No part of this excerpt may be used or reproduced in any manner whatsoever without the prior written approval of Lerner Publishing Group, Inc.

Excerpt from *Just Like Josh Gibson* by Angela Johnson. Simon and Schuster. Copyright © 2004 by Angela Johnson. Reprinted by permission of the author.

From *Ella Fitzgerald: The Tale of a Vocal Virtuosa* by Andrea Davis Pinkney. Copyright © 2002 by Andrea Davis Pinkney. Illustrations © by Brian Pinkney. Reprinted by Permission of Hyperion Books for Children.

Jazz Age Poet: A Story about Langston Hughes by Veda Boyd Jones and illustrated by Barbara Kiwak. Copyright © 1996 by Veda Boyd Jones. Reprinted with the permission of Millbrook Press, a division of Lerner Publishing Group, Inc. All rights reserved. No part of this excerpt may be used or reproduced in any manner whatsoever without the prior written approval of Lerner Publishing Group, Inc.

CHAPTER 10

From *The Story of Ruby Bridges* by Robert Coles. Copyright © 1995 by Robert Coles. Reprinted by permission of Scholastic Inc.

From *Mississippi Trail, 1955* by Chris Crowe, copyright © 2002 by Chris Crowe. Used by permission of Phyllis Fogelman Books, A Division of Penguin Young Readers Group, A Member of Penguin Group (USA) Inc., 345 Hudson Street, New York, NY 10014. All rights reserved.

Excerpt from *Watsons Go to Birmingham—1963* by Christopher Paul Curtis. Delacorte. Copyright © 1995 by Christopher Paul Curtis. Reprinted by permission of the author.

CHAPTER 11

CHAPTER 13

Index

Morrison, Toni, 197–98, 273
Moses: When Harriet Tubman Led Her People to Freedom, 59–60, 273
Moses, Shelia P., 149–50, 273
Mrs. Katz and Tush, 223, 228, 229
Muslims. *See* Nation of Islam
My Brother Martin: A Sister Remembers Growing Up with the Rev. Dr. Martin Luther King, Jr., 195
My Dream of Martin Luther King, 200
My Heroes, My People: African Americans and Native Americans in the West, 112–13
My Man Blue, 223
Myers, Walter Dean, 4, 45, 48n5, 82, 101, 126, 138, 141–42, 173, 183, 198–99, 212, 268–69; awards, 273, 275, 276, 278, 279, 280, 281

NAACP. *See* National Association for the Advancement of Colored People
Nation of Islam, 199, 206, 212
National Association for the Advancement of Colored People, 151, 203, 212, 290
National Association of Base Ball Players, 180
National Negro Business League, 137, 290
Native Americans: alliances with African Americans, 15, 84, 109–10, 112; as slaves, 2, 29; Choctaw Nation, 83–84; conflicts with government, 18, 117, 118; early years with settlers, 1, 11; Seminole, 111; use of term, x; with Lewis and Clark Expedition, 250–51
Negro, as synonymous with slave in 1680, 23
Negro Baseball League, 159, 175–80, 186, 227

Negro League: All-Black Baseball, 177–78
Nelson, Marilyn, 45–46, 212–13, 255, 273, 374, 275
Nelson, Vaunda Micheaux, 56–57, 204–5, 274
New Orleans, 27, 85, 165, 168, 207
Night Golf, 140–41
No More! Stories and Songs of Slave Resistance, 82–83
Nobisso, Josephine, 133
Nolen, Jerdine, 228
Now Is Your Time: The African-American Struggle for Freedom, 101, 269, 278

Ohio, 58, 64, 97, 115, 267
Ohio River, 54, 57, 61–62, 64
The Old African, 42–43
omission of Black history: from curriculum, 11, 12; from children's literature and other books, 67, 121, 244–56, 270
Only Passing Through: The Story of Sojourner Truth, 83, 275
Onward: A Photobiography of African-American Polar Explorer Matthew Henson, 137
Orbus Pictus Award, 256–57
Orgill, Roxane, 165
The Other Side, 229–30
The Other Side: Shorter Poems, 237, 276
Our Gracie Aunt, 230
Out of the Darkness: The Story of Blacks Moving North, 1890–1940, 182–83

Palmer, Colin, 14
Parks, Rosa, 187, 193, 195–96, 199, 200–201, 209
Pea Island Life-Saving Station, 145–46, 291
Peacock, Judith, 102

About the Author

Rose Casement is associate dean of education at the University of Michigan–Flint. She lives in Flint with her partner and their two youngest children. They enjoy summers at their coastal Nova Scotia cottage and spending time with her five grown children and six grandchildren, who live from the coast of California to the coast of Maine.

The likelihood that many students may never learn the extraordinary history, contributions, and challenges of African Americans, despite the fact that these experiences are woven into the tapestry of this country, provided the passion that propelled this book forward. It is Dr. Casement's hope that children's literature can help provide a venue to bring this history into its rightful place in the curriculum of American history.